Rivers of Fire

Published and Forthcoming by New Academia Publishing

SUPER/HEROES: From Hercules to Superman
Wendy Haslem, Angela Ndalianis and Chris Mackie, eds.

NATIONALISM, HISTORIOGRAPHY AND THE (RE)CONSTRUCTION OF THE PAST, Claire Norton, ed.

FROM THE HOLY LAND TO THE NEW JERUSALEM: Specialness, Utopia, and Holocaust
by Arthur Grenke

GOD, GREED, AND GENOCIDE: The Holocaust through the Centuries
by Arthur Grenke

TURKEY'S MODERNIZATION: Refugees from Nazism and Atatürk's Vision
by Arnold Reisman

VISUAL CULTURE IN SHANGHAI, 1850s-1930s
Jason C. Kuo, ed.

ON THE ROAD TO BAGHDAD, or TRAVELING BICULTURALISM: Theorizing a Bicultural Approach to Contemporary World Fiction
Gönul Pultar, ed.

IMAGING RUSSIA 2000: Film and Facts
by Anna Lawton (CHOICE Outstanding Academic Title 2005)

BEFORE THE FALL: Soviet Cinema in The Gorbachev Years
by Anna Lawton

HERETICAL EM[PIRICISM
by Pierpaolo Pasolini; Ben Lawton and Louise K. Barnett, eds., trs.

RUSSIAN FUTURISM: A History
by Vladimir Markov

WORDS IN REVOLUTION: Russian Futurist Manifestoes 1912-1928
Anna Lawton and Herbert Eagle, eds., trs.

SLAVIC THINKERS OR THE CREATION OF POLITIES: Intellectual History and Political Thought in Central Europe and the Balkans
by Josette Baers

ASPECTS OF BALKAN CULTURE: Social, Political, and Literary Perspectives
by Jelena Milojković-Djurić

To read an excerpt, visit: www.newacademia.com

Rivers of Fire
Mythic Themes in Homer's *Iliad*

C. J. Mackie

New Academia Publishing, LLC
Washington, DC

Copyright © 2008 by C. J. Mackie

New Academia Publishing, 2008

All rights reserved. No part of this book may be reproduced or transmitted in any form or by any means, electronic or mechanical, including photocopying, recording, or by any information storage and retrieval system.

Printed in the United States of America

Library of Congress Control Number: 2007941735
ISBN 978-0-9800814-2-8 paperback (alk. paper)

New Academia Publishing, LLC
P.O. Box 27420, Washington, DC 20038-7420
www.newacademia.com - info@newacademia.com

Contents

Preface vii

Introduction 1

Chapter 1: Monsters 21

Chapter 2: Horses 63

Chapter 3: Archers 93

Chapter 4: Fire 155

Conclusion 191

Bibliography 201

Notes 213

Preface

This book was written over a long period of time that included several periods of study leave. I am grateful to the Universities of Glasgow and Edinburgh, Clare Hall Cambridge, and La Trobe University, for generously offering their research resources during this time. The University of Melbourne supported this project in many different ways, not least of which was a publication grant to assist in the final preparation of the material. A draft of the book was written at Cambridge in 2003-4 where I received every kind assistance from the staff of the Classics Faculty Library. I am also very grateful to Richard Hunter, John Davidson, Michael Osborne, and James Stratford. I owe the greatest debt of gratitude to Peter Toohey at the University of Calgary, who, with characteristic generosity, read through an earlier draft of the MS and made many cogent comments and criticisms. Finally, a dedication to my family, Karen Block, Rachel Mackie, and Naomi Mackie, for all their love and support over the years.

Melbourne
July, 2007

Introduction

This book is concerned with the use of myth in Homer's *Iliad*. Its central subject is the notion of generational transition in the conduct of heroism, from the earlier periods through to the generation of Achilles at Troy. It will focus on the repeated allusions to heroic encounters in the times before the Trojan war, including the 'quests' of the renowned heroes of old (Heracles, Perseus, Bellerophon, Jason, and Pirithous). There is a very different level of detail provided in the *Iliad* for the lives and deeds of these earlier men. A detailed narrative of Bellerophon's adventures occurs in one extended passage; whereas Heracles tends to be alluded to in less complete passages. Other early heroes, like Perseus and Jason, are referred to in the very barest of ways. The combined effect of these references is the notion of a distinguished heroic past that lies behind the war at Troy. In some cases the participants in the war have a direct genealogical connection to the heroes of old (as Glaucus does to Bellerophon, and Tlepolemus to Heracles). And in the case of the old Pylian king Nestor, we can identify an actual participant in earlier conflicts, somebody who is more than prepared to talk about his experiences in the days of his youth. The Trojans too have a distinguished heroic past in which they take a great deal of pride (note especially Aeneas at 20.206ff.). And they too have an old man, king Priam, who once lined up against the Amazons when they appeared at Troy (3.188ff.).

A memory of earlier times and people is therefore a fundamental characteristic of the *Iliad*, one that is revealed both in the narrative of the poem, and in speeches made by Greeks and Trojans. The nature of these reminiscences, and the earlier world that they reveal, means that there is some considerable emphasis placed on the notion of generational change in heroic conduct; and one of our principal tasks in this book is to explore this. Most of the references reveal that the world of the heroic past was very different from the setting of the war for Priam's Troy with which the poem is primarily concerned. The main warriors of the *Iliad* operate in a martial context that is fundamentally new and different from earlier times, even from one generation beforehand when Heracles sacked the city of Troy. References to the heroic past in the *Iliad* signal the distinctive character of the two wars, and the fact that Troy will be treated very differently by the Greeks when they eventually take the city the second time around. Most significantly, Achilles seems to dominate the heroic world of his generation in an entirely different way from Heracles in the previous era. As we shall see, Achilles is a remarkable epic hero partly because of what he is not, as well as what he is. The struggle for Priam's city is a new kind of war dominated by a special hero who is quite different from the great men of the past.

The notion of generational change will be explored by reference to four symbolic themes - monsters, horses, archers, and fire. These particular subjects are dealt with because they help to reveal the way that the world changes across one generation in the *Iliad*. The traditional feats of monster-slaying are the subject of Chapter 1, especially the distinctive achievements of Heracles and Bellerophon. These earlier heroic tasks, which are referred to throughout the *Iliad*, are compared in the first chapter with the 'world of Achilles', in which the monsters, as far as we can tell, have disappeared. The conflict for Priam's city is described as taking place in an entirely different kind of environment from the sack of his father's city; and it is in this context that heroic endeavor takes a distinctively different form. The absence of monsters from the new world of heroes means that organized conflict against other human societies is the only apparent means of acquiring imperishable renown. Participation in war seems to have become the single avenue to heroic achievement for Achilles and his comrades-in-arms in the world of the *Iliad*.

Similarly, the two wars for Troy are fought out in different ways over different objects of possession. In Chapter 2 we examine the roles of horses in the poem, their close association with Heracles and Achilles, and their part in the whole story of Troy from the earliest times. The argument will be put that on the one hand horses represent continuity across the generations in the *Iliad*. In some ways this marks them out from the other three symbolic themes dealt with in this book. Special horses were the prize over which Heracles fought the Trojans in the previous generation, and they are much sought after within the action of the *Iliad* itself (especially by the Argive prince Diomedes).

But whereas the *Iliad* points to a continuing Trojan affection for horses from the earliest times, it also suggests that the later generation of men conduct their conflicts over women, not over horses. The poem implies (as does the *Odyssey*) that it is principally women who are fought over in the later generation of warriors (Helen, Briseis, Chryseis; and Penelope in the *Odyssey*). Helen's role in the later period corresponds to the role of Laomedon's splendid horses in precipitating the sack of the city the first time around. The arguments in the first two chapters therefore are concerned with the apparent transition that the *Iliad* reveals in the heroic life through time, from the world of nature (ie. doing battle with monsters, and sacking the city for special horses), to the world of humans (ie. a monumental war between two different peoples over a special woman).

Chapters 3 and 4 continue to focus on the notion of generational change, except that in these two chapters our concern is with the actual conduct of the war for Troy in the two main heroic eras. Weaponry is the subject of Chapter 3, and the fact that the *Iliad* places great emphasis on the use of the spear by the leading Greek warriors at Troy. Achilles is the quintessential Greek spearman, and much is made within the poem of the lethal effect of his characteristic weapon. Likewise the other Greek princes, without exception, all favor the spear, and they use it to devastating effect. Only the spear turns the tide of battle towards the Greeks, because of its deadly impact against leading warriors on the Trojan side. Archery, by contrast, is usually a much less effective mode of fighting in the *Iliad*, and the use of the bow on the Greek side is associated with illegitimacy of birth. Weaponry is an important signifier of class within the Greek army, and we will be exploring the implications of this.

In contrast to the practice of archery among the Greeks, the bow is used as a weapon of war at the highest levels of Trojan society, right up to the royal house itself. The difference in class of the Greek and the Trojan archers is significant, and it helps us to draw an important distinction between the two sides. This is further reflected in the support given to Troy by the two divine archers, Apollo and Artemis. Troy is therefore associated with the bow and arrow at the divine and aristocratic levels, whereas this is not the case with the Greeks. Given the role of the spear as the weapon of choice among the Greek princes, and the acceptance of the bow at the highest levels of Trojan society (esp. Paris), it is very significant that the Iliadic Heracles was an archer. He sacked Laomedon's city with his characteristic bow (as we find in later sources), and there has been a fundamental change in heroic weaponry through time. In his world of war in the *Iliad* Achilles faces no sea-monsters, as Heracles once did; but he does put his life on the line in a different way from Heracles by using a lethal weapon at a much closer distance than the bow and arrow.

The war for Priam's Troy in the *Iliad* therefore offers us a vision of something more modern, and something quite distinct from the old days of Heracles and Laomedon. The effect of the new conduct of war, at least where Troy and the Troad are concerned, is that human civilian society is now more vulnerable to heroic violence than it was in the past. The text makes it clear that the present war will be concluded in a more ruthless and unforgiving way than was the case with Heracles' sack of the city; and this is the subject of Chapter 4. Whatever Heracles did when he took Troy in the earlier generation (and the poem is not really very clear about this), the city was able to renew itself and to become a great and wealthy place again within a fairly short space of time. There is no sense of a residual collective trauma among the people at Troy as a consequence of Heracles' defeat of the place.

The different treatment of the city in the two generations is symbolized by the use of fire in the poem. References to fire in the *Iliad* convey the notion that the city will ultimately be obliterated by the army of Agamemnon. The war is not some kind of competition between two opposing sides, as we might see in a contest between heroes. Just as Achilles and Hector run in single combat for the life of Hector, not for a prize (cf. 22.157ff.), so it is for the very life of the city that the war for Priam's Troy is conducted. When it is defeated it will be burnt to ashes, just like the great warriors after their deaths.

The graphic presence of fire's destructive power in the narrative of the *Iliad* (and especially its association with Achilles after his return to the fighting), is a signifier of what the city can expect when the Greeks finally win the day.

The chapters of this book therefore, follow, more or less, the order in which events unfold in the two wars for Troy, especially the first sack of the city. Thus the sea-monster that attacks Troy in the earlier period is viewed, as far as the structure of this book is concerned, as a preliminary to the dispute between Laomedon and Heracles. And so it is dealt with in the first chapter. In any case, monstrosity is a signifier of earlier times in Greek myth, and so it is appropriate to begin with this subject. The killing of the monster precedes the dispute over the special horses, and it is this dispute that brings about the first war; and so the causes of the two wars (the immortal horses of Laomedon/Helen of Sparta) are dealt with, *inter alia*, in Chapter 2. This is then followed by an analysis of the different weaponry used in the struggles for Troy, which comes under the heading of 'Archers' in Chapter 3. And finally the sack of the city in both generations is dealt with under the heading of 'Fire' in Chapter 4. In this way the order of the four major symbolic themes dealt with in the book is meant to have a specific chronological relationship to the course of events as they unfold in the two campaigns for the city of Troy.

The central argument of the book therefore is that the *Iliad* needs to be read in the context of the heroic history alluded to within the poem itself. The references to earlier heroic conduct have a fundamental role to play in differentiating the world of the past from the poem's main story. The allusions themselves are scattered right throughout the text. The most complete accounts of earlier heroic conduct are situated in speeches made by the combatants in the war; but references also reside within speeches of gods, and within the narrative.[1] The speech of Glaucus to his opponent Diomedes on the battlefield is principally a long narrative of past heroic conduct (6.152ff.). Glaucus gives a detailed account of the heroic tasks performed by his grandfather Bellerophon in Lycia. As we shall see in the first chapter, this is a remarkable heroic narrative, not least because it provides a full account of a quest in which the monster (the Chimaera) is actually described. Other important narratives are told by the two old men on the Greek side at Troy.

Phoenix tells the story of Meleager's heroic 'deed' (*ergon*, 9.527) in which he saved his city from an invading force (9.527ff.); and Nestor also likes to talk about various military exploits in times past.

These sorts of narratives of past heroic conduct (sometimes called 'para-narratives') are important literary devices in the *Iliad*, and so they have been dealt with in some important recent studies.[2] The para-narratives give us a sense of the hero as storyteller, which is an important notion in both Homeric poems (cf. Achilles with his lyre singing of the 'glorious deeds of men' [*klea andrôn*, 9.189], shortly followed by Phoenix's account of Meleager [*klea andrôn*, 9.524]).[3] They tell us a lot about the interaction of the warriors in the armies, and so they can be important indicators of the 'political' climate within the two sides. And they have an important didactic function as mythical paradigms for the various participants in the conversations. It should be stressed at the outset, however, that the principal concern of this book is the function of mythological allusion to earlier generations of heroes in a broad sense, rather than the 'para-narratives' as literary devices *per se*. References to the first sack of Troy by Heracles, which are scattered throughout the poem, will have a particular importance in the pages that follow.

The deeds of earlier men, therefore, are evoked by the characters in the *Iliad* as heroic *exempla*, in order to convince the listener(s) of a particular point of view. Nestor's frequent rhetorical use of his past (like his speech at 1.254-84), and that of Phoenix (9.524ff.) fit into this category. Likewise, the memory of earlier heroic conduct is used to inspire a friend or to humiliate an enemy.[4] Agamemnon makes an attempt to encourage Diomedes by saying that he is not as good a fighter as his father was when he fought at Thebes. And he gives him an account of the glorious deeds of Tydeus in that particular conflict (esp. 4.387ff.).[5] Another battlefield episode which precipitates a reminiscence of earlier times is the encounter between Tlepolemus, the son of Heracles, and the Lycian chief Sarpedon. Tlepolemus uses the memory of the earlier generation of heroes to try to belittle his opponent in battle (5.633ff.). He compares his own father, an indisputably great son of Zeus, with his opponent Sarpedon, another son of Zeus. The comparison is between men of different generations, and the point of it is to show that Sarpedon is very much the weaker. It is here that Tlepolemus narrates the deeds of Heracles at Troy; and then Sarpedon gives his own reminiscence of the earlier war. There are occasions however when recent personal experience seems to have a more profound impact than stories from the distant past. The unfortunate Andromache in Book 6 does not need to reach out for the lives and deaths of earlier peoples in her plea to her husband. She needs only to talk about her own life and the loss of her family at the hands of Achilles to try to persuade Hector to stay within the city and defend its people from the walls (6.407ff.). Her suffering is recent and profound, but she is still unable to bring Hector around to her point of view.

Many of the important and memorable descriptions of earlier heroic conduct therefore are told in speeches uttered by the human participants in the war. They are an important part of the discourse of the human characters within the poem. But the gods too have an interest in the heroes of the past, and they seem to have a special interest in Heracles. His journey to Hades to fetch Cerberus from the Underworld is revealed to us almost in passing in a speech by Athena in a conversation with Hera (8.358ff.). This is the only reference to Cerberus in the *Iliad*, and it is an important one because it gives us a valuable early source for the '*catabasis*' (ie. 'descent to the Underworld') of Heracles (see Chapter 1). Similarly, the bow and arrows of Heracles, which he uses against the gods themselves, are alluded to in a speech by the goddess Dione on Olympus to Aphrodite, after the latter has been wounded by Diomedes (5.392ff., see Chapter 3). And the story of Heracles' earlier sack of Troy is alluded to briefly by the god Sleep to Hera (14.251). Sleep is not very keen to incur the wrath of Zeus a second time after what happened the last time that he used his powers against him (14.243ff.). On that occasion Hera took advantage of Zeus's sleep by attacking Heracles as he 'sailed from Ilios, after he had sacked the city of the Trojans' (*epleen Iliothen, Trôôn polin exalapaxas*,14.251). Allusions to earlier heroic conduct sometimes lie in the narrative of the *Iliad* too. It is the narrative of the poem, not the speeches, that tells us that Heracles had to contend with a monster at Troy when he was there in earlier times (20.144ff.).

The *Iliad* therefore reveals to us in a fairly general way, both through the mouths of the characters, and through the narrative itself, that Heracles was an active hero in the previous generation. The fact that his exploits are alluded to by gods and mortals in their speeches, and within the narrative itself, seems to reinforce the notion of his status as the earlier Greek hero *par excellence*. The whole world seems to have a good knowledge of the heroic deeds of Heracles.

In keeping with the style and character of mythical allusion evinced more generally in the *Iliad*, the references to the earlier sack of Troy vary from the explicit, where we are told quite clearly what happened in earlier times, to the very obscure. These suggest that there was a widely known myth that Troy was sacked in earlier times by Heracles and a small band of men (*hex oiêis sun nêusi kai andrasi pauroteroisin*, 'with only six ships and fewer men', 5.641). Tlepolemus and Sarpedon give us some precise details, although not very expansive ones, of what happened to Troy in earlier times, and why it happened (5.633ff.). Despite the fact that they are enemies on the field of battle, and that they have quite a hostile verbal encounter before they fight, they are both able to agree on the bare details of the first sack of Troy. Later in the poem too we get further brief but explicit references to the role of Heracles in the story of the sack of the earlier city (14.251; 20.144ff.).

In addition to these short but explicit references, there are also very obscure allusions to the story. Teucer is described by Agamemnon as a 'bastard' (*nothos*, 8.284), despite the fact that he is doing exceptionally well with his bow at the time that the comment is made. It is likely, although by no means certain, that an audience of the *Iliad* would understand the use of the word here as a reference to the story (found only in post-Homeric sources, such as Soph. *Ajax*, 1299-1303) that Teucer's mother is Hesione, the sister of Priam. It is she who, in later sources, is the intended victim of the sea-monster that besets Troy. She survives that particular encounter only to end up as a concubine to the Salaminian hard-man Telamon. It is in this relationship that she gives birth to Teucer. An alert audience of the poem might well have put together the single-word references to *kêtos* ('sea-monster', 20.147) and *nothos* ('bastard', 8.284) to understand that the story of Hesione is being alluded to in these passages.

So we can identify very different levels of detail in the mythical allusions of the *Iliad* - long narrations by human characters, short but explicit references, and oblique allusions. And sometimes there are different kinds of allusions even in the case of the same basic narrative, like the reign of Laomedon as king of Troy, and the sack of his city by Heracles. One of the questions that usually presents itself to scholars of the poem is what lies behind these allusions. There are numerous episodes where an argument can be put forward that the poet has incorporated material from earlier poems, which he then uses and adapts for his own poetic purposes. These earlier works may include poems that deal specifically with the exploits of earlier generations of heroes.[6] There is a distinct possibility, for instance, that an epic, or epics, on the subject of Heracles' exploits lie behind the Iliadic references to him, although in the end this must remain a matter of speculation.[7]

Another major question is what is the part played by the poet in the creative process of mythical allusion? It is possible that the poet invents a particular story himself as a mythical parallel for what is going on in his own poem. Malcolm Willcock has argued that many of the allusions referred to are actually the inventions of the poet, including some parts of the reminiscences of Nestor, and some of the Meleager story.[8] 'Homer' he writes 'has a genial habit of inventing mythology for the purpose of adducing it as a parallel to the situation in his story'.[9]

We can also assume that there was a large corpus of myth at the poet's disposal - that is, not specifically *poetic* versions of myth - and that this too has a role to play in the allusions to earlier generations of heroes.[10] All of our evidence for myth in early Greek antiquity comes from the surviving written texts and from the material remains (especially from vase painting). We have no actual evidence for the 'body of myth' out there in early Greek life; although it must have had a massive presence in the society of the time. In Heracles' case it has been argued, not least by Nilsson, that myths about his exploits may go back to the Mycenaean world.[11] And certainly the broad range of allusions to him in Homeric epic, not to mention Hesiod, give us the clear sense that his adventures are widely known in the world of the poet and his audience.[12]

Much is written on all of this, but it is not the task of this book to enter into the various levels of critical discourse on the subject of what lies behind the *Iliad*, and precisely what the audience knows, or does not know. The task of uncovering the pre-Iliadic corpus of verse and myth, and the audience's knowledge of it, inevitably involves a significant amount of informed hypothesis. But it is worth making the point that even if we could identify unequivocally a poetic 'source' or 'sources', for, say, the first sack of Troy by Heracles (which unfortunately we are unable to do), then we still need to ask some basic questions about what the allusions are doing in our text, and what function they have within the poem itself. For the most part, the working assumption of this book is that the poet, and probably his audience too, know the main stories about the earlier generations, or at least most of them, in some basic form (Ruth Scodel's view is that the 'main narrative of both the *Iliad* and the *Odyssey* expects a general, fundamental knowledge of earlier epic stories but does not rely on the audience to know many details').[13] They may know them from earlier texts (written or oral, depending on how one enters into that particular debate), or they may know them in some other way, from a more general exposure to myth. The poet presumably knows the stories in a more precise way than his audience; and some narratives are probably more familiar than others. But the evidence does seem to point to a fairly general awareness of the hero myths of the earlier generations to which the poem alludes.

Despite the general scholarly interest in the early figure of Heracles, and the likelihood that Heraclean epic lies behind the *Iliad*, the allusions in the poem to the first sack of Troy have never really attracted great attention among Homeric scholars. The exploit is often mentioned in passing as one of the many adventures of Heracles in earlier times.[14] And certainly the encounter between Tlepolemus and Sarpedon (which is the major allusion to it in the poem) is an important episode in its own right. But the story has never really captured the imagination of Homeric scholars.

The reasons for this are not very hard to identify. The Iliadic allusions to the Heracles-at-Troy story are scattered throughout the poem. By my count the combined number of lines devoted to the preliminaries of the earlier war (ie. the snatching of Ganymede, the horses of Tros/Laomedon, Poseidon and Apollo at Troy, the monster that terrorizes the city), and to the actual sack of the place by Heracles, is around about sixty-three. And these allusions are situated in at least eight different places throughout the poem (5.265-73; 5.638-51; 7.451-3; 8.284; 14.249-51; 20.144-8; 20.231-8; 21.441-60). This kind of scattered process of allusion is quite different from some of the more complete single narratives of heroic conduct (especially Bellerophon in Lycia, or Meleager's final defense of

Calydon, or the Pylian exploits of Nestor *etc.*). Indeed the first sack of Troy is scarcely a narrative at all in the *Iliad*, as much as a series of allusions to a complex mythical episode, which we then have to put together using later sources to fill in the gaps.

Even though the story of Heracles' defeat of the city is never told in a detailed and dedicated narrative, it does have a crucial role to play in providing an earlier temporal context for a similar kind of heroic endeavor to the main story of the *Iliad*. It is an account of a sack of Troy by Greeks within another story of a sack of Troy by Greeks. Thus the fall of Laomedon's city has a more specific relevance to the war for Priam's Troy than most of the other narratives of earlier heroic conduct in the *Iliad*. One recent and important book by Maureen Alden on the main para-narratives in the *Iliad* (see n. 2) offers an assessment of the main phases of the story and its importance (especially at 24 and 157-61). Alden's main concerns in her book lie elsewhere, but she deals with the allusions to the first sack of Troy in a basic way (in the Introduction and under the heading 'Genealogy as Paradigm'). The conclusion reached however seems rather narrow and disappointing from my perspective: 'although the information concerning Heracles' sack of Troy is let out in a piecemeal fashion by the poet and his characters, the cumulative effect of the snippets is to build up an impression of the Trojans as habitual cheats and deceivers. The city which defended a bad cause and fell to Heracles in the previous generation could fall again to the Greeks in the present generation' (24).

There is no doubt that Trojan perfidy is a central theme in the destruction of Laomedon's city, first in his dealings with the gods Poseidon and Apollo, and then with Heracles himself. And the same theme has its importance for the way that the later generations of Trojans are presented (on this subject, see Chapter 3). But it will be one task of this book to show that the allusions to the earlier sack of the city do a lot more work than Alden suggests here. Most of all, the scattered references seem to reflect some fundamental distinctions in the heroic landscape and in the nature of war across the two generations. Monsters in particular are consigned to the past in the *Iliad*, and the various references to them help to identify the character of the generational change that has taken place.

It has long been realized that the *Iliad* has quite a different attitude to the world of monsters and the supernatural from many other hexameter epics. In a very influential article on the subject Jasper Griffin highlighted many of the most important differences between Homer and the poems of the Epic Cycle.[15] His task in the article was to demonstrate the ways in which the fragments and summaries of the Cyclic epics reveal a fundamentally different character from the *Iliad* and *Odyssey*. He argues his case by systematic reference to a range of different subjects - 'the fantastic' (40), magical powers and miracles, life after death, the 'mythological exuberance' of the Cycle (45), and so forth. The general conclusion reached in the article (53) is that 'the strict, radical, and consistently heroic interpretation of the world presented by the *Iliad* made it quite different from the Cycle, still content with monsters, miracles, metamorphoses and an un-tragic attitude towards mortality, all seasoned with exoticism and romance, and composed in a flatter, looser, less dramatic style. The contrast helps to bring out the greatness and uniqueness of that achievement'. As far as accounts of monsters and 'exotic types' (40), like Amazons, are concerned, the article takes the view that the *Iliad* keeps them at a safe distance, partly by putting references to them into the mouths of the characters.

It would be hard to disagree with the main thrust of Griffin's paper, that the *Iliad* has a very different way of dealing with the fantastic from the Cyclic poems (although the path is not so smooth in the case of the *Odyssey*). The inter-textual approach of Griffin's article offers us some important insights into early epic; but it needs to be complemented by an extensive analysis of allusions to the subject within the *Iliad* itself. This book therefore takes Griffin's arguments further by exploring the way that the *Iliad* constructs the past (and, in some cases, the future), and manages to distinguish the generations from one another. It is certainly true to say that compared to the Cycle supernatural elements, like Centaurs and Amazons and sea-monsters, have been marginalized within the *Iliad*. But there is also an argument that they have been creatively included within the text as a foil for the poem's main story. The case will be made throughout this book therefore that there is more to the allusions to monsters and hybrids, and indeed to earlier heroic conduct generally in the *Iliad*, than Griffin deals with in his article.

The *Iliad*'s concern with the notion of generational change has its parallel in other early Greek hexameter poetry. One significant parallel is the evolutionary process in Hesiod's *Theogony* by which the cosmos unfolds, and the part that monsters have in representing an earlier era. The generational transferal of power within the cosmos culminating in the hegemony of the Olympians, from Gaea to Uranus to Cronus to Zeus, is characterized by an increasing prominence of the human form and the use of weapons like intelligence and fire (see Chapter 4). Zeus's defeat of the monster Typhoeus by fire (*Theog.* 820-69) is the sign of his final victory, and parallels his use of the same weapon against the Titans earlier in the text (687-735). The use of fire in the *Theogony* is a defining characteristic of Zeus's acquisition and retention of power against older or more primitive enemies.

Moreover Zeus's defeat of primitive monstrosity at the cosmic level parallels the defeat of the monsters on earth by the heroes (see especially Perseus, Heracles and Bellerophon at 270-336). The victory of the heroes over the monsters thus re-enacts a cosmogonic pattern, and has important implications for the cosmos as a whole. As Jenny Strauss Clay writes in a recent book on Hesiod 'the monsters arise early in the cosmogonic process and represent a kind of wild efflorescence whose continuation might imperil the final stability of the cosmos. The heroes, on the other hand, come into being at a later stage, after Zeus accedes to the kingship over the gods and after the Promethean settlement separating gods and men'.[16] Both the *Theogony* and the *Iliad* therefore recall the defeat of the monsters in different ways, with the *Iliad* in particular situating their defeat in a period of time that is quite distinct from its own main concern.

The same interest in generational transition is clear in Hesiod's *Works and Days* in the so-called World Ages (106-201). In this section of the poem there is a vision of five ages of human existence, four of them represented by metals - gold, silver, bronze and iron (the iron age is the poet's own day). Between the ages of bronze and iron is placed the age of heroes (156-73), which is therefore the fourth age, the 'race before our own' (*proterê geneê*, 160). The men in this group are characterized by their martial prowess, and specific reference is made to those who fought at Thebes, and at Troy for Helen's sake. Hesiod conflates the two main sites of epic conflict in the Greek tradition, Thebes and Troy, and brings together the various generations of heroes into one age. This is a very different vision from what we find in the *Iliad*. As we shall see in Chapter 1, the *Iliad* presents three different periods of human activity; first the 'earlier generations' of men (that is, heroes from different periods of the past, like Perseus, Bellerophon and Heracles); second, the men who fought in the war for Priam's Troy; and third, the men of the poet's own day (*hoi nun*). The gap between the poet's world and the world of heroes is apparent both in the *Iliad* and in Hesiod's World Ages. But it is noteworthy that the *Iliad* makes a significant distinction between the period of Achilles at Troy, and the world of earlier heroes.

The *Odyssey* too is concerned with the passage of time and with notions of generational change. It certainly does not state explicitly that the men of the poet's day (*hoi nun*) are inferior to the men of the past, as the *Iliad* does. And indeed many scholars are comfortable with the idea that the world of Odysseus probably bears a resemblance to the world of the poet. But there is an important distinction made between the generation of Odysseus, and the men who lived in the era before them. In Chapter 3 we will examine the implications of Odysseus' statement to the Phaeacians that earlier men were better with the bow than the current generation (8.223ff.). Odysseus says that he would not want to compete with the men of earlier times, Heracles and Eurytus, in an archery contest. These two men seem to represent a fundamentally higher level of skill with the bow, meaning that Odysseus himself is the weakest of the four archers whom he names (the order seems to be Heracles, Eurytus, Philoctetes, and Odysseus). But the point that he is making here is that there is no shame attached to coming fourth in this group, because the other three are all magnificent archers. Thus there is a strong sense of generational decline in the speech, at least as far as archery is concerned (cf. the steady decline in human fortune in the 'World Ages' of Hesiod). This notion of decline through time bears comparison with other speeches in Homer, especially the speeches of Nestor in the *Iliad* (see Chapter 1).

The men of the past may have been better archers than Odysseus, but the mere fact that the hero of the *Odyssey* is an archer at all signals a significant distinction in the use of weaponry from the *Iliad*, in which the leading Greeks are all spearmen. Odysseus in the *Odyssey* seems to re-enact the roles of the earlier generation of heroes. It has long been recognized that an early story of Jason seems to lie behind the wanderings of Odysseus, and this likelihood may go some way to explaining the character of some of Odysseus' adventures on his journey home.[17] Moreover, the many parallels between Odysseus and Heracles in the *Odyssey*, including their shared skill in archery, signal the fact that Odysseus moves through a world that has more in common with the adventures of Heracles than with the Trojan war of the *Iliad*. To some degree Odysseus is a kind of 'rival' to earlier heroes like Jason and Heracles. It will also be argued in Chapter 3 that the *Odyssey* draws on the more recent past too, on the story of Philoctetes' part in the defeat of Troy, in order to describe the breaking of the siege in Odysseus' own house on Ithaca.

The *Odyssey* therefore is very conscious of earlier heroic achievement, and proceeds to re-enact it in its own heroic context. The poem also has a fundamental interest in the life cycle and the passage through time of Odysseus and his family. The periods of time through which Odysseus moves in the course of his adult life are distinctly defined within the text – his earlier time on Ithaca, the war at Troy, the magical world of his maritime journey from Troy, and Ithaca again after his return. The fact that Odysseus cannot re-trace his steps and move back to the world of the fantastic is made clear by the loss of his various means of transport. The raft on which he sails from Calypso's island is abandoned (5.339ff., 365ff.); the veil that Leucothea gives him to get to Scheria is cast backwards into the sea (5.346ff., 458ff.); and the Phaeacian ship that transports him on the final leg of his journey from Scheria is turned into stone (13.153ff.). The Ithacan home of Odysseus and his family is set apart and made quite distinct in some significant ways from the realms of his earlier adventures. Thus for the most part, the *Odyssey*, like the *Iliad*, is concerned with the more human sphere of activity at Ithaca by separating it from the earlier legendary world of Troy and the magical world of his adventures.[18]

Another distinction between the two Homeric poems is that the *Iliad*, unlike the *Odyssey*, offers us a sense of *future* heroic action, one that is quite distinct from the present world of heroic conduct. The reference to Philoctetes in the Catalogue in *Iliad* 2 (724-5) foreshadows his eventual arrival at Troy, and his crucial role in helping to bring final victory to the Greeks. It will be argued in Chapters 3 and 4 that this reference plays an important part in conveying the notion that the ascendancy of the spear has its defined temporal limit. The 'world of Achilles' in the *Iliad* is entirely dominated by the spear; but the poem looks backwards (to Heracles) and forwards (to Philoctetes), to periods when the bow is a supreme weapon in the defeat of Troy. The *Odyssey* by contrast has no real interest in the notion of future heroic action beyond the resolution of the crisis in the house of Odysseus and his family.

It is worth noting, finally, that the *Odyssey*'s structure seems to correspond to the lifespan of a man. It is sometimes pointed out that the poem as a whole seems to be constructed around the passage through life of a man, beginning with a young man, and ending with an old one. The first four books, and most of the fifteenth (the so-called *Telemacheia*), deal largely with Odysseus' son Telemachus and his movement from the domestic world of his mother into the wider world of men (which means, in practice, becoming involved in counsel and armed conflict). The next eight books are concerned with Odysseus in the prime of his life - both his adventures at Troy and the various challenges that he faces in getting home. And then the second half of the poem deals in some important ways with old age and death. Indeed the resolution of the family crisis takes place, for the most part, with Odysseus in disguise as an old man who is maltreated by men of a younger generation who show him no respect (the disguise is first mentioned at 13.397ff.; cf. 13.429ff.). At the very end of the *Odyssey* the representatives of the three generations of the family all stand together in triumph - Laertes, Odysseus and Telemachus. The long-suffering Laertes in particular finds joy in the return of his son, and the fact that his grandson has come of age. In response to a discussion between Telemachus and Odysseus, in which the young man says that he will bring no disgrace to the line of his fathers (24.511ff.), Laertes verbalizes his delight when he says 'what a day is this for me, dear gods? I am extremely happy. My son and my son's son are having a quarrel about courage' (*tis nu moi hêmerê hêde, theoi philoi; ê mala chairô:/ huios th' huiônos t' aretês peri dêrin echousi*, 24.514-5).

Thus we are in a position to say that the surviving poems of Homer and Hesiod are very concerned in different ways with notions of the passage of time, and with generational change - at the cosmic level and within the human sphere. There is also the sense that this interest in the process of chronology and genealogical evolution operates across poetic texts as well as within them. Clay argues that Homer, Hesiod and the four longer Homeric Hymns need to be interpreted together, rather than in isolation, because they have a common interest in establishing the chronology of the cosmos throughout the generations. She makes a case that the four long Hymns fill a temporal gap between *Theogony* and the stable cosmos that we see in Homer: 'The Homeric poems show us the fully perfected and stable Olympian pantheon in its interaction with the heroes; the *Theogony* reveals the genesis of the Olympian order and ends with the triumphal accession to power of Zeus. Between theogonic poetry and epic there remains a gap, one that is filled by the Olympian narratives of the longer hymns'.[19] The concern of early Greek texts with evolution and generational change may therefore operate inter-textually, and even across genres, as well as within specific poems. The Epic Cycle's apparent concern to fill chronological gaps in the story of the Trojan war may have parallels in other early Greek hexameter poetry.

Despite the undoubted scope for further inter-textual analysis of generational change, both within the *Iliad* and outside it, I have undertaken in the following pages to focus largely on the *Iliad* itself.[20] The main task of this book is to explore the internal function of allusions to myths of earlier periods, rather than how these operate vis-à-vis other hexameter works. I have certainly brought the *Odyssey* and other literature into the discussion at various points in the book where I have felt that some benefit may be gained in doing so. But the *Iliad* presents us with a vision of war in the time of Achilles that is quite distinct from the earlier period, and we need to be very clear about what this means for the way that we read the poem.

This vision of war is inextricably linked to the choice of Achilles as the great spear-bearing warrior hero. The inclusion of stories about earlier individuals, especially Heracles, means that the two great heroes, past and present, are brought into relief; and this appears to be a deliberate poetic strategy. This vision of an earlier heroic background to the poem's main story raises the question of whether changes in actual military conduct in Greek history are reflected in the *Iliad*. The apparent transformation in the conduct of war within one generation may of course have its parallel in changes to fighting practices through time in Greek history (see

Chapter 3 on weaponry). Historical wars, both ancient and modern, are fought very differently through time, and the *Iliad* seems to be conscious of this in its own portrayal of the periods of Heracles and Achilles (not to mention the appearance of Philoctetes with his bow at the end of the war). It would be foolish to deny the possibility that the *Iliad* responds to historical changes in fighting practices in the early Greek world. But my own view is that this connection to Greek military history, if it can be established, is probably at the general level, not specific to a change in fighting practices within one identifiable generation.

Likewise the emphasis on generational change in the poem may tell us something about the broader evolution in the genre of early heroic epic. The *Iliad*'s apparent desire to make a significant distinction between the heroic conduct of Achilles and Heracles may be suggestive of some kind of wider distinction, even a rivalry, within the epic genre itself. Richard Martin argues that references to Heracles (and especially his connection with Oechalia) reveal that the *Iliad* is in direct competition with the poetic tradition dealing with Heracles: 'When Homer says that a poet returning from Oechalia was deprived of his art (ie. the treatment of Thamyris by the Muses at *Il.* 2.594-600) he can hardly be more explicit: this is a claim that the Herakles tradition is faulty, that it suffered a break in historical transmission from the event itself'.[21] The view put forward in Martin's book is that both Achilles as the poem's hero, and the *Iliad* as a whole, rival the traditions of earlier heroes, especially Heraclean epic. This is an important idea, especially in view of the way that Odysseus in the *Odyssey* seems to adopt characteristics of earlier generation heroes, and to re-enact some of their heroic tasks (as above). One might reasonably come to the view that the two heroes of the two Homeric poems both compete with the Heracles of earlier epic, but that they do so in very different ways. Odysseus is a kind of latter-day Heracles, whereas Achilles is essentially an un-Heraclean rival. The problem is, unfortunately, that we lack the evidence of earlier Heraclean epic to come to any definitive answer on this. This book is concerned in any case with the *internal* function of references to the previous generations of heroes in the *Iliad* itself, and so I have generally avoided speculating on broader questions of the evolution of earlier heroic epic.

My own view is that the emphasis on generational change in the *Iliad*, and the new level of devastation wrought on the Trojans in the later conflict, is the vision of a poet with a unique perspective of war, and the tragic dimension that it has for human society. He incorporates allusions to heroic history (and to other stories of life at Troy before the coming of the Greeks), to emphasize the suffering of the city as it lives out its final days. The force of fire in particular seems to symbolize the new level of destruction that organized military conflict on a large scale brings, or will bring, to the world of Troy - to the landscape (the burning Scamander), to the human participants in the war (especially Hector and his family), and to the city itself. Many readers of the *Iliad* have felt that this grim vision of a new world of war has resonances in the modern world, where the forces of fire and technology have been brought to bear in inventive and devastating ways against many different societies.[22] There is a certain timelessness about war, even though the conduct of it may change from generation to generation. The *Iliad* seems to have an unrivalled capacity to inform the various transitions that war undergoes through time, and the perennial human suffering that is its consequence.

Chapter 1
Monsters

"Fish also eat their food raw, *ômêstai* and *ômophagoi*, like lions, wolves and Achilles."[1] (E. Vermeule)

This chapter is mainly concerned with the revenge of Achilles, and the way that various quest myths seem to lie behind the narrative in the later books of the *Iliad*. The argument is put that the poet has adapted traditional myths to tell a story of warriors who operate in a very different kind of heroic context from the monster-slaying generations. The first part of the chapter briefly considers the evidence within the *Iliad* for the lives and quests of five heroes from earlier times: Pirithous, Heracles, Perseus, Jason and Bellerophon. These are all prominent hero figures from earlier generations in the corpus of Greek myth, and so it is no real surprise to see them referred to in the *Iliad* (albeit very succinctly in most cases). As we saw in the Introduction, it will not be the task of this chapter to enter into questions about what kind of earlier poetic corpora may lie behind these references, important though such questions are. The emphasis rather is on the myths themselves within the internal evidence of the text. What function do the references to earlier heroes have in the workings of the poem? Why do we receive such a different level of detail in each case? How do the textual references to the names of earlier heroes and their quests affect our reading of Achilles' actions, and those around him, within the poem?

To this end, the second part of the chapter is focused on the subject of how the different generations are dealt with in the poem. It is argued that the *Iliad* reveals two competing notions; one that the men of earlier times were superior to those at Troy because they had to fight against non-human creatures in remote parts of the world. This is stated emphatically by Nestor in his first speech in the poem - at the very moment that the men of earlier times are first mentioned (1.254-84). The extent of the support for this view among the leading Greeks at Troy is not clear, however; and it does seem to be important that the younger warriors do not make this assessment. The second notion, which is never explicitly stated, is that the transition in heroic conduct through time has taken place in such a way that the later generation is not inferior to earlier men. Different challenges and different weaponry reveal a different heroic milieu, but it is not one that is necessarily inferior to times past. The case is made that Nestor's view runs counter to the treatment of the generations of heroes within the poem itself. Despite the many differences in the world of heroes through time, and the different demands and expectations of the new breed of young men, the best warriors at Troy do not admit inferiority to anyone, be it to Heracles or Pirithous or Tydeus. Nestor does not necessarily speak for his younger comrades when he draws unfavorable comparisons with the men who went before them.

The central argument of the chapter is that the traditional heroic quest of monster-slaying is a dominant mythic theme that lies behind the story of Achilles' defeat of Hector in the final part of the *Iliad*. The case will be put that an inversion takes place in the final books in which Achilles is an epic hero of such monstrous violence that he bestows great heroic status on those who have to confront him. References to earlier heroes and monsters have the function of informing the transformation that Achilles undergoes within the course of the poem. In short, Hector's task of confronting the furious Achilles is a conscious response to the quest narratives of the older generations of heroes. His is a 'modern day' quest against a great warrior, but the violence of his enemy is informed throughout by reference to monsters. Likewise the ransom mission of Priam to bring his son's body back is constructed around the traditional quest myth in which death is confronted every step of the way. The heroic tasks of the son (Book 22) and the father (Book 24) in confronting Achilles are modeled on the same core mythic theme, although both are adapted in significantly different ways. The body of Hector, the young victim of the first failed quest, becomes the object of the following successful quest of his father, the old man Priam.

1. Monster-slayers

We start with the old man Nestor who straddles the generations (1.247ff.), and who indulges in frequent reminiscences of earlier times (cf.1.254ff.; 4.308f.; 7.124ff.; 11.670ff.; 23.629ff.). His age and his role as a counselor and political operator often have him evoking the world of the past, and so he plays a major part in revealing how the world has changed between the generations. And when he makes an intervention into the dispute between Achilles and Agamemnon at the very beginning of the poem, he pleads for peace by evoking the earlier generations of men (1.254-84). He states that Achilles and Agamemnon are younger than he is, and then claims that he himself has mixed with, and been respected by, better men than they are (1.259-61). He then supports his claim by referring to six earlier warriors: Pirithous, Dryas, Caeneus, Exadius, Polyphemus, and Theseus (1.262-5).

Nestor argues that these six men represent the highest qualities of heroic might and courage.[2] And he is quite clear about how to measure such a claim - the fact that they fought and defeated the beast-men of the mountains.[3] He says that the earlier generation were 'the mightiest of men reared on the earth, mightiest they were, and they fought with the mightiest, with the mountain-dwelling beasts, and terribly did they destroy them' (*kartistoi dê keinoi epichthoniôn traphen andrôn:/ kartistoi men esan kai kartistois emachonto,/ phêrsin oreskôioisi, kai ekpaglôs apolessan*, 1.266-8). Nestor's intervention in the dispute provides us with the first references in the *Iliad* to the men of the past.[4] A major theme within the speech is that Agamemnon and Achilles are not as great as they think they are when one brings the earlier warriors into the picture ('with them [*sc.* the earlier warriors] could no man fight, of they who are mortal and are now upon the earth', *keinoisi d' an ou tis/ tôn hoi nun brotoi eisin epichthonioi macheoito*, 1.271-2; cf. 1.260-1).

So Nestor tells us that the earlier warriors were the mightiest (*kartistoi*), and that the creatures which they fought are now gone, after the triumph of the humans against them (*apolessan*). It seems that the later generation could not hope to emulate the deeds of these earlier men, even if they wanted to, because the beasts themselves - these particular beasts anyway - have gone forever.

And yet, despite the warrior greatness that these six men are supposed to evince, most of them are not referred to very significantly in the *Iliad*. Dryas, Exadius, Polyphemus and Theseus are not mentioned again, and Caeneus' name (in patronymic form) recurs only once, as the father of Coronus, and therefore the grandfather of Leonteus (in the Catalogue, 2.746).[5] It is only the Lapith Pirithous about whom we really learn something within the *Iliad* itself, and we never really learn very much at that. In the Catalogue (at 2.740ff.) we are told that Polypoetes, a co-commander (with Leonteus) of forty ships from northern Thessaly, is the son of Pirithous and Hippodamia. The passage points out that Pirithous is the son of Zeus, which means that Polypoetes can claim Zeus as his grandfather. Polypoetes himself was conceived to Hippodamia 'on the day when (Pirithous) got his vengeance on the shaggy beasts, and threw them out of Pelion, and drove them to the Aethices' (*êmati tôi hote Phêras eteisato lachnêentas,/ tous d' ek Pêliou ôse kai Aithikessi pelassen*, 2.743-4). This probably refers to the most renowned encounter of Pirithous - the fight between the Lapiths and the Centaurs at the wedding of Pirithous and Hippodamia. The brawl broke out when the Centaurs got drunk and tried to rape the women at the wedding, including the bride Hippodamia herself. Pirithous is also named (and described as 'equal of the gods in counsel') in the long list of Zeus's previous affairs with women. He is the first offspring named in the list (at 14. 317-8), as the product of Zeus's earlier lust for Ixion's wife (*oud' hopot' êrasamên Ixioniês alochoio,/ hê teke Peirithoon, theophin mêstôr' atalanton*).

So we can say in the first instance that Pirithous and his adventures seem to be well known to the poet and his audience - so well known that important details of the story are left out.[6] The tribal name Lapithai is not used in the references to Pirithous in Books 1 and 2 (although it is at 12.181), which is probably an indication that the story is very well known. Likewise it seems to be significant that the word 'Centaurs' is not used of Pirithous' battles: they are just called *'phêres'*, 'beasts', either 'mountain-dwelling beasts' (*phêrsin oreskôioisi*, 1.268), or 'shaggy beasts' (*phêras lachnêentas*, 2.743). Thus the poet alludes to traditional mythic narratives of Pirithous in the barest possible way, and he seems to be working on the audience's awareness of the main features of the story. As with most of the reminiscences of earlier heroes by the characters in the *Iliad*, we can make the observation that poetic versions of Pirithous and his adventures may lie behind these references to him and the Centaurs. Kirk argues, on linguistic grounds, that hexameter poems with an Aeolic character might lie behind the allusions.[7] It is equally possible that mythical narratives of the story – not specifically poetic versions of them – form the main background to the references. Of particular interest to me in this chapter is the nature and content of the allusions to the earlier heroes, and the fact that in this case there is so little interest in describing the actual physical form of the Centaurs whom Pirithous confronts. This is also true of most other monsters and hybrids referred to in the *Iliad*, and I will address this issue in a moment.

The most distinguished hero of the generation before the Trojan war is Heracles whose activities are referred to throughout the *Iliad*. Even though Heracles' own son Tlepolemus fights at Troy (5.628ff.), and therefore, chronologically speaking, he is not very distant at all, in essence he seems to represent a world that is long gone.[8] Emphasis is placed on his heroic encounters in diverse parts of the world, including fighting with gods. There are two specific confrontations with monsters; first, the journey to the Underworld to fetch back Cerberus (8.358-69), and second, his defeat of the sea-monster, the *kêtos*, that terrorized Laomedon's Troy (20.144ff.). There is not much in the way of detail about either of these stories in the poem, but their inclusion, even in an abbreviated form, is still worthy of note.

The Cerberus quest is mentioned only in passing by Athena, who has her own axe to grind against Zeus. She refers to the story in response to Zeus's support for the Trojans who have pushed the Greeks back towards the ditch (8.335ff.). Hector is very prominent in this conflict, and is described as 'having the eyes of a Gorgon or of Ares, plague of mortals' (*Gorgous ommat' echôn êde brotoloigou Arêos*, 8.349). When Hera wants to support the Greeks in the conflict (8.352ff.) Athena complains that Zeus has forgotten the goodwill that she herself had shown to Heracles at the request of Zeus himself. She refers specifically to Eurystheus' sending of Heracles to the house of Hades of the gates 'to lead the dog of hateful Hades from Erebus' (*ex Erebeus axonta kuna stugerou Aïdao*, 8.368). Heracles himself 'would not have escaped the steep-flowing waters of Styx' (*ouk an hupexephuge Stugos hudatos aipa rheethra*, 8.369) without her help. Cerberus is not even named in this passage (just called the 'dog', 'kuna', 8.368), which again suggests rather strongly that the story is well known in the poet's world (*Theogony* 311 is the only place where Cerberus is actually named [and called 'flesh-eater', *ômêstên*] in the whole of Homer and Hesiod; cf. the further description of him at *Theog.* 769ff.).

The other Heraclean exploit involving a monster in the *Iliad* is part of the story of the first sack of Troy. We saw in the Introduction that the story of the first attack on the city is alluded to in a scattered way in the *Iliad*, rather than as a more complete paradigm narrative.[9] The basic account of this Heraclean expedition, much of which is told in post-Homeric sources, is that, on Zeus's command, Poseidon and Apollo did menial work for a year for Laomedon, king of Troy. Poseidon (or Poseidon and Apollo, *Il.* 7.446ff.) built the wall, and Apollo tended the cattle on Mt. Ida (*Il.* 21.441ff.).[10] When the year was completed Laomedon broke his word and refused to pay them. He even threatened to tie their hands and feet and sell them off to islands far away, and chop off their ears (21.450ff.). In response to this outrageous threat, Apollo sent a plague, and Poseidon sent a monster to ravage the city. Poseidon's monster is alluded to, but not described, in the *Iliad*: it is simply a sea-monster (*kêtos*, 20.147) that once terrorized the place. The Trojans and Pallas Athena built a wall for Heracles for 'when (the monster) drove him from the sea-shore on to the plain' (*hoppote min seuaito ap' êïonos pedionde*, 20.148). The Trojans try to appease the monster by roping Laomedon's daughter Hesione to a rock and presenting her as an offering (Hesione is not named, nor is this episode explicitly alluded to in the *Iliad*). Heracles makes a timely arrival in the Troad and volunteers to free the girl and kill the monster if he receives Laomedon's horses in return (the horses are referred to at 5.648ff.). These are probably the horses that Tros received from Zeus in recompense for the taking of Ganymede (5.265ff., cf. 20.230ff.).

After Heracles performs his feats Laomedon again breaks his word, and refuses to give over the horses (5.648ff.).[11] An expedition is then mounted by the Greeks led by Heracles to sack the city, which they duly complete 'with only six ships and fewer men' (5.633ff.; cf.14.251). Part of the process of sacking the city and distributing the booty is that Hesione is then given over as a prize of war to Telamon, the Salaminian (cf. Sophocles' *Ajax* 1299-1303). Telamon and Hesione then produce Teucer the archer figure, the half brother of Ajax (which may explain the reference to Teucer as a 'bastard' in the *Iliad* [*nothos*, 8.284; on which see below, Chapter 3]).[12] If one assumes that Hesione is Teucer's mother in the *Iliad*, then he fights against his mother's city now ruled by Priam, his maternal uncle. Teucer is a human 'product' of an earlier conflict between the two same peoples who now endure a second and larger struggle outside the city walls. Heracles' sack of Troy therefore lies behind the poet's narrative of the more renowned siege, but we only get glimpses of this story in the *Iliad* itself.[13]

Thus a major part of the renown of Heracles in the *Iliad* is his confrontation with monsters - Cerberus in the Underworld, and the sea-monster at Troy. These confrontations complement references to his other heroic encounters, including shooting arrows at Hera and Hades, which causes great pain to both gods (5.392-404).[14] Monster-slaying, fighting with gods, descent to the Underworld, and archery are germane to the earliest Heracles (his famous club probably being a post-Homeric invention). The *Iliad* quite clearly distinguishes these Heraclean attributes from the profile of Achilles who operates in an entirely different landscape and heroic context. It seems to be in keeping with the *Iliad*'s general focus on human form and human limitations that there is absolutely no attempt to give any kind of full detail of the monsters that Heracles confronts, just the bare allusions to them (ie. *kuna* [8.368] / *kêtos*, [20.147]).[15]

Essentially the same sort of bare allusive process is at work in the case of Perseus and his great opponents the Gorgons. Perseus is not actually mentioned in the same context as the Gorgons in the *Iliad*, and in fact he is named only once in the whole of Homer (although the patronymic *Persēiadao* is used to describe Sthenelus at *Il*.19.116 and 19.123). The reference to Perseus himself is in the long list of Zeus's affairs where he is mentioned as the child of Zeus and Danaë, and where he is 'pre-eminent over all men' (*pantôn arideiketon andrôn*, 14.320).

The gorgon on the other hand is referred to three times in the *Iliad*. The first of these is the description of the *aegis* worn by Athena (5. 741-2). On this is set, *inter alia*, the 'head of the terrible monster, the Gorgon, terrible and awful, a sign of Zeus the aegis-bearer' (*en de te Gorgeiê kephalê deinoio pelôrou,/ deinê te smerdnê te, Dios teras aigiochoio*, 5.741-2; cf. *Od*.11.633-5). Then in Book 8 Hector, who is carrying all before him, 'has the eyes of a Gorgon or Ares, plague of mortals' (*Gorgous ommat' echôn êde brotoloigou Arêos*, 8.349, a description which precedes Athena's allusion to Heracles and Cerberus). And then in Book 11, as he arms himself for battle, Agamemnon's shield 'has on it the grim-eyed Gorgon glaring terribly, and around her were Terror and Rout' (*têi d' epi men Gorgô blosurôpis estephanôto/ deinon derkomenê, peri de Deimos te Phobos te*, 11.36-7). The Iliadic references to this particular quest, therefore, such as they are, are much more concerned with the Gorgon herself and with the fundamental terror which her image is supposed to inspire in men. As a consequence of Perseus' quest the gorgon has been transformed from being a 'real' threat to humans in earlier times, to a mere image or device to evoke or to inspire fear. As with the Centaurs mentioned by Nestor, she is a threat no longer. Moreover she is never actually called 'Medusa' in the *Iliad*, which is in keeping with the reluctance of the poem to go into much detail about the creatures who are confronted in these sorts of quests.

So we can say in the first instance that the stories of Pirithous, Heracles, and Perseus seem to be very well known within the world of the warriors at Troy in the *Iliad*, and within the world of the poet himself and his audience. It is also perfectly clear from the implicit comparison made in the text (and from the explicit comparison of Nestor at 1.254-84), that the current world of the war at Troy is a very different kind of heroic environment from these earlier times. There also seems to be a conscious desire on the poet's part to limit the attention devoted to the monsters; hence the Centaurs whom Pirithous fought are merely wild beasts (*phêres*), Cerberus is an unnamed Underworld dog (*kuôn*), and the sea-monster at Troy is just a *kêtos* without any description of its physical form. Likewise the Gorgons are menacing creatures for mortals, the sorts of figures that might properly bedeck a shield; but there is no clear description of their physical forms and their powers, and no explicit connection in the text with Perseus at all.

The pattern of poetic composition is clear: allusion to the earlier quests of heroes is made without the revelation of much in the way of specific detail about precisely what form the confrontations took. And we can come to the same conclusion in the case of Jason who is alluded to three times in the *Iliad* (7.467ff.; 21.40ff.; 23.740ff.). In his case again there is a bare minimum of detail, and no reference at all to his Colchian encounters. The closest Iliadic reference to the Argonautic expedition is the mention made of Hypsipyle on Lemnos as the mother of Euneus by Jason (7.467ff.).[16]

The bare and allusive way in which the feats of earlier heroes are recalled serves only to emphasize the description of Bellerophon's adventures in Greece and Lycia, which are told in much greater detail (6.145-236). In the case of Bellerophon we have a reasonably complete account of his heroic adventures, although the length and detail of it are presumably limited by the fact that it is narrated in the midst of battle.[17] The story is told when the Argive Diomedes and Lycian Glaucus meet in battle (6.119ff.). The initial exchange between them is all about identity. Diomedes' superior profile as a warrior, which has been demonstrated to us in Book 5 where he even wounds the gods Aphrodite and Ares, is suggested by the fact that he is unsure who Glaucus actually is (6.123-5, although he may be saying this an insult to his opponent). Glaucus, by contrast, knows Diomedes well enough and he is quite prepared to acknowledge his identity (6.145).

It is significant, given the different character of heroic conduct between the generations referred to in his speech, that Glaucus begins his answer with a reflection on the nature of generational change (a reflection, which, it must be said, involves no qualitative difference from one generation to another): 'great hearted son of Tydeus', says Glaucus, 'why do you ask about my lineage? Just as is the generation of leaves, so is it also of men. As for the leaves the wind scatters some to the ground...so too of men, one generation springs up and another ceases' (*Tudeïdê megathume, tiê geneên ereeineis;/ hoiê per phullôn geneê, toiê de kai andrôn./ phulla ta men t' anemos chamadis cheei...hôs andrôn geneê hê men phuei hê d' apolêgei,* 6.145-7 and 149). Glaucus then provides the story of his own lineage, which culminates in the recognition that he and Diomedes have a historic guest-friendship relationship. This remote and unexpected relationship is commemorated by the exchange of armor between the two of them, in which Diomedes receives gold for bronze.

Glaucus' account of his ancestry focuses largely on his grandfather Bellerophon whose adventures led him from Greece to Lycia. The story again reveals the memory of a world whose characteristics were very different from that of Glaucus himself. Bellerophon is sent by the Argive king Proetus to his father-in-law, the king of

Lycia, after charges of sexual misconduct are made against him by the king's wife Anteia (6.156ff.). In keeping with the usual pattern in this kind of heroic narrative (and in keeping with the pride that Glaucus reveals in his grandfather) Bellerophon is innocent of the charges made against him (6.160ff.). After his arrival in Lycia, and a period of nine days of entertainment, the Lycian king reads the folded tablet signs that Bellerophon brought with him, which state that he should be put to death there (6.172ff.).

The king then sends him out on various quests in the hope that he will be killed; and so Bellerophon has four separate encounters against different enemies. First of all he has to confront and kill the Chimaera (6.179ff.); next he fought with the Solymi (the 'mightiest battle', *kartistên…machên*, 6.184-5); then he killed the Amazons ('equals of men', *antianeiras*, 6.186; cf. Priam at 3.189); and finally he killed all the best men of Lycia when they ambushed him upon the king's command (6.187-90). The Lycian king then recognized that Bellerophon, having succeeded in all the tasks thrown up at him, was a 'noble offspring of a god' (*theou gonon êün*, 6.191); and so he kept him there and gave him his daughter and half his kingdom (6.191ff.).

The first task of Bellerophon, to kill the Chimaera, is of most interest to us in this chapter, and the description of this creature runs as follows:

prôton men rha Chimairan amaimaketên ekeleuse
pephnemen: hê d' ar' eên theion genos, oud' anthrôpôn,
prosthe leôn, opithen de drakôn, messê de chimaira,
deinon apopneiousa puros menos aithomenoio.
kai tên men katepephne theôn teraessi pithêsas.
(6.179-83)

'First he commanded him to kill the raging Chimaera.
She was of divine stock, and not of men,
a lion at the front, a snake at the back, a goat in the middle,
and terribly she breathed out the force of blazing fire.
And he killed her trusting in the signs of the gods'.

So the Chimaera is distinct in three ways, and these correspond to the three lines 6.180, 181, and 182. First, she is of divine stock (*theion genos*); second, she is a hybrid of three different animals - lion, snake and goat; and third, she uses as her weapon the terrible force of fire. These three elements combine to make her the most formidable of creatures, and this therefore is the first and most terrible challenge that Bellerophon must confront (*prôton men*, 6.179). The characteristic adjective *amaimaketê* (6.179, 'raging' [Janko] or 'invincible' [Kirk]) helps to reinforce the terror that it inspires (cf. 16.329 where the same adjective is used of the Chimaera again).[18] Bellerophon defeats the creature, trusting in the signs of the gods (*theôn teraessi pithêsas*, 6.183), and is then confronted with his other challenges.

Much of the scholarly interest in this story is directed towards how it operates as a literary device (a 'para-narrative'), and what it is telling us about the two individuals who meet and talk. The combatants exhibit very different temperaments and attitudes, and the culmination of the meeting is the unequal exchange of armor between them, where gold is handed over for bronze (6.232ff.). The encounter between them is a kind of verbal contest that actually ends up replacing the need for physical fighting. Diomedes obviously gets the better of Glaucus in terms of the relative value of the armor (6.234-6), but the verbal exchange between them is played out at a much more subtle level.[19]

In some ways therefore the story of Bellerophon and his Lycian adventures plays a secondary role to the actual encounter of the two warriors on the field of battle. Moreover, the whole episode is an important early account of cross-cultural contact between east (Lycia) and west (southern Greece), and there may be significant historical implications to this contact.[20] But our concern in this chapter is with the myth itself, and the fact that we have here a clear and unequivocal description of an entire heroic quest against a monster, together with an explicit statement of the tasks that were set. The Bellerophon narrative is a noteworthy inclusion in the *Iliad*, not least because it represents our only 'complete' monster-quest from the earlier generations of heroes.

It is equally significant that this is the only complete description of an exotic hybrid. The passage (6.179-83) might be thought of as the 'exception that proves the rule' that Homer is keen to avoid explicit images and descriptions of monsters in the *Iliad*. Geoffrey Kirk rightly points out in his Cambridge commentary that 'such monsters (*sc.* as the Chimaera) are rare in the Homeric Epic which steers clear of animal mixtures (Centaurs are the exception) and other Near Eastern *exotica*'.[21] As we saw in the Introduction, the *Iliad* is very different from the Epic Cycle in this regard, but the fact is that Kirk could have been even more emphatic about how significant the present passage actually is. For the Centaurs in the *Iliad* (1.268; 2,743) are really treated quite differently in the text from the Chimaera, in so far as there is no explicit statement of precisely what their physical form is. And even Chiron's physical form is not made clear to us in the four references to him in the *Iliad* (4.219; 11.832; 16.143; 19.390). I am not arguing that a different physical form from the usual hybrid one lies behind the references to Centaurs in the *Iliad* (although Leaf did in his commentary).[22] In fact the absence of any reference to a particular physical form probably implies that the poet has no interest in departing from the usual one in the ancient sources.[23] But the point is simply made that the appearance of Centaurs is left unelaborated, which is not the case with the Chimaera, whose physical features are presented to us with considerable clarity.

We are dealing therefore with a unique passage in the *Iliad*, but one that also raises a lot of questions. There is the usual issue of what might lie behind the narrative, and the extent to which Homer might have adapted earlier accounts.[24] It is certainly possible that the passage is an abbreviated version of a longer poetic version of the story. Linked to this is the question of why there is no room for the winged horse Pegasus in the story? Explicit reference to the hybrid form of the Chimaera might have provided a fine opportunity for the inclusion of Pegasus into the narrative. But he is left out of Glaucus' story, and there are probably important implications to this.[25]

So is it possible to identify a rationale for the detail provided of this particular myth - including the monster - when no other such quest in the poem receives anything like the same treatment? In an attempt to answer this question, the argument will be put that this narrative is described in full detail because it helps to inform the central conflict of the poem between Achilles and Hector in Book 22. It will be argued in section 3 of this chapter that the placement of the quest of Bellerophon (6.152-211) *within the wider narrative* of Hector's brief return to his family at Troy (6.116-8 and

237-529), points to the kind of task that Hector will have to confront at a later stage in the action of the poem.[26] The foreshadowing of Hector's looming confrontation with Achilles (in his conversation with Andromache, 6.407-93) has an integral and unusual structural connection with Bellerophon's quest in the distant past (6.152-211).

But, before proceeding with these arguments, a few brief comments to conclude what we have seen so far. First, the stories of the earlier generations of heroes, and the monsters which they confronted, are widely known, although perhaps not universally known, by the characters in the poem. We cannot say with any certainty how much Agamemnon is supposed to know about Pirithous and the Lapiths and the Centaurs when he listens to Nestor talking about them (1.254-84); but we can certainly assume that he knows all about Perseus and the Gorgon from the fact that he has her on his shield (11.36-7). Likewise Diomedes, as an Argive, may know the story of Bellerophon and the Chimaera well enough, but he may only just discover that he has a historical connection with Glaucus and his family (6.215ff.). Tlepolemus and Sarpedon both know the story of the first sack of Troy so well that they offer to each other complementary - but not contradictory - accounts of what actually happened at the time (5.633ff.). There is a widespread consciousness among the men at Troy of the stories of earlier men, and it is not only old Nestor who is aware of them through personal experience. Second, the audience appears to know these quest narratives so well that bare allusion to them is a standard technique on the part of the poet. This means, amongst other things, that many of the individual allusions to monster-slaying in the *Iliad* (not including Bellerophon and the Chimaera) have little light to shed on our knowledge of these mythical narratives as a whole.

We could conclude, therefore, that these allusions are not very important in the poem, because of the economical way with which they are usually dealt. The focus of the *Iliad* is firmly on human form and human limitations, not on monsters, or monster-slayers. And it is true that, individually, many of these brief references may not have great importance in the poem as a whole. But collectively they convey the sense of a recent past that was fundamentally different from the world of Agamemnon and Achilles and Hector. In a time prior to the war at Troy great individuals confronted fearsome creatures, the likes of which seem no longer to roam the earth (note *kai ekpaglôs apolessan*, 1.268, and the killing of monsters by Bellerophon and Heracles). The first sack of Troy seems to have been a *personal* triumph of one man against a monster, and also of a man (with a small force, 5.641) against a city.

But the new breed of heroes must acquire their renown through war alone, as part of a huge collective expedition (cf., on the size of the expedition, Priam at 3.182-90). Individual ambition, even among the mightiest warriors at Troy, must now be satisfied within the more complex structures of a vast Greek expeditionary force. The changes in the heroic landscape mean that war is a very different kind of heroic pastime from what it was in Heracles' time. This 'new world of war' suits some more than others, and the *Iliad* has a central concern with a crisis that arises in the Greek army between two men of very different heroic temperaments and two very different fates.

2. The Generations of Heroes

Broadly speaking the *Iliad* identifies three periods or phases of human activity.[27] These can be listed as follows: first of all there is the world of earlier heroes and warriors, the pre-Trojan war generations, the likes of whom we have just been examining. These are not all contemporaries: Bellerophon is the grandfather of Glaucus, whereas Heracles is the father of Tlepolemus. Likewise Perseus is a much earlier figure than Heracles and Jason and Pirithous (cf.19.114ff.). The Trojans too have a clearly defined line of kings from Dardanus on Mount Ida to Laomedon in the previous generation. But for our purposes in this chapter all these men may be grouped under the heading of the 'earlier generations'.

Then there is the generation of those who are fighting the war at Troy, those with whom our poet is chiefly concerned. Clearly within this group too, some, like Achilles, are younger than others, like Agamemnon. Achilles is also younger than Odysseus, who says to him that 'I am older-born and I know more'(*proteros genomên kai pleiona oida*, 19.219). These in turn may be younger than Idomeneus, if the grey fleck in his hair is anything to go by (13.361). The actual ages of people are never mentioned in the *Iliad*, but there seems to be a general consciousness of the relative ages of the individuals who take part in the conflict. Nestor's son Antilochus, like his father, is one who is very conscious of age: 'for Ajax is only a little bit older than I, but this man (Odysseus) is of an earlier generation and of earlier men' (*Aias men gar emei' oligon progenesteros estin,/ houtos de proterês geneês proterôn t' anthrôpôn*, 23.789-90).

Then, last of all, there is the world of the poet himself, the men of today (*hoi nun*). This last generation is sometimes compared with the warrior figures in the poem, and they do not shape up well. Thus, at 12.381ff., Telamonian Ajax's capacity to lift a huge rock with which to kill Epicles is duly compared with the capacity of today's men (*hoioi nun brotoi eis'*) to lift such a rock. The passage is quite emphatic that the men of today could certainly not perform this feat, not even a young man who used both of his hands (12.381-3; cf. Hector shortly afterwards at 12.445ff.). Likewise Aeneas picks up a stone to throw at Achilles, 'one which two men could not carry, such as men are now' (*ho ou duo g' andre pheroien,/ hoioi nun brotoi eis'*, 20.286-7; cf. Diomedes at 5.302ff. where exactly the same language is used [5.302-4, of Diomedes =20.285-7, of Aeneas]). The poet's unfavorable comparison of men of his own time with the men of the Trojan war offers a parallel to the point made by Nestor in his first speech in the poem (1.254-84). A central aspect of Nestor's speech is the unfavorable comparison made between the warriors embarked on the current war (*hoi nun*, 1.272), and the great men of earlier times (including, presumably, Nestor himself!): 'and I fought as my own man; but with these (*sc.* the 'beast-men', or Centaurs) could no man fight today, of those who are mortal upon the earth' (*kai machomên kat' em' auton egô: keinoisi d' an ou tis/ tôn hoi nun brotoi eisin epichthonioi macheoito*, 1.271-2).

Thus, the men of the two later periods (the Trojan war generation, and the men of the poet's day) are both explicitly compared with the generations that precede them, and they usually come off the worse. Homeric epic is retrospective and idealized, and so generational transition sometimes means generational decline. Nestor (1.254ff.), and the poet himself (5.302ff.;12.381ff.; 12.445ff.; 20.286ff.), are both suggesting a declining scale in the physical prowess of men through the ages, with privilege and preference given to those who went before. A similar idea comes from Agamemnon who chastises Diomedes for not being the equal of his father (4.370ff.). Tydeus fought and killed a whole force of Cadmeians on his own, and Agamemnon refers to this to inspire the son to greater things (cf. Athena at 5.800ff.).

Diomedes himself does not offer a reply, out of respect for Agamemnon (4.401ff.), but his charioteer Sthenelus has plenty to say (4.404ff.). 'Son of Atreus, don't tell lies when you know how to speak the truth. We claim that we are much better than our fathers: we took the seat of seven-gated Thebes, leading a smaller army under a greater wall (*sc.* than our fathers), placing our faith in the signs of the gods and in the help of Zeus. But they perished through their own recklessness. So do not ever set our fathers in equal honor with us' (*Atreïdê, mê pseude' epistamenos sapha eipein:/ hêmeis toi paterôn meg' ameinones euchometh' einai:/ hêmeis kai Thêbês hedos heilomen heptapuloio,/ pauroteron laon agagonth' hupo teichos areion,/ peithomenoi teraessi theôn kai Zênos arôgêi:/ keinoi de sphetrêisin atasthaliêisin olonto/ tô mê moi pateras poth' homoiêi entheo timêi*, 4.404-10).[28]

The stridency of the challenge to older authority from somebody of Sthenelus' secondary rank leads us to anticipate a rebuke of some sort. And so it happens that the charioteer is quickly put in his place by Diomedes (4.412ff.). It is very significant however that Diomedes does not actually disagree with anything that Sthenelus says about the respective qualities and abilities of the generations of warriors. 'Good friend' he says 'stay silent, and obey my word; for I will have no resentment against Agamemnon, shepherd of the people, for urging on the well-greaved Achaeans to fight. For glory will follow for him, if the Achaeans slaughter the Trojans and take holy Ilios' (*tetta, siôpêi hêso, emôi d' epipeitheo muthôi:/ ou gar egô nemesô Agamemnoni, poimeni laôn,/ otrunonti machesthai euknêmidas Achaious:/ toutôi men gar kudos ham' hepsetai, ei ken Achaioi/ Trôas dêiôsôsin helôsi te Ilion hirên*, 4.412-6). Thus Agamemnon has good reason to make his exhortation, and it is quite understandable to Diomedes himself. But certainly at no point does Diomedes agree with what he has to say about the respective qualities of him and his father.[29] It is a reasonable inference that Sthenelus' views on the subject of generational merit may be widely held by the *promachoi* of the day, including Achilles and Diomedes themselves. But it is also significant that none of them ever offers explicit support for the kind of view that Sthenelus puts forward in this passage.[30]

There is an obvious danger for the poet of the *Iliad* in privileging the earlier generations of warriors in this way. If the audience takes Nestor at his word that the earlier heroes surpass those at Troy, then the logical conclusion is that our poem is populated with figures of the second rank. They may be preeminent in their own time, but they are still inferior in a wider temporal context. And this includes Achilles himself, who is on the receiving end of the comparison made by Nestor. It would obviously be intolerable if circumstances were created within the epic where Achilles was viewed by the audience as a poor man's Heracles, or a second-rate Pirithous.[31] And yet that is precisely what Nestor seems to be saying to the disputants in Book 1 (esp. 271-2).

This raises a problem, which may interrogated like this: if we take Nestor at his word that confronting hybrid monsters is the ultimate heroic challenge, then where does that leave the generation with no monsters to kill? Is Achilles' heroic excellence diminished by the fact that in the *Iliad* he lives his life in a world where the organized violence of large-scale war is the only heroic *modus operandi*? In short, how great is the 'best of the Achaeans' really when one brings the earlier heroes into the picture?

The first answer to these questions is that the *Iliad* is very careful not to scrutinize with any degree of precision the comparative worth of *individual* heroes across the generations (unlike Odysseus in the *Odyssey*, 8.219ff., who explicitly compares his own archery skills with those of Heracles and Eurytus [and Philoctetes]). The bare allusions to earlier quests provide no real scope for specific comparison between the generations, just a vague sense of a time when a different kind of heroic regime prevailed. The text implies a general consciousness of the comparative worth of individual warriors who fight in the *same* campaign at Troy (eg. 'Telamonian Ajax was by far the best of the warriors whilst Achilles continued to rage', *andrôn au meg' aristos eên Telamônios Aias,/ ophr' Achileus mênien*, 2.768-9 [cf.17.278-80; 18.192-3; and *Od*.11.550-1]. And indeed a comparison is made even of the best horses that they drive (those of Achilles and Eumelus at 2.763-7).

But the same sort of comparison in individual ability does not usually operate through time. As we have seen, sons are sometimes compared with their fathers, as Agamemnon does in the heavy-handed piece of battlefield rhetoric with Diomedes and his father Tydeus (4.370ff.).[32] And Tlepolemus compares Sarpedon, the son of Zeus, unfavorably with his own father Heracles, also a son of Zeus. But these rhetorical encounters in battle are clearly designed either to inspire or to infuriate the warrior on the receiving end of them. Nestor too indulges in his comparison primarily to make the most out of a bad situation within the Greek army. And he does so with some degree of caution by not embarking on a specific comparison between individuals across the generations. It is significant that Nestor's comparisons in Book 1 are made at the *general* level, and there is no attempt to move beyond this.

But more important still is the fact that the different generations are perceived to have weaponry that is appropriate to the specific tasks which individuals must confront. We shall examine weaponry in much greater detail in the third chapter of this book, but it is appropriate to make just a few general comments here. The main transition in the use of weapons through time in the *Iliad* is from the bow (esp. of Heracles) to the spear (esp. as a weapon of Achilles). This is neither a complete nor a universal transition. The bow and the spear were both used in the past, just as they are both used in the second attack on the city, as described in the *Iliad*.[33] But as far as the greatest heroes are concerned, Heracles and Achilles, and the two wars that are fought for Troy, there has been a fundamental change in weaponry. This change is in keeping with the more extensive transformation in the nature of the world within the same period. The weapons of these two individuals in the *Iliad* help to symbolize a fundamentally different heroic climate between the generations. The apparent smoothness of this transition in weaponry has the effect of establishing a continuum in heroic conduct between the generations in the midst of a changing landscape and social context. The core elements of the heroic life remain essentially intact, despite the very different challenges with which individuals have to deal. The spear is appropriate for Achilles in his world, just as a bow was appropriate for Heracles in his. There is no shame attached to Heracles in the *Iliad* at the fact that he used to fight with a bow in earlier times. And there is no element of weakness attached to Achilles because he fights no monsters, or because he fails to embark on some kind of descent into the Underworld. Both heroes operate in the appropriate way within their own heroic milieus. In this sense there is a continuity in heroic excellence across the generations, although it manifests itself differently in each case.

Thus, Nestor's speech notwithstanding (1.254-84), there is no need to think of a general decline in heroic excellence in the *Iliad* between the first and the second phases.³⁴ But rather, we can identify a process of adaptation where core heroic values are retained amidst changing heroic contexts and landscapes. Putting one's life on the line is still the keynote of heroic conduct in the later generation, as it was earlier, but the character of it in the *Iliad* changes very significantly through time. The *Odyssey*, as an epic poem based on heroic adventures at sea, offers us a return to the world of monsters and archery, which the *Iliad*, as a 'land epic', leaves well behind.³⁵ Odysseus embarks on a whole range of challenges that require numerous weapons appropriate to the tasks involved (including the bow). But again this kind of weaponry is seen to be appropriate to the heroic context in which he operates (cf. below, Chapter 3).

Thus the transition in the *Iliad* from the world of monsters in the immediate past to the world of mass organized violence in the present, involves two competing ideas. The first is that the previous generations are fundamentally superior, especially those who had to fight with non-human creatures like Centaurs (this is the view of Nestor in his speech). The second is that the world has changed in many ways, which means that the conduct of a heroic life is different from beforehand, but not necessarily inferior to it. Nestor may certainly subscribe to the former, but there is no great sense in the poem that it is held by the younger generation of warriors. Diomedes is not prepared to give an inch to Agamemnon on the subject of his own ability, vis-à-vis that of his father Tydeus (4.401ff.). And Sthenelus' challenging view about the superiority of the younger warriors at Thebes might even receive quiet support from those around him (4.404ff.). And even Glaucus tells his story without any sense of a decline in heroic worth across the generations. Glaucus' concern is to link himself to a great family line, not to diminish the heroic nature of the war in which he finds himself.

The *Iliad* manages, through isolated allusions, to portray a distinctive and distinguished heroic past, one that precedes the Trojan war, without allowing it to overshadow the current generation of warriors and their feats in battle. The gap however between the second and third phases of human activity, between the men of Achilles' time and those in the poet's own world, is definitely real, not least because the poet himself is quite explicit about it (5.302ff.; 12.381ff.;12.445ff.; 20.286ff.). In this case there is no attempt made by the poet to establish a continuum of talent and worth among men from the time of the Trojan war. Indeed the epic operates on the basis that things were grander, and men were bigger and braver, in the time of Achilles than they are in the poet's day.

3. The Quest: Hector and Achilles

We have been examining the way that the reader of the *Iliad* is presented with the idea of a continuity in basic heroic conduct in the midst of the many changes that are envisaged to have taken place across the generations. Heroes in the world of Achilles still chase after great material prosperity, and acquire undying renown, as they did in earlier times; but they do so in a different social climate, and within a very different value system. Another manifestation of this in the *Iliad* is that monstrosity, or the nearest thing to it, now resides within the human form, not in the outer world of nature, as it once did. As we have seen, the individual quest - brave man against terrifying monster - was the hallmark of earlier heroic conduct. It was clearly not the only *modus operandi* of earlier heroism: Bellerophon battled Amazons, and fought whole armies of men; and Heracles fought gods and attacked Pylos and sacked Troy. Earlier heroes had a variety of challenges to confront, and this diversity of experience comes through in the *Iliad* itself. But the battle with the monster is the principal measure of heroic greatness in earlier times, as Nestor himself points out (1.262ff.).

The *Iliad*, therefore, with its focus fixed firmly on human aspirations and human suffering in the struggle for the life of a city, could have dispensed entirely with this sort of old-fashioned personal quest by consigning it to the dustbin of mythical history. The *Iliad* could speak to us with a message that 'the monsters of the past and the heroes who fought them are irrelevant in this new vision of heroic conduct based solely on the conflict of man against man in warfare'. But rather what we find is that the old quests are alluded to within the text and then woven into the description of the struggle between the invaders and the defenders of the city. The text is clear that a monster (*kêtos*) beset Troy in the previous generation (20.147); and one may be said to do so again in the new campaign, within the course of the *Iliad* itself, although he is a human being in brilliant Olympian armor. It is the fundamental terror that Achilles inspires, the fact that he is a *deinos anêr* (a 'terrible man', 11.654) that lies behind the new kind of quest with which the *Iliad* is concerned. The final books of the poem describe two very different personal quests from the ones that we have been examining. Hector's confrontation with Achilles in Book 22, and Priam's mission to get his son's body back in Book 24, both appear to be conscious responses to the various quest-narratives of the past to which the *Iliad* repeatedly alludes. The principal Iliadic quests are man against man, Trojan against Greek, but the heroes and monsters of the past help to inform the main action in the last part of the poem.

Early Greek mythical narratives of heroes and monsters, therefore, enhance the description of Achilles' awesome physical presence, and the frenzy of his return to the battlefield. In the cultural context of early Greece, and within the tradition of heroic poetry, there is no better way to convey the terror that Achilles inspires in his enemies than by a conscious response to the quest-myth of man against monster. Like most things of dread in the *Iliad* Achilles is '*deinos*', 'terrible', 'fearsome', 'dire' (cf. *deinon* in the description of the Chimaera's fire, 6.182). It is actually his friend Patroclus who describes him in this particular way, in a speech to Nestor, well before the return of Achilles to the fighting: 'you know well, old man nurtured by Zeus, what he is like, a terrible man' (*eu de su oistha, geraie diotrephes, hoios ekeinos/ deinos anêr*, 11.653-4). Achilles is a man of extremes, and Patroclus knows this better than anyone (cf. 16.33-5 in which Patroclus accuses him of being pitiless [*nêlees*], and being born from the grey sea and towering rocks). The narrative of Achilles' return to the fighting pays considerable attention to his emotional, and even to his physical, transformation. The implicit notion running through the last part of the *Iliad* is that no-one in the war has ever seen anything quite like Achilles when he returns to the fighting after the death of Patroclus. This is a special moment in a long conflict, not just another day in battle.

So the Trojans in general, and Hector in particular, now have to confront something much more and much less than a man. Achilles brings against them Olympian power and an otherworldly capacity for violence. His special background as the child of Thetis, and his awesome prowess in battle, enable him to marshal powers from the different spheres of the world for the sake of his revenge. He is a kind of hybrid in one sense - a mortal man who can bring to bear against the Trojans a range of different weapons, from Olympian fire and immortal armor and a special spear made by a Centaur, to the ferocity and cruelty of wild, flesh-eating animals.

This mixture of various elements seems to suggest a rather different kind of hybrid status from the hero figures in Hesiod, who are quite distinct from the monsters in being a combination of two different elements, the mortal and the divine. Jenny Strauss Clay has recently explored the hybrid nature of monsters and heroes in Hesiod, and stressed the need to analyze their roles within the cosmogonic process as a whole: 'while the monsters come into being spontaneously in their exuberant disorder, the heroes are the products of a distinctive divine intervention that momentarily blurs the boundaries between gods and men. Yet for all their differences, these two hybrid species are linked in so far as the heroes are the instruments of the monsters' destruction'.[36] The remarkable thing about Achilles in the later books of the *Iliad* is that he is a hybrid just like Hesiod's heroes (and like Sarpedon and Aeneas), but that he acquires, within the course of the poem, the added element of monstrosity.

Thus it is partly for this reason, as it seems to me, that the poem alludes repeatedly to monsters - the fact that collectively they enhance the vision of precisely what the Trojans have to confront in the person of Achilles in the later books of the poem. The idea of the monster is never allowed to disappear from the reader's consciousness. It is probably not a matter of chance that the *kêtos* which terrorized Troy in the previous generation is referred to in the very book in which Achilles makes his return to the fighting (20.147). Hector says that Achilles is the greatest bane to the Trojans (*su gar sphisi pêma megiston*, 22.288; cf. 22.421-2), and so he effectively replaces the real sea-monster which afflicted the city in earlier times (cf. Patroclus to Achilles at 16.33-5). The emphasis in the *aristeia* is on the eating of raw flesh (esp. 21.22ff.; 21.122ff.; 21.203ff.; 22.345ff.) and the fact that he feeds on the blood and suffering of his enemies (cf. 19.209-14). Achilles' rejection of food and drink (19.206-14; 19.303-8; 19.319-21; 19.342ff.), and the emphasis on raw flesh, are really different sides of the same coin after his decision to return to the fighting. Even the flight of Hector from Achilles in his Olympian armor (22.131ff.) seems to bear resemblance to a man running from a monster (Perseus running from the Gorgon sisters?).[37] Likewise, the triple nature of the Chimaera bears comparison with Achilles: a divine background (*theion genos*) = 6.180;[38] a fearsome and animal-like nature = 6.181;[39] and the use of blazing fire as a major weapon = 6.182 (on the subject of Achilles and fire, see below, Chapter 4). The tripartite form of the creature seems to have a special relevance to Achilles; and the explicit description of it in the text may be explained by this connection.[40]

And so in a general and implicit way, Achilles, as he returns to battle, seems to bear comparison with other terrifying creatures, notably the sea-monster at Troy, the Gorgon, and the Chimaera. But this association is not as textually explicit as we find in some later literature, or indeed in early Greek art. Given the frenzy that grips Achilles after the death of Patroclus, and the ferocity of his *aristeia*, one might have expected some kind of direct comparison with a monster; or perhaps a description of him carrying an image of an appropriate monster somewhere on his armor. Either of these techniques could have been used to offer quite emphatic and explicit indications of just how violent and cruel he is in these particular books.

In later post-Iliadic sources the armor of a warrior often helps to inform the man who wears it in some important ways. In Vergil's *Aeneid* the Rutulian hero Turnus, an individual who is modeled partly on Homer's Achilles, bears a graphic image of the Chimaera on his helmet:

> *Ipse inter primos praestanti corpore Turnus*
> *uertitur arma tenens et toto uertice supra est.*
> *cui triplici crinita iuba galea alta Chimaeram*
> *sustinet Aetnaeos efflantem faucibus ignis;*
> *tam magis illa fremens et tristibus effera flammis*
> *quam magis effuso crudescunt sanguine pugnae.*
> (*Aen.* 7.783-8)

> And Turnus himself among the leaders with an excellent
>   physique
> goes forth in his armor, taller by a whole head.
> His helmet bedecked with triple plume
> has high aloft an emblem of a chimaera,
> breathing Etna's flames from its jaws,

roaring and spreading terror with its destructive breath
more and more as the battles grow grimmer and the blood
flows freer.
(R.D. Williams, trans).

Vergil makes it abundantly clear at the outset of the Iliadic *Aeneid* that the Chimaera's fiery nature informs Aeneas's new opponent in Italy. The reference is appropriately placed as the new war commences to anticipate the role of Turnus within the rest of the poem. Turnus has only just been blasted by the fury Allecto (7.445ff.), who uses a torch, a whip, and two snakes to drive him into the war against the Trojans. The Chimaera, an image of which also appears in the Underworld of the *Aeneid* 'armed with flames' (*flammisque armata Chimaera*, 6.288), is an eminently suitable creature to express the kind of *furor* that besets Turnus after his demonic infection. Further to this is the sense in which Turnus is 'the other Achilles in Latium' (*alius Latio...Achilles*, 6.89; cf. 9.742) prophesied by the Sibyl, against whom Aeneas will have to fight a new 'Trojan war'. The fiery nature of Turnus as he prepares himself for the looming war is therefore quite an explicit Vergilian parallel to the figure of the Homeric Achilles in his *aristeia*. Moreover, the figure of the monster helps graphically to convey Turnus's state of mind.

There are other literary descriptions of apparel or armor which inevitably associate the bearer of the image with the creature/s depicted on it (cf. *Od*.11.609-14 [Heracles' belt]; the pseudo-Hesiodic *Shield of Heracles*; and Aeschylus' *Seven Against Thebes*, 359-652 [the shields of seven generals]). As with the helmet of Turnus in the *Aeneid*, these images help to inform the men who bear them. And indeed Achilles himself in some later post-Homeric sources is depicted carrying images of monsters. This is certainly the case in the visual sources from an early period, in which Achilles frequently bears the Gorgon and other such creatures on his shield.[41]

Similarly, the later description of the arms of Achilles in the *Electra* of Euripides (452-75) alerts us to the terror that he brings to Troy (for the effect on the Trojans of Achilles and his armor, note *Elec.* 456). In the first stasimon of the *Electra* the chorus describes the creatures that are pictured on Achilles' armor: Perseus on the rim of the shield with the Gorgon's head and a pastoral Hermes (457ff.); in the center of the shield, the sun with his winged horses, and Pleiades and Hyades (464ff.); on his helmet, sphinxes with their prey (470ff.); and finally on his breastplate, the 'fire-breathing lioness' (= Chimaera, *purpnoos... leaina*, 473-4), and Pegasus.[42] It is worth noting here the variety of the creatures on Achilles' armor. As with the shield of Agamemnon in the *Iliad* (11.32ff.), the terror which the armor is meant to inspire is certainly not limited to just one creature.

So the representations of monsters (including the Gorgon and the Chimaera) occupy central places on the arms of Achilles in early Greek art and in the *Electra* of Euripides, just as the image of the Chimaera is carried by Turnus, the 'other Achilles', in Vergil's *Aeneid*. These post-Homeric representations have their parallel in the *Iliad* itself with the shield of Agamemnon (11.32ff.). This has the Gorgon and other formidable figures on it, and its presence within the poem at least reminds us that the *Iliad* is quite prepared to present such images on the shield of a warrior if it has an interest in doing so. Agamemnon's shield prepares us, appropriately enough, for his *aristeia* to come. It seems to anticipate the effect that he will have on the field of battle until he is wounded and has to make a departure from it.

But nothing like this happens in the case of Achilles, who has a much more extensive and brutal *aristeia* than Agamemnon. The images on Achilles' shield in the *Iliad* (18.478ff.) include just about everything other than monsters. It has five circles with a diverse series of images on it: cosmological representations (earth, heavens, the sun and moon, stars etc., 18.483-9); the city at peace (two cities, with descriptions of marriage celebrations and a legal case, 18.490-508); the city at war (a siege of a city by two armies, the ambush of a herd and its consequences, 18. 509-40); the farming year (18.541-72), cattle and sheep herding (18.573-89), the dance (18.590-606); and finally Oceanus on the shield's outermost rim (18.606-7). The whole world seems to be on the shield of Achilles, but there is not a single monster in sight. The disappearance of monsters from the heroic landscape within one generation in the *Iliad* seems to be reflected in the images on the shield of Achilles itself. The emphasis is on the lives and societies of human beings, and their place in the world.

The complex character of the images on Achilles' shield provides a challenge for the most determined of literary scholars.[43] The ecphrasis has inevitably precipitated a diverse range of critical responses, some of which draw on the internal evidence of the Homeric poems themselves, others drawing on evidence from outside of the text, including the material remains of early Greek antiquity. In light of the preceding discussion, it is important to bear in mind what is *not* on the shield, as well as what is on it. A conscious effort seems to have been made in the composition of the poem to offer something completely different from what Agamemnon has on his shield (11.32-7), and from what Athena has on the aegis (5.741-2).[44] The description of Achilles' shield seems consciously to avoid the representation of a monster or monsters by focusing on more complex images of human society and the cosmos. This apparent avoidance of monsters is all the more significant because a violent image would seem so appropriate for the forthcoming fury of Achilles. As Oliver Taplin puts it: 'the joys of civilization and fertility on our shield are peculiar. Why all this and not the usual horrors?'[45]

One answer to this is that the horrors are not necessary because they are there in the man. The association of Achilles with monsters has been woven into the image of the hero in other ways. There is no monster on Achilles' shield in the *Iliad* because there is no need of one, because traditional hero myths have been adapted in different ways throughout the poem. The extended description of the shield therefore focuses on other aspects of the world, and it is generally in keeping with the human focus of the poem, and with the Olympian manufacture of the armor. The early vase painters, who often present Achilles with a Gorgon on his shield, have no real scope to deal in the adaptation of myth in the same complex way that Homer does in his epic.[46] Their shield images have to convey the terror that Achilles inspires in his enemies in a single frame. So they offer something quite distinct, and quite different from the *Iliad*, but more appropriate to their own medium. And even Euripides in his *Electra* uses the armor of Achilles in a single extended passage to convey something of his formidable presence in the battles at Troy.

Homer however conveys this kind of terror in different ways throughout the whole poem, including much earlier than the presentation of the shield to him in Book 18. We see this in one important way as early as Book 6 where there is a fundamental textual connection established between the quest of Bellerophon in Lycia, and that of Hector against Achilles at Troy. The unusual structure of Book 6 points to the notion that Hector's looming confrontation with Achilles will be a kind of latter-day quest of the sort that Bellerophon once conducted against the Chimaera.

Book 6 of the *Iliad* is really dominated by two heroes and the very difficult challenges that they face. These challenges are confronted in two different generations against very different kinds of enemies. The first narrative describes the adventures of Bellerophon in times past (two generations before the war at Troy), and deals with the tasks that he undertook on the instructions of the Lycian king (the Chimaera, the Solymi, the Amazons, and the ambush of Lycian men, 6.145-231). He overcame everything that was thrown up at him, including the Chimaera, and he was rewarded with a royal wife and a kingdom of his own. But even he ultimately encountered the hostility of heaven (although we never learn why in the *Iliad*). The emphasis therefore is on the triumphant nature of Bellerophon's life, not surprisingly seeing that his grandson tells the tale in a proud speech to a prominent enemy warrior.

The other quest, that of Hector against Achilles, is yet to come, much later in the poem, but the anticipation of it hangs over the lives of the Trojan participants in Book 6 (esp. 6.390ff.). In keeping with the *Iliad*'s principal focus on the human form, this quest will be against a man, not a monster. And even though at this early stage of the poem there is no explicit statement against whom Hector will fight his great battle, Andromache's anxiety seems to make it quite clear.[47] Despite Hector's great success earlier in the book in lifting morale among the Trojans (at 6.108ff. the Greeks think that some god has come from heaven to rouse them!), Andromache meets him and immediately enunciates her fear of his imminent death (6.407ff.). She tells him that his might (*menos*) will be his death (*phthisei se*, 6.407).[48] She then narrates all of the terrible actions that Achilles perpetrated against her family (6.408ff.): he killed her father, her seven brothers, and he even enslaved her mother before accepting ransom for her. Achilles has brutalized her and her family, and Andromache is concerned to remind Hector of the fact as soon as they meet.

Hector himself in reply (6.441ff.) is in no position to offer her any confidence that he will survive what is coming up for him. His concern for his wife and his son matches her concern for him; but there is no confidence whatever that he and Troy will overcome the challenges that they face. It may have been Diomedes who was the prominent warrior in the recent fighting (esp. Book 5, *passim*); and indeed it is Diomedes' dominance in battle that is the ostensible reason for the return of Hector to the city in the first place (cf. 6.96ff.; 6.277f.; 6.305ff.). But it is Achilles whose presence hangs over the life of the family as they meet for the only time in the narrative of the poem.

Iliad Book 6 therefore looks back to Bellerophon and the Chimaera (etc.), two generations before the current conflict, and it looks forward to Hector's fateful confrontation with the awesome killer of Andromache's family. It is also significant that these two quests have an integral connection within the structure of Book 6. At the beginning of the book the Trojans are not doing well in the fighting (6.1-71), and in response to this Helenus urges Aeneas and Hector to get them to hold their ground (6.77ff.). He then urges Hector to go inside the walls to get the women of the city to make prayers and offerings to Athena. Obviously Helenus could do this second task for himself, and there is no need to take the best warrior on the Trojan side out of the fighting. But the scene is being set for a series of meetings between Hector and his family, and especially with Andromache and Astyanax. After rousing the Trojans for the fight (6.102ff.) Hector duly turns around and goes back into the city (6.116-8). It is at this point that Glaucus and Diomedes meet on the battlefield (6.119ff.), an encounter which is quickly followed by the story of Bellerophon and his adventures in Lycia (6.145ff.).

Thus it is very important that the story of Bellerophon's quest (6.145-231) resides within the narrative of the meeting of Diomedes and Glaucus (6.119-236), which in turn lies within the account of Hector's return to the city (6.102-18 / 6.237ff.). Or, to put it another way, the account of Hector and his return to his family 'frames' the meeting of Diomedes and Glaucus, which in turn 'frames' the narrative of Bellerophon and the Chimaera. The narratives of Diomedes and Glaucus, and Bellerophon in Lycia, could have been placed quite separately from Hector's return to the city. There is no specific need for them to sit within the narrative of Hector. The obvious alternative to what we find in our text (with a need only for a minor linguistic adjustment), is to describe the episodes one after the other; first of all Hector's return to Troy (continuing at

6.119), and then Glaucus and Diomedes / Bellerophon in Lycia.[49] It seems clear that the structure of the text as we have it is consciously *connecting* (not just *juxtaposing*) the stories of Bellerophon and Hector. The placement of one narrative within the other seems to point to a fundamental connection between the actions and the lives and deaths of the two heroes.

So the argument here is that Hector will have to fight his own 'Chimaera' later in the poem, just as Bellerophon did in time past; and that this is being signified by the unusual connection of the two main parts of Book 6. The story of Bellerophon and the monster is therefore an important part of the 'foreshadowing' of the doom of Hector with which *Iliad* 6 has a major interest.[50] It informs the kind of task that awaits Hector by connecting it to an earlier heroic context. Whilst Bellerophon and Hector are alike in the virtuous natures that they exhibit, they certainly conduct quests that have very different outcomes. In Hector's case there will be no triumph, not least because the gods abandon him when he most needs them (22.166ff.). In the account told to us by Glaucus, Bellerophon could count on the gods to support the tasks that he is set, both in his journey to Lycia (6.171), and in his actual fight with the Chimaera (6.183). But this is not the case with Hector in his quest, despite his courage and his piety. Athena, who is the recipient of Trojan prayers and offerings in Book 6, plays a crucial role in his eventual defeat and death (esp. 22.177ff.). The power of Achilles, and the weapons that he can bring to bear, make this ultimately a very uneven contest. The contrast in human fortune could scarcely be more stark than between the parallel heroic quests of Bellerophon and Hector in *Iliad* 6 and 22.

Book 6 therefore has an important role to play in foreshadowing Hector's task against Achilles; and the text links this challenge to the quests of Bellerophon in times past. Mythological allusion to monster-quests within the poem seems to take the place of more direct allusion to monsters (such as we might have found on the shield of Achilles). My own view, therefore, is that the detailed description of the Chimaera is specifically included in the text of the *Iliad* at this point and in this way because it has fundamental relevance to the looming task of Hector in facing Achilles. The divine stock of Achilles, his wild animal nature, and the fire with which he is associated, parallel the essential attributes of the Chimaera, and they give a clear sense of what kind of challenge Hector is going to have to confront later in the poem.

It has been stressed in this part of the chapter however that the text at no point explicitly links the warrior to the monster in the way that some later ancient sources do. And yet the audience of the poem may have known a narrative that gives added meaning to the essential attributes of both Achilles and the Chimaera. There is a story, one that is not referred to in Homer, that Thetis was a shape-shifter, and that Peleus had to wrestle with her in her different appearances so that he could marry her.[51] He finally managed to do so and was then married to her, although probably still against her will (cf. *Il*.18.429-34). It does seem to be significant that the forms that she takes on to escape his advances are the shape of a lion and a serpent, as well as the physical force of fire. These elements are strikingly close to the features which help to define the Chimaera of the *Iliad* (6.180-2): she is of divine stock, a hybrid of three animals (lion, serpent and goat), and she breathes out as a weapon the terrible force of fire. The story of the shape-shifting of Thetis, first mentioned in the fifth-century BC by Pindar (*Nem.* 4.62ff.), seems to convey the notion that these same features are, so to speak, 'in Achilles' blood' through Thetis. The *Iliad* of course prefers to dispense with explicit versions of these sorts of stories, and we are not even in a position to say with any certainty that Homer was aware of such narratives.[52] They may however lie behind the poem, and give added meaning to the notion of Achilles as a kind of hybrid of man, god, and monster, one who brings an otherworldly kind of terror to his opponents on the battlefield.

4. The Quest: Priam and Achilles

We can infer from all of this that allusions in the *Iliad* to earlier heroic encounters with monsters have a specific thematic connection to the main single combat between Achilles and Hector in Book 22, and that this connection is established as early as Book 6. The comparatively few important passages in which the exploits of the earlier heroes are narrated, and the complete absence of monsters from the later world of Troy, can sometimes make us assume that the poet has entirely left behind the patterns of action of hero myths of the former generations. But, as we have seen, the monsters may have disappeared, but the basic patterns of heroic action have not. A man can become a monster if certain things happen to him in life - and they happen to Achilles when he loses Patroclus. Monstrosity of form need not necessarily accompany monstrosity of action, just as a god in Homer can seem, to all intents and purposes, human. All the different levels of existence can operate within an outwardly human appearance. In the final books of the poem Achilles is both an epic hero himself, and one whose violence and cruelty also bestow heroic status on those who have to confront him. As we have seen, the first such quest ends with the death of Hector and the mutilation of his body. But the final books of the *Iliad* deal with two quests to confront Achilles, not just one. We now turn briefly to the second quest, the ransom journey of Priam to retrieve his son's body in the final book of the poem.

It is one thing for a young warrior like Hector to confront the violence and cruelty that Achilles perpetrates on his enemies, but quite another for an old man to do so. After Hector fails in his quest against Achilles, it falls to Priam to embark on one of his own. The physical remains of one failed quest (ie. Hector's body) now become the object of the second quest. The aim of most quests is to bring something back, and this is certainly the task for Priam. The body of Hector requires burial, and so Priam's aim is to get it back, and thereby unite the Trojans in an appropriate funerary ritual. It falls to Priam to heal the suffering of his entire community. But Hector's recent fate only increases the desire of the Trojans that their king should not follow in his son's footsteps. Andromache, Priam and Hecuba had all pleaded with Hector not to go and face Achilles (6.407ff.; 22.38ff.; 22.82ff.). Better to stay inside the walls and try to fight off defeat from there. But Hector will not be denied, even if he eventually runs away at the sight of Achilles in his Olympian armor (22.131ff). In Priam's case the mission seems so foolhardy to his fellow Trojans that serious questions are raised about his state of mind: 'Alas' says Hecuba 'where has that wisdom gone for which you used to be renowned among strangers and among those over whom you rule?' (*ô moi, pêi dê toi phrenes oichonth', hêis to paros per/ ekle' ep' anthrôpous xeinous êd' hoisin anasseis*; 24.201-2; cf. 22.408ff.). Hecuba's funereal wailing (*kôkusen*, 24.200) at the thought of Priam's departure signals her initial perception that the venture will end in certain death for her husband (cf. 24.206ff.).

Hecuba does not actually say it in as many words, but old men are not really meant to undertake quests like this. It is a young man's task, and it is not for those who are unable to meet the physical demands involved (cf. Vergil's response to this, with his account of Priam and Hecuba in *Aeneid* 2.515ff.). The heroes Jason, Bellerophon, Perseus *et al.* are usually young, and the confrontation with the monster is a youthful rite of passage in many cases. But the *Iliad* has a way of turning up surprises, and of radically adapting traditional mythic themes. Old age, as it turns out, proves to be an advantage for Priam in his mission (24.486ff.), not least because of the impact that it has on Achilles himself (24.507ff.). It is really love and courage and the favor of the gods that help in the success of this quest. The physical power of youth was not much use to Hector in the face of Achilles' wrath, especially when the gods turn from him. In the final book of the *Iliad* old age succeeds where youth has just failed. Priam, trusting in the signs of the gods (as Bellerophon did, 6.183; cf. 6.171), is able to undertake a successful mission. The poem ends with a powerful and poignant adaptation of the traditional quest myth in which Achilles, the creature who was so loathed and feared by all the Trojans, becomes an agent of goodwill for them. The figure to be supplicated in Priam's quest is completely transformed within the narrative of the quest itself.

Quest myths of the earlier generations usually involve a journey: Bellerophon to Lycia, Jason to Colchis, Heracles to Hades, Perseus to a land in the remote west, and so forth. Confronting the unknown by physical movement outside of one's own world is the keynote of quest narratives. The *Odyssey* is based around two quest-journeys, that of the father Odysseus to get home, and that of the son Telemachus to get news of his missing father. One significant similarity in the two Homeric poems is that parallel quests are undertaken by fathers and sons - Hector and Priam in the *Iliad*, and Odysseus and Telemachus in the *Odyssey*. In the *Iliad* the attempt to reunite the family (in death) is undertaken by the father (in Book 24), whereas in the *Odyssey* it is the son who goes out to get news of the father, in the hope ultimately of getting him back (in Books 1-4 and 15). The fundamental urge for communion with one's family in the face of fear and suffering is a common theme in both Homeric poems. The physical movement involved in the quest is often driven by elemental human impulses of love for one's kin.

At first glance the *Iliad* seems to stand apart from this notion of physical movement, in that on the whole the poem is not very concerned with 'journeys' in the usual sense of the word. In fact this is one of the things that distinguishes the two Homeric epics, that the *Odyssey* is very concerned with physical movement by sea (and to a lesser degree by land in Book 4) in different parts of the world; whereas the *Iliad* describes a siege in which movement, by definition, is limited. The earlier generations of heroes in the *Iliad* seem to have been free to roam the world, but the current crop all seem to be 'stuck' at Troy. In *Iliad* 6 Bellerophon goes first to Lycia, and then (presumably) he goes outside of the kingdom, or at least outside of the king's city, to confront the Chimaera. Hector, by contrast, in Book 6 just walks out of the gates on to the field of battle; and the next description of his return is when he is dead.

Despite this fundamental difference in the two Homeric epics we do find important journey narratives in the first and last books of the *Iliad*, in each of which a father is re-united with a child from whom he has been separated.[53] These are very different kinds of journeys, not least because one father, Chryses, is re-united with his daughter still alive (although a recent victim of forced captivity), whereas Priam in the final book goes on a ransom mission for the body of his son. The first journey (1.308ff.), which is conducted by sea during the daytime, describes the Greek mission to return Chryseis to her father. This follows Agamemnon's decision, under no small pressure from various quarters, to let the girl go. Chryseis is conducted back by Odysseus and twenty rowers.

The details of their movement there are conveyed in two parts, first the arrangements for the loading of the ship and the departure (1.308-11), and second, their arrival at the harbor (1.430-35). They disembark, hand Chryseis back to her father, and then conduct the ceremonies to Apollo including the offer of a hecatomb (1.435-66). Chryses urges Apollo to cease his anger against the Greeks, which the god agrees to do. They then feast, drink, and sing to Apollo (1.467-74). When darkness comes they sleep beside the ships (1.475-6), and then return the next morning (1.477-87). Having sailed back they disperse immediately to their various camps (1.487). The description of the journey 'frames' the taking away of Briseis from Achilles (1.318-48), and Achilles' impassioned discussion with Thetis in response to this (1.348-427). The narrative of the girl's return to her father is not greatly concerned with the detail of the journey itself. Some details of the passage of the ship are set out in the narrative (esp.1.432-9; 477-83); but the emphasis is largely on the solemn rituals that placate the god Apollo (esp. 1.447-68).[54] The description of the actual journey (that is, the movement to and fro over the sea) seems to have no particular symbolic importance of the sort that we see in some quest-narratives in early epic.[55]

The ransom journey of Priam for Hector's body in Book 24, could scarcely be more different from this earlier one. Whereas the Greek sailors in Book 1 undertake a collective mission within the known world, within their own sphere of control, by day, Priam passes virtually alone, with only an old herald to accompany him, from safe territory, from within the walls of Troy, into a realm that is fundamentally hostile.[56] Thus, in keeping with the basic danger of the mission, this is a night journey.[57] The heroism of the journey is also founded upon the recent fate of Hector, who was not only killed by Achilles, but whose body is now the object of a terrible cruelty not seen elsewhere in the poem.[58] Despite the fact that the gods precipitate the journey, Priam still risks death every step of the way (note esp. *Il.* 24.203ff.; 328; 337ff.; 353ff. 364ff.; 519ff.). Divine goodwill in the mission, and the prompting by the gods to undertake it in the first place (24.74ff.), do not diminish the fear of the old man. There is usually no heroism without fear, and this is certainly the case with both Hector and Priam.[59] In keeping with the danger of Priam's journey, the narrative has some striking symbolism usually associated with the heroic passage to the Underworld (the so-called *catabasis*).[60] In many ways Priam's journey is much more obviously drawing on traditional quest narratives than Hector's encounter with Achilles. This is largely because of the movement involved in the description, and the fact that we can identify with ease some of the core elements of the descent myth to the Underworld.

Thus Priam first descends from his home on the citadel, down through the city, out through the gates, and on to the plain (for the downward movement, *kata astu*, 24.327 and *kateban*, 24.329). Moreover, added emphasis is given within very few lines (24.349-53) to various 'otherworldly' elements: the tomb of Ilus that they drive past (*hoi d' epei oun mega sêma parex Iloio elassan*, 24.349); the river at which they stop so that the mules and horses can drink (*stêsan ar' hêmionous te kai hippous, ophra pioien/, en potamôi*, 24.350-

1); the darkness that suddenly comes upon the land (*dê gar kai epi knephas êluthe gaian*, 24.351); and the fact that they encounter Hermes, the divine guide and psychopomp (*ton d' ex agchimoloio idôn ephrassato kêrux/ Hermeian*...24.352-3). Similarly, the emphasis on liminality in the description of their journey (that is, the guards and gates through which they must pass, 24.440ff.), has much in common with the journey to the afterlife in the *Iliad* (cf. Heracles in the Underworld at *Il*. 8.366ff. and Patroclus' ghost at 23. 71ff.). Hermes puts the guards of the Greek camp to sleep (not unlike the way that Aeneas's guide, the Sibyl, puts Cerberus to sleep in the Underworld in *Aeneid* 6.417ff.). The central description of Priam on his mission, therefore, bears comparison with other narratives in which heroes encounter monsters or journey to the Underworld.

In keeping with the nature of Priam's mission, Achilles no longer occupies a rough camp on the fringe of the Greek army. In earlier books (cf. 1.326ff.; 9.182ff.; 11.599ff.; 16.1ff.; 18.1ff.) we have seen Achilles in his 'domestic' setting when he refuses to fight, but the poem has shown little interest in what his camp is actually like. Were we to ponder the question earlier in the poem of what his camp actually looks like, one would probably think of it (there being no particular evidence to the contrary), as a fairly makeshift arrangement constructed next to his ships at one end of the Greek army (for the position of Achilles' structure at the end of the line of Greek ships, see 8.222-6=11.5-9).

This vague picture of a temporary camp all changes in Book 24. The camp of Achilles is the final destination for Priam in his quest, and therefore important attention is given to a description of it. The different mood and setting of Book 24 help to transform it into a large structure (*all' hote dê klisiên Pêlêïadeô aphikonto/ hupsêlên*, 24.448-9), characterized most especially by its huge doors (24.453ff.; cf. the notion of it as a house, not a camp, 471, *oikou*; 512, *dômat'*; 572, *oikoio*; 647, *megaroio*). It would usually take three men to lift the bolt to open the door, although Achilles (like Hermes, who lets Priam through, 24.457ff.) can do so on his own (24.453-6). The size of the structure therefore, at the very least, informs the greatness and power of Achilles, and the affection in which he is held by his men who had built it for him (24.449ff.). Whereas previously we have seen Achilles sitting outside in the light, in the final book he occupies a space behind a huge door in the gloom of night.

A close Homeric parallel for the door of Achilles' camp is the cave of Polyphemus in *Odyssey* 9 where great emphasis is given to the entrance to the cave (*Od.* 9.240-3; cf. 9.313 and 340). In this case however there is no real door as such, but rather a huge boulder that effectively operates as a door (twenty-two fine wagons could not lift the boulder from the ground!). On his return to his cave Polyphemus blocks the entrance with this huge rock, thereby locking the Ithacans inside. To the horror of Odysseus and his men when they introduce themselves, Polyphemus rejects both Zeus and his ritual practice of *xenia* ('guest-friendship', 9.273ff.). Polyphemus is not a human, but a monstrous cannibal, who almost immediately eats two of Odysseus' men, and then plans the same fate for all the others whom he has captured (9.287ff.; 9.310ff.; 9.343ff.; 9.369f.). His response to the gift of wine by Odysseus is to offer to eat him last. The quest for Odysseus is now to get out of the cave by circumventing the great boulder; something which he is able to achieve through his characteristic *mêtis*. The cave and the boulder therefore help to signify the kind of inhabitant who lives within. The habitat helps to point to the primordial nature of Polyphemus' existence (cf. 9.116ff.; 9.181ff.). The cave and its 'door' are a kind of a polar opposite to the highly civilized palaces that kings like Menelaus or Alcinous occupy in the *Odyssey* (4.43ff.; 4.71ff.; 6.297ff.; 7.81ff.).[61]

In a similar way, the vast structure which Achilles occupies in *Iliad* 24 has the effect of conveying some of the power and greatness of the inhabitant, and, presumably, a sense of the awe and menace that greets the old wayfarer who arrives there. It helps to give Priam's supplicatory journey an otherworldly air, like a journey into the labyrinth or into the Underworld itself. But there is no Polyphemus lurking behind Achilles' doors, even if Priam might have expected to find a similarly fearsome 'flesh-eater' there (cf. 22.408ff.; 24.200ff.; 24.328) . Despite his fears of what might await him, Priam encounters a man who does precisely what Zeus and the gods tell him to do. Far from rejecting Zeus (as Polyphemus does, *Od.* 9.273ff.) Achilles accepts immediately the need for the ransom exchange to occur. As an audience, we know from early in the final book (24.139-40) that Achilles will do what Zeus has told him to do, and that he will accept the ransom. But the *manner* of the exchange has not been ordained by Zeus. This is left entirely to Achilles. And the fact that it is Priam himself who conducts the quest (unbeknownst to Achilles, for Thetis made no specific reference to this, 24.128ff.), seems completely to surprise and disarm him (24.477ff.).

The ransom of Hector's body is conducted with the highest level of humanity and compassion, not least because Thetis tells Achilles in no uncertain terms where he stands in relation to his own destiny (24.128ff). Death (*thanatos*) and fate (*moira*) stand right beside him, and he should get on with living again for the brief time that he has left. The encounter between Achilles and Priam is constructed on the fact that the two of them have much in common. Not only have they both endured the recent bereavement of loved ones, but they also have a short time left to live. There is great emphasis in Book 24 upon Achilles' renewal, the fact that he takes up again the major elements of life - the things that he rejected after Patroclus' death: sleep, sex, food and drink, and compassion for human suffering. Thetis tells him quite explicitly (24.128ff.) not to spend his brief time remaining in a state of grief and lamentation. Achilles' most cruel moments in the poem coincide with his conscious rejection of the things of life in response to Patroclus' death by Hector (cf.19.206-14; 19.303-8; 19.319-21; 19.342ff.). With the intervention of the gods these things are taken up again (this is signaled initially by his eating at 24.475-6); and Priam, at the climax of his quest, finds himself with a very different kind of person from the one who had dragged his son's body around.

The ransom is completed with alacrity, and there is at the same time a genuine mutual awe and respect between the two. The culmination of this is an offer by Achilles, out of the blue, to hold up the fighting so that Priam can conduct the funeral for Hector. He asks the old man (24.656ff.) how many days he intends for the funeral of his son; for he will hold back the Greeks for the period required. Priam replies (24.660ff.) that they would mourn him for nine days, make his funeral on the tenth, and then feast on the eleventh. The fighting would therefore resume on the twelfth day if it must. And so Achilles, in his last words in the *Iliad*, agrees that this is the way it will be, for he will hold back the battle for the due length of time. Hector will be released to his final resting place whilst Achilles will restrain the Greeks, who are no doubt restless for the conflict (cf. Hermes at 24.403-4). After this final exchange between the two, and the brief sleep that they have (Achilles with Briseis [24.676], in keeping with his mother's speech), Hermes wakes Priam and then leads him back to the city as the sun rises (24.671-95). They duly emerge from the darkness, and only Cassandra on the acropolis recognizes them. As they come back through the gloom it is almost as if they emerge from the Underworld itself.

As we have seen therefore, the *Iliad* concludes with two separate quests to confront the same individual; first Hector, and then Priam face up to Achilles. The one leads directly to the other, but, for all that, the two quests could not be more different. One is by a warrior bearing weapons in his prime of life, the other by a very old man with nothing really in the way of a physical presence to protect him. One is conducted in the bright light of day, the other in the gloom of night without a hint of any torches or lights or stars to help show the way.[62] Hector encounters Achilles at the peak of his ferocity, with all the brightness and power of Olympian fire, whereas his father receives a level of compassion, and even altruism, seen nowhere else in the *Iliad*. The failure of one quest and the success of the other have everything to do with the role of the gods, who ensure the destruction of Hector and the survival of Priam. The support of the gods and the power of Priam's love for his son provide him with the necessary resolve to succeed in his mission. As with the tasks of many other great hero figures, the success of Priam's quest brings great relief and solace and unity to his people. Priam helps to restore his community's proper processes by ensuring that the appropriate funerary ritual takes place. The restoration of proper ritual means that it is really a sense of reintegration and healing with which the *Iliad* ends.[63]

We can see therefore from the poem's isolated references to the earlier generations of heroes that the poet and his audience are immersed in traditional tales of personal quests into wild and dangerous locations. The journey to the Underworld and the confrontation with monsters were presumably a central part of the corpus of myth that the poet must have had at his disposal, be it in the form of earlier hexameter poems, or as part of myth in a more general sense. Some allusions to these stories of the earlier generations are included within the poem to give a context to the later war being fought out for Troy. When one thinks of other epic heroes from surviving poems, Gilgamesh, Odysseus, Jason, Aeneas, Beowulf, among others, it does seem to be important that within the *Iliad* Achilles should neither meet a monster nor undertake a journey to the Underworld. Nestor almost calls Achilles' heroism into question by suggesting that the challenges of earlier men are not available to the modern day hero, who is therefore not really as good as those great men of earlier times.

But the remarkable thing about the *Iliad* is not that the challenges of confronting monsters and of descending to the Underworld have disappeared from the heroic landscape. That certainly seems to make Achilles an unusual or an 'un-traditional' type of epic hero, in so far as it differentiates him from the earlier epic figure of Gilgamesh, and many later epic heroes. But it is probably not so remarkable in itself. The truly remarkable thing is that the *Iliad* incorporates myths of monsters and Underworld journeys into the patterns of action of the poem itself. Narratives of monster-quests and Underworld journeys are given a human appearance. Rather than dispensing with monstrosity altogether the poem reveals an inversion of the traditional quest pattern, in which the hero himself has an otherworldly capacity for violence and cruelty. Achilles embraces both ends of the traditional epic quest in the *Iliad*: he is both the hero of the epic, the 'best of the Achaeans', and the figure of fundamental violence who himself has to be confronted.

Chapter 2
Horses

"Horses have always captured the mythic imagination through their ability to symbolize a number of related phenomena: power, wealth, divinity, sexuality, flying, and the tension between taming and freedom."[1]
(W.D. O'Flaherty)

Whereas monsters in the *Iliad* were a threat to human society in earlier times, one that subsequently disappeared as a consequence of the deeds of heroes against them, horses are described as a valuable and much sought-after possession across the generations. The food that these two creatures eat helps to spell out the difference between them: monsters are eaters of raw flesh, but horses are herbivorous. Monsters have to be confronted and put to death, but horses can be controlled and managed. The one is a menace to human society, the other a special friend. Two of the fundamental human desires - to avoid and to possess - come to the fore in hero myths about monsters and horses. And sometimes the two creatures coexist in some important ways in the one narrative. As we have seen Laomedon's Troy was terrorized by a sea-monster sent by Poseidon; and the only hope for the city lay with the wandering hero Heracles. The king's splendid horses were the prize on offer, if Heracles was able to do the job; and they should have been handed over to him by the king when the monster was eventually killed. But Laomedon's desire to hold on to his horses got the better of him, and he broke his promise, thereby bringing about the sack of his own city (5.648ff.).

This story tells us a lot about Troy, and about the pattern of destruction that afflicts the city in the two generations with which the *Iliad* is concerned. It is fundamental to the wider story of Troy that the city's desire for things of beauty proves twice to be its ruin. In the earlier generation it was the desire for the fine horses, but the second time around it is a beautiful woman. Just as the monsters have disappeared from the landscape within one generation, thereby changing forever the character of the heroic life, so the second war for Troy is fought over a beautiful woman, not beautiful horses. One aspect of the focus on human form in the *Iliad* is that the war is being fought out for the possession of a human being. If this is not remarkable enough - to fight such a vast war over one woman - then the strident conflict among the Greeks themselves over the captive women Chryseis and Briseis seems to give it even more emphasis. Comparison with the first sack of Troy, and the earlier world of the heroes, seems to suggest a changed emphasis on the possessions over which men fight. The *Iliad* seems to be saying that it is women, first and foremost, over whom this new breed of men contend.

The two wars for Troy therefore are both fought principally over objects of beauty: in both cases the Trojans fight to keep what they have (the horses/Helen), and the Greeks, who have their own claims to possession, attack the city to take them away. And yet despite the fact that the focus of the later war is fixed principally on the possession of Helen, there is no doubt that horses are still much sought-after possessions across the generations. Indeed, in contrast to monsters, the figure of the horse is associated with a *continuity* of heroic conduct through time in the *Iliad*. Horses are very prominent in the poem, not least because everybody seems to have an affection for them: gods and mortals, Trojans and Greeks, the heroes of earlier times, and the later generation of warriors present at Troy. Horses help to connect the different realms of the world, not just as a means of transport for gods like Zeus or Athena or Hades, but as objects of gift-giving and exchange between heaven and earth.[2]

The giving over of horses from Olympus to earth means that Heracles and Achilles, the two principal heroes of their generations, are both informed by the immortal horses that they possess, and this seems to provide a sense of continuity between the two periods in which they live and fight. Indeed the desire for breeding and owning fine horses informs heroic life more generally through the ages in the *Iliad*: Erichthonius and Tros, Heracles and Laomedon, Priam, Achilles, Diomedes and Hector, all seem to love the horse and to be associated with it in various ways. Horses help to define the special identity of the city of Troy, its beauty, wealth, and divinity; and they also inform the wealth and power of the warriors who fight to capture, loot, and destroy it. The Greek superiority in the war is reflected in their capacity to acquire the best horses from their Trojan opponents within the *Iliad*; but the affection of the warriors for their horses is common to both sides of the conflict. And, as we will see, this affection even extends to verbal communication between horsemen and horses.

Most especially, horses play a crucial role in representing the wealthy aristocratic world with which the *Iliad* is chiefly concerned, be it on the Greek side, where most of the leading warriors possess fine horses, or on the Trojan side where affection for horses is described as having a long and prominent history that goes right back to the city's foundation.[3] In short, horses help to convey a sense of the brilliance and aristocratic glory of the main individuals who fight in the wars for Troy.

Quite apart from the principal day-to-day role of the horse as a means of transport for warriors and gods to and around the field of battle (about which we will have only a little to say in this chapter), most readers of the *Iliad* can probably think of important episodes in the poem in which horses play crucial roles. In fact a diversity of roles really characterizes the figure of the horse in the *Iliad*. They are sometimes named characters in their own right, not just anonymous possessions of the princes. To get a sense of the importance of horses in the *Iliad*, here is a list of some of the most important episodes in which they have a central involvement. I am not thinking here specifically of battle-scenes, as much as other episodes in which the horse plays an important role in some way. The list is reasonably long, but by no means complete:

- the best horses are strongly sought after and acquired as objects of possession by leading warriors (both in earlier times and in the course of the Trojan war itself);
- horses are sometimes hit in battle;
- the beautiful horses of Rhesus become the object of a Greek night-quest that involves the brutal killing of men as they sleep;
- horses mourn and weep out of love for a lost master (Patroclus);
- in one episode a horse (Xanthus) actually talks and offers

prophecy;
- immortal horses drag the dead body of Hector around to assist in the process of mutilating it;
- horses are crucial players in the grand funeral of Patroclus;
- they are sacrificial victims at the funeral pyre;
- they are major participants in the most important of the athletic contests at the funeral;
- and in the final book they take the old man Priam on his dangerous night ransom-mission to try to get his son's body back.

I have chosen these particular episodes because they came instantly to mind as graphic and memorable passages of the *Iliad* which involve horses in some important way. I will be making some comments in the following pages about most of these episodes. The list itself, or one like it, makes it clear just how important the horse is in revealing some of the central themes and concerns of the *Iliad* – mortality and immortality, the life and death of the hero, the cruelty of war, the importance of ritual to the life of human society, and love and friendship in the face of fear and death.

Horses therefore have a central role in the actions described in the *Iliad*, and it is clear that their importance goes right back to the earlier generations of men. The concern of this chapter is to examine the role of the horse in the *Iliad*, including the wider temporal context beyond the war for Priam's Troy. The first section deals with horses and Achilles, and the second section is concerned more widely with horses in the life and identity of the city of Troy. It will be argued that Troy at the level of the monumental city, and Achilles, at the individual level, as the greatest warrior, both have a fundamental connection with the horse that goes right back to their earliest times. As far as my list of prominent 'horse episodes' is concerned, it is worthy of note that most of them (the later ones anyway) involve Achilles in some way.

Accordingly, it will be argued in the first section of the chapter that Achilles' imminent return to the field of combat fundamentally changes the earlier role of the horse in the *Iliad*. One might even say that horses take on a central role in the poem, and even become characters themselves, only when Patroclus and Achilles return to the centre of the action. Horses play an important role in helping to define the heroic identity of Achilles, even among a class of warriors who are themselves closely associated with horses (I think here especially of other individuals like Diomedes and Hector, who, as the leading Argive and Trojan warriors respectively, and as 'breakers of horses' [*hippodamoi*], have their own claims to a special affinity with the horse).

The special relationship of Achilles with horses not only signifies his role as the best warrior, which almost goes without saying, but also that he operates at a 'higher' level, spiritually speaking, than those around him. His conversation with his horse Xanthus, and the capacity of the horse to offer prophecy as well, sets Achilles quite apart from all the other heroes involved in the war. It parallels some of the other discourse that he is involved in within the poem, with his mother, with the gods, with the dead (Patroclus), and even with the king of the enemy city. Moreover it is clear that horses have accompanied Achilles in a special way throughout his life, from his earliest times as a student of the Centaur Chiron, and then right through the war at Troy (Xanthus and Balius). There is an implicit sense too that horses will accompany him in death as sacrificial victims at his funeral, as they do at the funeral of Patroclus.

So, in short, Achilles in the *Iliad* is the best horseman with the best horses on the field of battle, something which clearly complements his profile as the best spearman and warrior. Significantly, of the men involved in the war, it is only Achilles who is taught by a Centaur (which is usually half-man, half-horse, although the *Iliad* does not specify this). Only Achilles has immortal horses; only he holds a conversation with his horses; and only he sacrifices horses. Indeed, one may say that Achilles is far and away the most 'horsy' of the warriors at Troy, and the first section of the chapter will be concerned with this subject.

It is equally significant that horses also help to signify the mythic identity of Troy itself. The horse is a dominant figure in the story of Troy, and the various struggles to take the city. Horses have a central role in the story of the life and death of the city. The early 'history' of Troy (and in fact its 'pre-history', before its actual foundation) is narrated with horses as a central concern. Troy is renowned for its horses, including in earlier times when it was the recipient of immortal horses from Zeus himself. The landscape around Troy in the *Iliad* gives it a special identity as a good place for horses (like Argos and Thessaly in the Greek world); and so it is their presence that helps to signify the wealth and beauty of the city.

Similarly the figure of the horse is fundamental to the destruction of Troy, once in the previous generation (by Heracles), and then in the final sack and death of the city by the later warriors. The second sack of the city (in post-Iliadic sources) is led by Odysseus who devises the scheme of the wooden horse as a means of taking and then destroying the place. After it has fulfilled its usefulness this carved image of a horse stands in silent accompaniment to the fire that destroys the city (cf. *Aen*. 2.327ff. and below, Chapter 4, 'Fire'). Thus, as we shall see in the second section of the chapter, Troy is informed by the horse right throughout its existence, from its origins to its destruction. The city's identity as a great and special city, its beauty, wealth, power and divinity are all signified by an important and continuous association with the horse. And at the same time it is also the figure of the horse that has a central role in the eventual destruction of the city.

Before commencing our examination of Achilles and his association with horses, a few brief and rather basic comments on the role of horses in the *Iliad*.[4] Because of the costs of acquiring and keeping horses, they are firmly associated with the aristocratic princely class who are the main figures in the *Iliad*. Thus in early Greek literature, as in Greek history generally, the horse is the possession of a social and military elite. On the Greek side in the *Iliad* (apart from Achilles) some individuals like Diomedes and Eumelus have a special connection with the horse in the various narratives;[5] but this is also true, to varying degrees, of most of the Greek princes (like, for instance, the other participants in the chariot race at Patroclus' funeral in Book 23).

Similarly, on the Trojan side, in addition to Hector, who is a great horseman in his own right, special mention is made of Aeneas and the Thracian Rhesus who have magnificent horses with them in the fighting at Troy. Both of these, however, lose their horses (and Rhesus loses his life) within the course of the poem to the Greeks.[6] Diomedes captures Aeneas's horses in battle (in Book 5), and those of Rhesus are taken at night while he sleeps (in Book 10). The princely class of warriors on both sides of the conflict uses the spear as their main weapon, and so we may say that both the spear (ie. heavy weaponry) and the horse are two fundamental signifiers of princely status. Right throughout the *Iliad* there is an integral connection between the spear and the horse, because the chariot-owning class is also the spear-bearing class.[7]

One classic encounter involving two such spearmen is the meeting in battle of Lycian Glaucus and Argive Diomedes in *Iliad* 6 (119ff.), which we discussed in the previous chapter. The long discussion between these two, including the narrative of Bellerophon, takes place when they are standing on their chariots, even before they have had a chance to take up their fighting positions. The chariot here seems to function as a kind of elevated speaking platform above the flurry of battle. The two of them come close to one another (drawn by their horses, 6.119-20), and then they hold their discussion whilst still standing on their chariots. At the end of their long conversation they jump down from them (*hôs ara phônêsante, kath' hippôn aïxante*, 6.232), not to fight, as would normally happen, but to shake hands and exchange armor. Thus the horses and chariots which they both possess, and from which they speak, seem to enhance in many ways this scene of aristocratic gentility.[8]

For the most part therefore the heavy-armored spearman is also the possessor of horses and chariots. There are exceptions to this however on the Greek side, like Odysseus and Ajax, who do not appear to have chariots at Troy, although they still fight with the spear. The absence of horses in their cases can probably be explained by the fact that they come from small islands, Ithaca and Salamis, rather than from more spacious landscapes, like many of the other Greek princes. In Odysseus' case this is spelt out in the *Odyssey* in which Telemachus rejects Menelaus' offer of horses as a gift because of Ithaca's topography (*Od.* 4.590 and 4.601ff.). Telemachus tells his host that, unlike the land around Sparta with its plains and meadows, his island of Ithaca is better suited to goats than horses. Later in the *Odyssey* Athena tells Odysseus that Ithaca is a 'rough island, and not good for driving horses, but is it not completely poor, although it is not wide' (*ê toi men trêcheia kai ouch hippêlatos estin,/ oude liên luprê, atap oud' eureia tetuktai*, 13.242-3). Athena goes on to say that there is plenty of grain for bread, and it is good for wine, and the fertile nature of the place also makes it a good place for goats and cattle.

These statements about the character of Ithaca in the *Odyssey* seem to have relevance to the *Iliad* too, in which Odysseus does not own horses at Troy, and seems to have no particular interest in doing so. Although he plays a major and enthusiastic part in the dangerous theft of Rhesus' horses from the Trojan camp (*Il.* 10.272-579), it is the horseman Diomedes, not Odysseus, who seems to acquire the horses at the end of their quest ('when they came to the well-built hut of the son of Tydeus, they tied up the horses with shapely thongs at the manger, where the swift-footed horses of Diomedes stood eating honey-sweet grain'; *hoi d' hote Tudeïdeô klisiên eutukton hikonto,/ hippous men katedêsan eütmêtoisin himasi/ phatnêi eph' hippeiêi, hothi per Diomêdeos hippoi/ hestasan ôkupodes meliêdea puron edontes*, 10.566-9).[9] Odysseus, by contrast, takes the spoils of Dolon and puts them on the stern of his ship in preparation for a sacrifice to Athena (10.570-1). This division of spoils is not greatly emphasized in the text, but it does seem to be in keeping with the superiority of Argos as a place for horses, and Ithaca as a small and rocky island.

On the Trojan side too, special mention is made of Pandarus who ignores his father's advice to take a leadership role in the fighting in defense of Troy. In his father's halls there are eleven fine chariots, newly made and furnished with two horses for each (5.192ff.). But, despite all his options, Pandarus leaves his horses and chariot at home to come instead on foot, bearing the bow and arrow as his weapon. Rather strikingly, and perhaps surprisingly, he came to this decision, or so he claims, for the sake of the horses themselves, in case they did not get enough food to eat when they came to the war (*hippôn pheidomenos, mê moi deuoiato phorbês/ andrôn eilomenôn eiôthotes edmenai hadên*, 5.202-3). As we will see in the next chapter, it is hard to imagine a Greek warrior of any importance coming to such a decision for such a reason in a poem like the *Iliad*. This narrative, therefore, plays its part in identifying the priorities and the character of a prominent foreign archer. The decision that he makes is tantamount to a rejection of the fundamental warrior value-system of the *Iliad*, based on horses, chariot and spear, and Pandarus comes very quickly to regret the decision that he made (esp. 5.188ff.; 5.274ff.).

In light of the horse's significance in the heroic value system of the *Iliad*, individuals will go to great lengths to acquire their opponents' horses, especially the prized horses on offer, like those of Aeneas, Rhesus, and Achilles. Indeed special horses inspire great warriors to risk everything. Heracles risked everything for Laomedon's horses in the first sack of the city, and Diomedes and Odysseus do the same for those of Rhesus within the poem itself. Dolon tells Odysseus that Rhesus' 'horses are the most beautiful and the greatest I have ever seen, they are whiter than snow, and run like the winds' (*tou de kallistous hippous idon êde megistous:/ leukoteroi chionos, theiein d' anemoisin homoioi*, 10. 436-7).[10] The figure of the horse is therefore a frequent prize in quest myths *across the generations* in which the hero puts his life on the line. The great value of the horse (although not usually the chariot itself) makes it an object of special pursuit for the ambitious and acquisitive hero. And even an inferior man like the Trojan Dolon tries to get his hands on the special horses and chariot of Achilles (10.319ff.; cf. 10.391ff.). But Dolon pays the ultimate price for having an acquisitiveness that surpasses his abilities in war (10.391ff.). Odysseus tells him (10.401ff.) that the horses of Achilles are hard for mortal men to control or drive, apart from Achilles, who was born from an immortal mother (*hoi d' alegeinoi/ andrasi ge thnêtoisi damêmenai êd' ocheesthai,/ allôi g' ê Achilêï, ton athanatê teke mêtêr*, 10.402b-4).

It is significant that Greek horse-quests in the *Iliad* are always successful, whereas Trojan horse-quests always end in failure. Dolon's is a most conspicuous failure, as one might expect from a man of his class; but even a warrior of Hector's stature cannot acquire the immortal horses of Achilles after the death of Patroclus (17.75ff [17.76b-78=10.402b-404].). Dolon and Hector, two Trojan individuals at very different ends of the scale of heroic worth, have to confront exactly the same kind of failure when it comes to acquiring the horses of Achilles. The success of Greek quests for Trojan horses (and the parallel failure of the Trojans and Thracians to keep what they have) is yet another sign of the fundamental dominance of the Greeks in the main fighting with heavy weaponry and horses and chariots. The capture of the horses of the Trojans and Thracians seems to play an important part in anticipating the taking of the city itself.

There is only a very limited tactical or strategic role for the horses and chariots in the *Iliad*. They tend, for the most part, to transport the warrior to a location where the spear-fight can commence, rather than operate in battle in a more strategic kind of way.[11] In fact the role of horses and chariots in the *Iliad* is often greeted with some element of bemusement.[12] It sometimes seems a bit silly that the charioteer drives into a part of the battle, and then stops the horses at the appropriate moment for the spearman to alight for single combat. We naturally assume that there might be a more developed tactical use for them in battle.

The absence of much in the way of strategy raises all sorts of questions about the poet's likely knowledge, or lack of knowledge, of the realities of early Greek warfare.[13] It may well be that the kind of role given to horses and chariots on the field of battle in the *Iliad* reveals an ignorance on the poet's part of the actual conduct of war. Similarly, the limited tactical use of horses in the *Iliad* should be seen in the context of the failure of the spear as a weapon to capture the city of Troy. The early epics devoted to the story of Troy, including the *Iliad*, make it clear that the use of the spear, for all its heroic virtue, is not really going to bring about the fall of the city itself. Even in the *Iliad* there is a sense of failure about the spear as a weapon to perform the main task of overcoming the imposing defenses of the city (on this subject, see Chapter 3). The Greeks have certainly had their successes in defeating other places in the Troad (cf., *inter alia*, 9.128ff. and 9.328ff.); and the spoils of these earlier encounters, and the stories resonating from them, play an important part in the *Iliad*.

But the sack of the city of Troy is a very different matter from the destruction of these other places. There is a sense that the Greeks meet their match at Troy, as far as horses, chariots and spears are concerned. The whole story of the siege of Troy is based around the monumentality of its defenses - its power, wealth, beauty, and so forth. The *Iliad* makes it clear that Achilles' spear will not bring about the sack of the place (cf. Apollo to Patroclus, 'it is not fated that the city of the lordly Trojans will be sacked by your spear, nor by the spear of Achilles, who is much better than you', *ou nu toi aisa/ sôi hupo douri polin perthai Trôôn agerôchôn,/ oud' hup' Achillêos, hos per seo pollon ameinôn*, 16.707-9). The explicit statement of Achilles' failure to take Troy with his spear clearly signals its inadequacy as a weapon of ultimate victory against a monumental city.

The other side of this inadequacy is the foreshadowed need for the archer Philoctetes to return from Lemnos so that Troy can be sacked (2.724-5, which is discussed in detail in Chapter 3). In later texts Troy eventually falls because archery and treachery are used against it; and so it is the bow and arrow, and a huge wooden horse - not real ones - that bring victory to the Greeks. It is no more silly to use horses and chariots as a means of transport to the scenes of combat than it is to fight with the spear in the first place, when this particular weapon will not breach the wall and bring about the main goal of the war. The tactical limits which define the use of the horse and chariot in the *Iliad* also define the use of the spear. Moreover, the absence of a strategic role for horses in the *Iliad* also serves to remind us of how important they are as symbols of the wealth and status of the social and military elite with whom the poem is fundamentally concerned.

1. Achilles and the Horse

In the *Iliad* much is made of the fact that Achilles is the hero most associated with the horse, and one aspect of this is that he is the only prince who is taught by the Centaur Chiron. As we saw in the previous chapter, the *Iliad* usually provides us with few details about monstrous figures like Centaurs; and so the inclusion of Chiron's name in the *Iliad* as Achilles' teacher (at 11.828-32) might be considered a remarkable allusion to an earlier pre-Iliadic tradition. We will explore this reference further in Chapter 3, where it will be compared with the important allusion to the archer Philoctetes in the Catalogue of ships (2.716ff.). The principal teacher of Achilles in the *Iliad* is the old man Phoenix, who plays a crucial role in the embassy of the Greeks in Book 9. Nevertheless, the Chiron tradition is not ignored entirely, even if the Centaur does not appear in the poem as such.

The central consequence of including the story of Achilles' upbringing with Chiron in the *Iliad* is that it helps to convey just how different the background of Achilles is from the other princes at Troy. All of these others have, as far as we can tell, human teachers in the normal fashion.[14] Nowhere in the *Iliad* is any specific attention paid to the physical form of Chiron, or the other Centaurs; and so we have to assume on the basis of later evidence that he is a hybrid (half-man, half-horse). One also assumes, given the nature of Chiron's physical form, that he is supposed to have instructed the boy Achilles in the area of horsemanship in earlier accounts.[15] This would obviously be an appropriate skill for the master Centaur to teach his young pupil. But Homer sheds no light on this aspect of Achilles' education. The only explicitly stated gift of Chiron to the young Achilles in the *Iliad* (apart from the indirect passage of the special spear) is that of medicine (11.828-32). And so we are left to wonder who is supposed to have taught Achilles all his skills with horses.[16]

There is however plenty of evidence for Achilles' dominance as a horseman. His status as the best horseman of the Greeks is indicated as early as the second book (2.763ff.), and is then re-affirmed by Achilles himself in the twenty-third book, prior to the chariot-race (23.274ff.). The Catalogue tells us that 'of the warriors, Telamonian Ajax was much the best, while Achilles continued his rage, for Achilles was mightiest by far, both he and the horses which carried the blameless son of Peleus' (*andrôn au meg' aristos eên Telamônios Aias,/ ophr' Achileus mênien: ho gar polu phertatos êen,/ hippoi th', hoi phoreeskon amumona Pêleïôna*, 2.768-70). As far as the comparative quality of the leading horses is concerned, Eumelus, the grandson of Pheres, another Thessalian, has the best horses in Achilles' absence from the fighting; for his horses are as swift as birds (*hippoi men meg' aristai esan Phêrêtiadao,/ tas Eumêlos elaune podôkeas ornithas hôs*, 2.763-4). The mares of Eumelus were bred by Apollo, and then (presumably) were given to his father Admetus, who passed them on to his son (much as those of Achilles were passed down from Peleus). The very best horses in the campaign at Troy are passed down from contact with the gods at earlier times, or were bred directly from divine horses. Despite possession of such special horses, Eumelus is unable to win the chariot race at Patroclus' funeral, even with Apollo's support, not least because Athena outdoes them both and causes Eumelus to crash his chariot (23.375ff.). It is Diomedes who prevails in this contest. His skill as a horseman, and his acquisition of the horses of Aeneas (bred from those of Tros, 5.221ff., 263ff.; 23.290ff.), and the support offered to him by Athena (23.388ff.), give him the victory in the race. But it is important to recognize that the chariot-race at the funeral is really a contest for the second-best place in horses and horsemanship after Achilles.

In his preparation for the chariot race Achilles first of all sets up the prizes including a woman and a tripod for first prize, and a pregnant mare for second (23.262ff.). He then addresses the assembled throng and tells them that if he himself were to compete he would surely win the contest because of the quality of his horses:

'if we Achaeans were now holding contests for somebody else, then surely I would win the first prize and take it to my camp. For you know how my horses are surpassing in excellence' (*ei men nun epi allôi aethleuoimen Achaioi,/ ê t'an egô ta prôta labôn klisiênde pheroimên./ iste gar hosson emoi aretêi periballeton hippoi*, 23.274-6). In this context he says that his horses are immortal, a gift from Poseidon to his father Peleus who passed them on to him (*athanatoi te gar eisi, Poseidaôn de por' autous/ patri emôi Pêlêï, ho d' aut' emoi eggualixen*, 23.277-8). Earlier in the text however they are described several times as a gift of the gods (16.381=16.867 *ambrotoi, hous Pêlêï theoi dosan aglaa dôra*; and 17.443ff.). Their names are Xanthus ('Bay') and Balius ('Dapple'); their mother is the Harpy Podarge ('Swift-foot' or 'Bright-foot') and their father is Zephyr, the west wind (16.148-51). They can run like the wind, and one of them, Xanthus, evinces special powers of speech and prophecy in the course of the poem (19.408ff.).

Thus the warrior virtue of fleetness of foot, which characterizes Achilles in the *Iliad*, is a principal characteristic of the special horses that he brings with him to Troy. It is obviously significant that both the hero and his horses are pre-eminent on the field of battle in the matter of their speed, which is a critical area of martial activity in the *Iliad*.[17] The superiority of the Greeks in general, and of Achilles in particular, is revealed both through their skill as warriors (ie. on their feet in battle with the spear) and through their superiority with horses.

All of this is very much as it should be: the best of the Achaeans should by definition be the best horseman with the best horses, because horses play an important part in helping to define the class of warriors with whom the poem is chiefly concerned. Achilles' horses however are not just the best of those in battle, which they obviously have to be in light of his role in the poem; but they belong to a different realm of existence, and there is much attention paid to this. One manifestation of their special immortal status is a verbal exchange between the warrior and his horses (19.400ff.). Achilles prepares for battle by telling his father's horses 'in terrible tones' (*smerdaleon*, 19.399) not to leave their charioteer behind this time as they did with the dead Patroclus (this earlier episode is described at 17.426-542): 'Xanthus and Balius' he says 'far-famed children of Podarge, in a different way mind that you bring your charioteer back safe to the host of the Danaans, when we have had enough of war, and do not leave him there dead as you did Patroclus' (*Xanthe te kai Balie, têlekluta tekna Podargês,/ allôs dê phrazesthe saôsemen hêniochêa/ aps Danaôn es homilon, epei ch' heômen polemoio,/ mêd' hôs Patroklon lipet' autothi tethnêôta*, 19.400-3).

This is not the only occasion when a warrior rebukes his horses in the *Iliad*. Earlier in the poem (8.185ff.) Hector shouts out to his horses, reminding them of the good treatment that they have received in the past from Andromache, who gave them honey-hearted wheat to eat, and wine to drink. Similarly, Antilochus and Menelaus, two of the participants in the chariot race at Patroclus' funeral, address their horses in turn (23.403ff.; 23.443ff.). The former tells his horses to go faster so that they can catch those of Menelaus; and the latter re-assures his that age is on their side and they are superior in the chase. It is noteworthy that in both cases the horses respond to the rebukes of their masters by running that little bit harder (*ôs ephath', hoi de anaktos hupodeisantes homoklên/ mallon epidrametên* ...23.417-8[a] = 23.446-7[a]). In the earlier fighting in Book 5, Aeneas tells Pandarus, who is rather despondent about his failure to inflict a mortal wound on Diomedes with his bow and arrow (5.180ff.), to get on to his chariot and take the whip and the reins (5.218ff.). Aeneas's horses are bred from those of Tros (cf. 5.265ff., see below, next section), and if Pandarus drives the chariot he will have an experience of what it feels like to drive such excellent horses, be it in pursuit or flight. Pandarus, however, tells Aeneas in reply (5.230ff.) to keep the reins himself and drive the horses because they will perform better with their accustomed charioteer. 'They might take fright' he says 'and run wild when they miss your voice, and not be willing to carry us out from battle' (*mê tô men deisante matêseton, oud' ethelêton/ ekpheremen polemoio, teon phthoggon potheonte*, 5.233-4).

Thus the close connection between the warrior and his horses frequently extends to verbal communication on the part of the horseman at key moments in the action (just as any horse-rider today might talk to his or her mount at an important moment). The affinity between the men and their horses is revealed both in the words spoken by the driver, and the special response of the horse. The rebuke of Achilles to his horses has a much more profound sense to it than these other cases because of the recent death of Patroclus, and the imminent return of Achilles to battle. The speech has an important function of anticipating the action to come with his return to the fighting. He is not going to die just yet, but the encounter with the horses gives a sense of the imminence of his death.

The really remarkable thing about this episode, however, in light of the rather austere nature of the *Iliad*, is for one of the horses to utter a reply. Xanthus responds to the rebuke from Achilles when Hera provides him with the power of speech (19.407).[18] The horse rejects strongly the thrust of Achilles' rebuke, and in so doing reveals himself to be very aware of his master's personal destiny. He mentions Achilles' fate twice in the speech, the fact that his time is near (*alla toi egguthen êmar olethrion*, 19.409). And then he provides him with the specific details of his death - the fact that he will be killed by a god and a man (19.409-10/19.416-7).[19] The encounter between the two of them is in every way a brusque exchange: Xanthus is not going to accept the blame for what happened to Patroclus. He prefers to place responsibility for this death to Apollo: 'nor was it through our slowness and indolence that the Trojans took the armor from the shoulders of Patroclus; but the best of gods, he whom lovely-haired Leto bore, killed him among the leading warriors and gave glory to Hector' (*oude gar hêmeterêi bradutêti te nôcheliêi te/ Trôes ap' ômoiin Patroklou teuche' helonto:/ alla theôn ôristos, hon êükomos teke Lêtô,/ ektan' eni promachoisi kai Hektori kudos edôke*, 19.411-4). Achilles then proceeds to give Xanthus a terse response to his prophetic utterance. He says that he knows from his mother what his fate is, and he then re-affirms his preparedness to die at Troy (19.420-3). After this speech he resumes his place in battle by driving his horses off into the foremost part of the fray.

The immortality of the horses is therefore a direct contrast to the imminent death of their master Achilles.[20] Different conditions of existence help to define the nature of the relationship between Achilles and his horses. Their immortal status, and their affection for their mortal master, run parallel to the relationship between Achilles and Thetis within the poem. The horses are a crucial link in the deaths of Patroclus and Achilles. When Xanthus utters his speech, they have already endured a great grief for Patroclus (17.426ff.); and it is clear that they will have to go through it all again with the death of Achilles (19.408ff.). The notion of immortal grief for mortal beings lies behind their sense of loss for their master.

Their mourning for Patroclus was graphically described—the fact that after his death they were standing apart from the battle, weeping and refusing to budge from where they were (17.426ff.). Then 'warm tears flowed from their eyes down to the ground as they wept for the loss of their charioteer' (*dakrua de sphi/ therma kata blepharôn chamadis rhee muromenoisin/ hêchiochoio pothôi*, 17.437-9). The beauty of their manes is sullied by their response to the loss of Patroclus (cf. 23.276ff.). The different conditions of existence of the horses and their masters, and the suffering that they endure, prompt Zeus to reflect upon the wisdom of giving them to Peleus in the first place: 'poor creatures' he says 'why did we give you two to lord Peleus, to a mortal, while you two are ageless and immortal? Was it that you too should have sorrows among unhappy men? For there is nothing more miserable than man of all the creatures that breathe and creep upon the earth' (*a deilô, ti sphôï domen Pêlêï anakti/ thnêtôi, humeis d' eston agêrô t' athanatô te;/ ê hina dustênoisi met' andrasin alge' echêton;/ ou men gar ti pou estin oïzurôteron andros/ pantôn hossa te gaian epi pneiei te kai herpei*, 17.443-7).

The role of the horses therefore precipitates some important reflections on the nature of mortal and immortal existence, a subject with which the *Iliad* as a whole has a fundamental concern. The close connection between the warrior and his special horses tends to typify later epic narratives from diverse cultures; but the presence in the poem of an immortal talking horse with a knowledge of fate is a remarkable phenomenon in any literature.[21] The conversation between Achilles and Xanthus is all the more remarkable in light of the 'severely unsupernatural' character of the *Iliad*.[22] The poem's caution in dealing with the fantastic was discussed in the Introduction and in Chapter 1 where we saw that monsters are usually alluded to with a minimum of detail and elaboration. It was argued that the explicit description of the physical characteristics of the Chimaera (6.179-82) was an exception to the general narrative pattern in dealing with monsters. And much the same sort of thing might be said of the oblique reference to the Centaur Chiron as Achilles' teacher (11.828-32; cf.16.141-4 = 19.388-91).

The episode of the talking horse Xanthus, however, surpasses anything seen elsewhere in the *Iliad*, because it takes place within the main temporal context of the poem itself, not in previous times. The discussion between horseman and horse firmly conveys the notion of Achilles' uniqueness as a warrior: nobody else in the *Iliad* has a talking horse![23] The brief conversation bears comparison with some of his other discourse in the poem - with the dead (Patroclus, 23.62ff.), with his goddess mother, with the Olympians (esp. Athena at 1.188ff.), and with the enemy king (Priam, 24.486ff.). Quite apart from the peculiarities of the language of Achilles within the poem (about which much has been written elsewhere),[24] it is important to recognize the very *range* of his discourse within the *Iliad*. His conversations cross various boundaries which usually limit human communication. The breadth of Achilles' communion with the world around him sets him quite apart from the other Greek princes at Troy.[25] But the price that he seems to pay for this is that he struggles to communicate effectively within his own warrior community in the wider Greek army. His undoing is the consequence of a fundamental breakdown in communication with his own allies at Troy. He struggles to find a satisfactory role for himself within the confines of the warrior society of which he is a part. The consequence of this is that, despite his role as the best fighter, he spends most of his time on the margins of the Greek army at Troy in the *Iliad*.[26]

A crucial aspect of Achilles' equine associations in the *Iliad* therefore is the way that the figure of the horse seems to accompany him through his life - from his early childhood (with Chiron), and through the war up to his death (Xanthus and Balius). As we have seen, the emotional attachment of a warrior to his horses (and vice-versa) is common in later epic traditions (cf. nn. 19 and 21), and we can also clearly identify it with Achilles in the *Iliad*. The hero and his horses accompany one another as they move through life and confront death on the field of battle. 'Horses' (ie. including Chiron) are virtually part of Achilles' family.

It is worth bearing in mind that an important aspect of heroic epic is its concern with the passage through life, and sometimes the death, of its principal characters (cf., for instance, the *Epic of Gilgamesh*). Neither Achilles nor Odysseus dies in the two Homeric epics devoted to their heroic deeds, but their passage through life is a central notion in both poems. In the *Odyssey* the notion of the transition through life is fundamentally associated with the physical journeys undertaken by sea. Both Odysseus and Telemachus venture out on sea-journeys, and it is this movement that allows a painful phase of their lives to come to an end. Telemachus in particular moves from the domestic sphere of the female (Penelope and Eurycleia) into the outer political and military world of the adult male (in the 'Telemacheia', *Od.* Books 1-4 and 15.1-300). This comes about with Athena in the role of the guide on a sea-journey, *in loco patris*; and so the figure of the ship is an integral part of this process. The conduct of his physical passage over the sea helps to inform his passage into manhood, whereupon he can stand as an ally with his father in the looming battle with the suitors.[27]

His father Odysseus has been thoroughly restricted in his movement too, in very different circumstances, and it is two sea journeys, one on a raft and a veil (5.228ff./ 5.333ff.), and one on a Phaeacian ship (13.70ff.), that eventually bring him back to Ithaca. Thus, as a maritime epic, the *Odyssey*'s main physical movement is obviously by sea, and it is the figure of the ship that helps to convey the notion of an important passage through life of Odysseus and his family. It is worth noting too the way that the ship and the sea help to define the later life and the eventual death of Odysseus, as told in the prophecy by Teiresias to Odysseus himself in Hades (11.119ff.).

When the *Odyssey* commences therefore Odysseus has been 'stuck' for a long time with Calypso, but within most of the poem itself he is a man on the move. The *Iliad* by contrast has a fundamentally static hero figure, physically speaking, for most of the poem, until he explodes back on to the battlefield to avenge the death of Patroclus. In response to the dispute with Agamemnon over Briseis Achilles situates himself solely in his camp, from where he does not move until he goes out in pursuit of vengeance against Hector and the Trojans. And once this has been accomplished he is again described as sitting in his camp when Priam comes to him to plead for Hector's body (in Book 24).

Despite the sedentary role of Achilles throughout most of the poem, there is a great deal of attention paid to his passage through life, and especially to his imminent death. In his case however it is the figure of the horse - not the ship - that helps to inform the notion of movement.[28] The horse is as closely associated with Achilles' passage through life as the ship is with Odysseus. The references to Chiron on the one hand, and the roles of Xanthus and Balius on the other, help to convey his movement through the two earlier phases of his life. The former accompanied him in his early life, and the latter have been there with him throughout the long years of the war. Linked to the equine role in his earlier life is the fact that in the final books of the poem horses are closely associated with his death; and they seem to inform his final rite of passage. The death prophecy by Xanthus (19.408ff.), the role of horses in Patroclus' funeral (23.1ff.), and the chariot-race after the cremation (23.257ff.), all seem to anticipate the death of Achilles himself, and the part to be played by horses at his funeral.

It is appropriate, given Achilles' horse associations, that his re-emergence on to the field of combat completely transforms the role of the horse in the *Iliad*. In the earlier books the horse is used largely a means of transport to, around, and from the field of battle; or else a much sought-after prize for enemy warriors. There is nothing really that is very exceptional about its role in these early books. Horses are certainly not characters in their own right, as Xanthus and Balius are with the return of Patroclus into the fray. In the final three books of the *Iliad*, the horse acquires, through the actions of Achilles, some strikingly different roles from earlier.[29] First, they are used to drag Hector's body around behind the chariot of Achilles (22.395ff.); second, they are used in formal funerary ritual, including their role as sacrificial offerings at the cremation of Patroclus; and third, they are principal players in the funeral games for Patroclus.

The dragging of Hector's body behind Achilles' chariot is obviously a new and brutal use of the horse in the *Iliad*.[30] Achilles binds him to the chariot with his face down to the ground: 'he then got up on to the chariot and lifted up the glorious armor, and cracked the whip to drive them, and not unwillingly did the pair fly off. And from Hector as he was dragged there was a cloud of dust, and on either side his dark hair spread out, and his head, which before was so attractive, lay all in the dust' (*es diphron d' anabas ana te kluta teuche' aeiras/ mastixen rh' elaan, tô d' ouk aekonte petesthên./ tou d' ên helkomenoio konisalos, amphi de chaitai/ kuaneai pitnanto, karê d' hapan en koniêisi/ keito paros charien*, 22.399-403). The mutilation of the body, so graphically represented for all to see, is obviously a terrible sight for the watching Trojans, and a most violent show of disrespect for the remains of a great warrior.[31] The immortal horses of Achilles are used to maximize the damage done to the body of Hector, and this is obviously a significant departure from their earlier role. Little wonder that Apollo is so affronted at the behavior of Achilles in trying to mutilate the body (24.33ff.).

Against the background of the dragging of Hector's body is the prominence of the horse in Achilles' conduct of Patroclus' funeral in Book 23. Horses are prominent in all aspects of the funeral; the mourning of the Myrmidons for Patroclus who drive their chariots three times around his corpse (23.6ff.); the funeral procession (*ecphora*), which is led by the Myrmidons in their chariots (23.128ff.);[32] the laying of sacrificial offerings, including four horses, on the pyre itself (23.161ff.; *pisuras d' eriauchenas hippous/ essumenôs eneballe purêi megala stenachizôn*, 23.171-2); and the chariot race in Patroclus' honor which is the central section of the whole book (23.262-652).[33] It goes without saying therefore that the funeral for Patroclus is a visually striking series of rituals in which the horse plays a crucial role.

Not the least significant of the funerary rituals involving the horse is the ostentatious destruction of wealth, including the ritual offering of horses that takes place prior to the lighting of the pyre. Achilles sacrifices sheep and cattle in whose fat he wraps the body, and then jars of honey and oil, four horses, two dogs, and twelve young Trojan captives whom he took earlier from the river (23.161ff. cf. 21.26ff.).[34] Immediately after the cremation has taken place, and the burial of the bones, Achilles organizes the first and most significant of the athletic contests, the chariot race in which Eumelus, Diomedes, Menelaus, Antilochus and Meriones all compete (23.257ff.).[35] The affinity and affection of the warriors for their horses is graphically represented throughout this contest, reminding us that the horse in the *Iliad* is more than just an accoutrement of war (cf. Pandarus at 5.197-203).

The role of the horse therefore at the various stages of the funeral (mourning, procession, cremation, and chariot race) helps to bestow a special dignity and prestige upon Patroclus. As Odysseus points out earlier in the text (19.228ff.), the normal mourning and funeral practice in such difficult times are much more perfunctory than they are here for Patroclus. This is obviously an exceptional funeral, and the notions of power, beauty, wealth and movement symbolized by the horse are central to it. More than anything else the spectacular funeral and the grandness of its scale tell us a great deal about Achilles and his relationship with Patroclus.[36] The dignity and prestige that the figure of the horse bestows upon

Patroclus in death, also fall upon Achilles in life.

But there is also a sense in *Iliad* 23 that the funeral for Patroclus anticipates a similarly spectacular funeral for Achilles himself after his imminent death (cf. 24.131-2). We know that Achilles himself will soon die, and we assume that he will be honored with a funeral something like the one that he himself gives to Patroclus within the text itself. An audience of the *Iliad*, regardless of its knowledge of any poetic accounts of Achilles' funeral outside the context of the poem,[37] would quite reasonably assume an equally grand funeral for Achilles himself. In other words we are provided with every reason to assume that horses will accompany Achilles in his death as they accompany Patroclus in his.[38] Thus, although Achilles' death is described outside of the Iliadic narrative, there is a strong sense in the final books of the poem that horses will accompany him in death as they have right throughout his life.[39]

2. Troy and the Horse.

Achilles therefore has a special connection with horses in the *Iliad*, one that helps to define his whole life and his presence as the 'best of the Achaeans'. It is important too that this horse association is also true of the city and the people against whom he fights, including Hector, his major opponent. There is great emphasis on the fact that Troy has a significant association with horses from the earliest days right up to the second siege and destruction of the city. Stories about horses seem to dominate the oral 'history' of Troy provided to us in various ways by Aeneas and Diomedes and Sarpedon. Allusions to the earlier generations of Troy in the *Iliad* seem to be bound up with stories of famed horses. A Trojan (Aeneas) provides us with details of Erichthonius' horses (20.215ff.); an Argive (Diomedes) alerts us to the renown and quality of the horses of Tros (5.265ff.; cf. Aeneas at 5.221ff. and 20.232ff.); and a Lycian (Sarpedon) tells us about the horses of Laomedon (5.648ff.). Moreover, Diomedes knows all about a current breed of Trojan horses - the splendid creatures owned by Aeneas (5.265ff.). The impression provided is that the fame of all these fine Trojan horses has spread throughout the world in very different directions. An important epithet for Troy is 'land of fine foals' (*eupôlos*), and this is precisely what is revealed by the characters in the poem itself.[40] The dominance of the horse in the reminiscences of early Troy means inevitably that this particular creature plays a major part in helping to define the city's background and identity.

The story of Troy's earliest association with horses comes from Aeneas who says to Achilles (20.215ff.) when they meet in battle that, even before the foundation of the city, Erichthonius, the son of Dardanus, was a man whose wealth in horses eclipsed all others. He became the richest of mortal men, and his wealth, as far as we can tell, is based on horses. He possessed 3000 of them, all mares herded in the marshland, who delighted in their tender foals (*tou trischiliai hippoi helos kata boukoleonto/ thêleiai, pôloisin agallomenai ataleisi*, (20.221-2). The mares capture the attention of the god Boreas, the North Wind, who fell in love with them, and so turned himself into a stallion. After coupling with twelve mares in his new form as a stallion he produced twelve foals. These horses would run over land and sea without trampling on ears of grain or touching the sea below (20.226ff.).[41]

Thus special horses identify the earliest occupation of the region around Ida, and they help to signify the wealth of the place in the days before the actual construction of the city (20.215ff.). Moreover, the emphasis in the *Iliad* is on the *continuity* of Trojan affection for horses right up to the period of Priam and Hector.[42] It is important that the Trojans are described as 'breakers of horses' (*hippodamoi*);[43] and, of the individual Trojans in the war, it is Hector, the great defender of the city, who is most frequently described in this way.[44] The use of the word (*hippodamos*) to end the whole poem seems to highlight the role that horses have played in the life of Hector and his city right up to the end: *hôs hoi g' amphiepon taphon Hektoros hippodamoio*: 'in this way they held the funeral for Hector, breaker of horses' (24.804). As far as topography and landscape are concerned, the emphasis is on the wide plains around the city, and the plentiful supply of water, which together provide good conditions for the keeping and breeding of horses.[45] In this sense Troy is a rather esteemed foreign parallel to Argos and Thessaly, which are similarly renowned for their horses within the Greek world in the *Iliad*.[46]

So the *Iliad* makes it clear that horses are an integral part of Trojan life from Erichthonius right through to Hector. Erichthonius however is five generations before Hector, and it is no surprise that we also find scattered allusions to the important role of horses in the various generations in between these two. In his long speech on the battlefield to Achilles about his ancestry (20.200ff.) Aeneas mentions the fate of Ganymede. This young Trojan, the son of Tros (and therefore the uncle of Laomedon) 'was the most beautiful of mortal men' (*hos dê kallistos geneto thnêtôn anthrôpôn*, 20.233), and he was taken up by the gods, specifically because of his beauty (20.234-5). In his new role he is to be Zeus's cupbearer, and so he will dwell among the immortals (*ton kai anêreipsanto theoi Dii oinochoeuein/ kalleos heineka hoio, hin' athanatoisi meteiê*, 20.234-5). In recompense for his loss Tros was given immortal horses by Zeus.[47]

This story too is so well known that it is told by the Argive Diomedes, a man with a keen eye for a fine horse. In response to the approach of Aeneas and Pandarus in battle, Diomedes points out that Aeneas's horses 'are of that stock from which wide-seeing Zeus gave to Tros as recompense for his son Ganymede, as they were the best of all horses that exist under the dawn and the sun' (*tês gar toi geneês, hês Trôï per euruopa Zeus/ dôch' huios poinên Ganumêdeos, hounek' aristoi/ hippôn, hossoi easin hup' êô t' êelion te*, 5.265-7; cf. Aeneas at 5.221-3= Diomedes at 8.105-7). A process of exchange took place three generations before the current war for Priam's Troy. A mortal boy was taken up to Olympus from earth; and then immortal horses were given in return to the Trojan king to dwell on earth. Beautiful horses are given for a beautiful boy. Tros presumably had no say in the deal that was put in place, and the *Iliad* says nothing about how he responded to the loss of his son (although the *Homeric Hymn to Aphrodite* does).[48] But, given the Trojan love for things of beauty in the *Iliad*, especially horses, he presumably took some pleasure in the recompense that he received from Zeus.

So the early Trojan affection for horses is revealed in the figures of Erichthonius and Tros who both seem to glory in their wealth and in the beauty of the horses that they own. Troy has an eye for equine beauty from the earliest days. Whilst there is no evidence in the *Iliad* as to whether Tros continued to mourn for the loss of his son after he received recompense, we can certainly say that his grandson Laomedon was not prepared to part with the horses once he had acquired them. The horses of Tros seem to have been handed down through his son Ilus to Laomedon (5.265ff.; 20.236), and it is probably these horses that Heracles sought as payment for his work in killing the sea-monster. The fame of Troy for its horses seems to have attracted Heracles in the first place (5.651), just as its fine horses continue to attract the attention of Diomedes himself. Heracles and Diomedes have much in common in *Iliad* 5 – not least their capacity to inflict wounds on gods (see Chapter 3), and their keen eye for a fine horse.

Sarpedon does not actually specify that the horses of Laomedon are the same ones that Tros received from Zeus (5.648ff.). But it does seem most likely that this is the version lying behind the reference (especially in view of the slightly earlier reference to Tros's horses at 5.265ff.). It seems to be clear from what Sarpedon says that the result of one earlier transaction (the exchange of Ganymede with Zeus's horses) should have formed the basis for a second transaction two generations later (the removal of the sea-monster by Heracles in return for Laomedon's horses). But reciprocity collapses in a fairly general way in the period of the kingship of Laomedon. It happens first of all when the king refuses to pay Poseidon and Apollo for their labors at Troy, and then the same trick is performed on Heracles. Laomedon appears to be stupid, as well as perfidious and greedy, if his choice of enemies is anything to go by. The breakdown in reciprocity and exchange that he perpetrates obviously has grave consequences: Laomedon himself is killed (together with most of his sons in later sources), his city is sacked, and his daughter Hesione is handed over to the Salaminian Telamon (although of these three important consequences, only the sack of the city is specifically referred to in the *Iliad*).

So Troy is associated with beauty and divinity through the figure of the horse from the earliest times. Boreas, the north wind, turned himself into a stallion and bred from Erechthonius' horses to produce twelve remarkable fillies (20.223ff.); and then Zeus's immortal horses are given to Tros (5.265ff.), thereby earning the city a further reputation for horses that seems to attract the interest of Heracles in the time of Laomedon (5.651). And the horses of Aeneas, which he loses to Diomedes within the course of the *Iliad* (5.321ff.), reveal that Priam's Troy still possesses beautiful horses bred from those special ones of earlier times (5.221ff.; 5.265ff.). The collective effect of all these allusions is to convey a sense of continuity about the identity of Troy. Horses have always been part of the city through the generations, from its origins around Ida right through to its crucial encounter with the vast Greek army now outside its walls. Troy is a special place with a great reputation for beauty and wealth, one that attracts the attention of gods and men alike. The city is wealthy, powerful, beautiful, fertile, and closely connected with the gods; and the role of the horse in the *Iliad* plays a significant part in revealing this.

On the one hand therefore the war for Priam's Troy reveals a continuing fascination and attraction for fine horses on both sides of the conflict. But it may also be significant that the war itself is fought directly over a different kind of beauty from that in the previous generation. The second conflict is fought over Helen, and other material goods of importance, rather than over Zeus's immortal horses. Immortal beauty seems to be the curse of Troy; and in both generations the Greeks sack the place to retrieve the beautiful creatures that they consider to be rightfully theirs. The many references in the *Iliad* to Helen's role as the beautiful woman over whom the men fight, clearly make her a special object of possession (cf. 2.160ff.; 2.356; 2.590; 3.67ff.; 3.100; 3.136-8; 3.156ff.; 3.351ff.; 6.326ff.; 6.354ff.; 19.324-5; 22.114ff.; 24.762ff. etc.).[49]

There is no need to read too much into the change in the causes of the wars. As we have seen horses seem to represent *continuity* across the generations in the *Iliad*. They were a highly valued commodity in earlier times, and they remain so in the campaign for Priam's city. And the *Iliad* seems to question whether any prize is worth fighting a war for, whether it be a beautiful woman or beautiful horses. But the focus on a human being as the object over whom men fight in the later war does also seem to run parallel to the increased focus on the human form through time that we saw in the previous chapter. Just as the men of the later generation fight only against other men, not against monsters, so the cause of war shifts from the animal kingdom to the human realm.

The focus on men fighting over women is given added emphasis by the 'internal' dispute between Achilles and Agamemnon over Briseis.[50] This dispute within the Greek army obviously operates within the context of the broader conflict between the Greeks and Trojans over Helen (a little bit like the way that the 'siege' of the Greeks at their ships is meant to take place within the greater siege of Troy itself). An 'internal' dispute over a woman exists within the context of a war over a woman. Naturally the circumstances of these two disputes are different in just about every conceivable way; most notably the fact that Helen is an aristocratic Greek wife, and Briseis is a captive foreign princess (and therefore a 'prize' (*geras*) to be handed out as part of the spoils from earlier conflict). But the common denominator is that we witness men disputing over women in two very important ways.

The *Iliad* seems to be conveying the notion that this kind of conflict informs the later generation in a more significant way than in earlier times.[51] The earlier generations of heroes fought *against* women, in the form of the Amazons. That kind of conflict happened in the days of Bellerophon (6.186), and even as recently as Priam's younger days (3.189). In the *Iliad* however the Amazons seem to have gone the same way as the monsters - wiped out by the glorious heroic deeds of earlier generations of men. Bellerophon certainly killed the Amazons that he confronted, just after killing the Chimaera and the Solymi (6.183ff.); but we hear nothing in the way of detail about the fate of Priam's Amazons (3.189).

The appearance of the Amazon Penthesilea at the Trojan war, as told in the Cyclic poem *Aethiopis*, only helps to signify what a different vision of the world Homer provides in the *Iliad*. The name and identity of the Amazons inform an earlier period in the *Iliad*, one that differs fundamentally from the context of the present war. The poem seems to be saying that just as men now fight exclusively in war with other men (rather than against monsters, hybrids, Amazons etc.), so women are now *fought over* in a very prominent and new kind of way. The desire to acquire significant material gain is a perennial impulse in the conduct of war across the generations. But the *Iliad* does seem to be suggesting a transition in the way that this is played out through time.

Horses therefore have always been valuable assets, and they are still objects of great worth within the course of the war for Priam's city. The two major social crises dealt with in the poem however, (the war itself, and the dispute between Achilles and Agamemnon), arise over the possession of women, not horses. The doom hanging over Priam's Troy therefore is obviously precipitated by a very different series of circumstances from the one that confronted his father. Priam is certainly no greedy and perfidious king like his father was, but, by not forcing the issue of Paris's possession of Helen, for whatever reason, he runs the risk of destroying his city just as surely as Laomedon did in the previous generation. Priam's dilemma, and that of his city, is how to stave off destruction by a powerful and determined force of invaders. Because of the basic change in the reason for the (second) war for Troy, horses do not enter into the discourse relating to the destruction of the city in the *Iliad* in the same way that Helen does. But it is significant that in post-Iliadic texts the figure of a horse - a wooden horse - does play a major role in the final defeat and destruction of the city.

Although the story is not specified in the *Iliad*, the wooden horse is referred to on three separate occasions in the *Odyssey* (4.271ff. [Odysseus' role inside the horse]; 8.492ff. [Demodocus sings the story of the horse, in reported speech, at the request of Odysseus]; 11.523ff. [Neoptolemus' part in the late stages of the war, including the wooden horse]).[52] Odysseus' request to Demodocus, and the subsequent song itself (8.492ff.), provide the most detail about the horse - the parts played by Epeius, Athena and Odysseus, the sailing away of the Argives, the torching of their camps, the debate of the Trojans, and the sack of the city itself. On the whole the references within the *Odyssey* tend to focus on Odyssean notions of Greek heroic conduct, rather than on the horse *per se*. The allusions to it naturally have important relevance to the figure of Odysseus within the poem. His kind of cleverness is able to overcome the monumental size and strength of the walls which stand in the way of the Greeks (note, most especially, the important comparison here with the exit of Odysseus and his men from the cave of the Cyclops in *Odyssey* 9).[53] Odysseus is a specialist in getting into and out of dangerous places, a bit like an escape artist, and the account of the wooden horse is a classic narrative of this kind of expertise.

Moreover in its fullest form the story also describes a victory by the whole Greek military community. There are certainly key individuals who acquire great renown for their parts in the defeat of the city (like Odysseus, Epeius, and Athena), but the wooden horse narrative represents much more of a *collective* victory than the one which Heracles perpetrated on the city in earlier times (*Il.* 5.633ff; 14.251). The destruction of the city in the two generations, which we will examine in Chapter 4, seems to reveal a transition from Heracles, a singular hero with immense physical prowess, to the involvement of a wider military community led partly by a new kind of hero with a reputation for cleverness. Raw individual physical power (*bia*) has been replaced by guile (*mêtis*), and a larger community of warriors. The sack of the city in the two generations in the *Iliad* speaks volumes about some fundamental changes in heroic conduct through time.

Whatever the rather obscure story of the wooden horse actually means, and there are many possible avenues of interpreting its role in the fall of the city, it does seem to have some important relevance to the wider association of Troy with horses that we can identify in the *Iliad*.[54] It goes without saying that it is a wooden *horse*, not a cow or a sheep or a ship, and this fact would surely seem to bear comparison with the *Iliad*'s emphasis on the horse traditions of Troy. Chapter 4 will explore the notion that the life of the city in the *Iliad* is akin to the life of a human being. There is a thematic connection established between Achilles and Troy, one that is built on the notion that both the hero and the city are about to reach the ends of their lives.[55] The life of a man ends in consuming fire, as with the grand funerals of Patroclus and Hector in the poem itself. Similarly references to the looming destruction of Priam's Troy by fire signify, as it were, the imminent death and cremation of the city (on Troy's 'cremation', *Il.* 20.315-7 = 21.374-6).[56] The poem places emphasis on the fact that Troy has a long and distinguished background, and also on the fact that fire is about to destroy it forever. As readers of the *Iliad* we are very conscious that Achilles too will soon die, and that he too will be placed in fire, much like Patroclus in *Iliad* 23. Troy and Achilles both await their fates at the end of the poem, and the role of fire in the *Iliad* helps to convey precisely what this fate is.

We have also seen in this chapter that Achilles and Troy both have a fundamental connection with the figure of the horse. On the one hand Achilles' passage through life seems to be linked to the special creatures who have accompanied him. Chiron helps to represent his early life, and Xanthus and Balius accompany him through his later life up until his death. And the parts played by the horses in prophesying his death and in the funeral of Patroclus seem to foreshadow the fact that horses will also 'accompany' him in his final rite of passage. Likewise the *Iliad* seems to signify that horses have 'accompanied' Troy from its earliest days right through to the current war. Erichthonius is mentioned solely in the context of horses. And the fame of Tros is based partly on the exchange that took place for Zeus's horses. Laomedon loses everything for the sake of his fine horses, including his own life. And the reputation and love for horses characterizes the Troy of Priam and Aeneas and Hector. If one thinks, therefore, of the city as being like a man, then horses accompany the life of Troy from the beginning to the end, just as they do with Achilles. Whatever else the story of the wooden horse may mean, it certainly seems to signify the continuing presence of the figure of the horse right up to the very end. The image of a horse is present as a kind of silent witness of the final burning of the city (cf. *Aen.* 2.327-30 and Book 2 *passim*), just as they are also present in some important ways at the cremation of Patroclus in the *Iliad*.

This chapter has mounted the argument therefore that horses on the whole represent *continuity* across the generations in the *Iliad*. This marks them out as quite distinct from the other subjects dealt with in this book - monsters, archers and fire, all of which seem to emphasize in different ways the notion of *generational change*. The previous chapter argued for a significant change in the character of the heroic life within one generation, largely because monsters and hybrids do not roam the earth in the present generations as they did in the recent past. The apparent eradication of monsters in the *Iliad* fundamentally affects the heroic landscape and the acquisition of fame and wealth, so that war against human society becomes the principal, or perhaps the only form of heroic endeavor for the present generation of heroes. And in the next two chapters we will witness a similar argument about the way war is conducted in the *Iliad*: that a fundamental transition in weaponry has taken place from the time of Heracles (Chapter 3); and that fire itself is going to be used to obliterate the city of Troy in a new kind of way (Chapter 4). The *Iliad* provides us with the very strong sense that the army of the Greeks will raze the city to the ground by fire, and enslave the women and the children, thereby conducting themselves in an entirely different way from Heracles and his force of men.

Horses however are so pervasive across the generations that they do not distinguish the present from the past in anything like the same way. Greeks and Trojans are both horse-owning cultures in the poem in the past and the present; and Heracles and Achilles are at one in owning immortal horses, even if Heracles had to acquire his by conquest. And the lesser men around them, both Greeks and Trojans, aspire to possess the best horses, even if the acquisition of them might bring about their own deaths. The principal difference in the role of horses in the two defeats of Troy seems to be as a cause of the war in the first campaign, but not the second. As we have seen, the extensive conflicts *over* women in the present generation within the *Iliad*, and the conflicts *against* women (ie. Amazons) in previous times (3.189; 6.183ff.) seem to signal a transition in the heroic landscape that we can identify in other ways. Moreover, the fact that Amazons make their 're-appearance' at Troy in the war for Priam's city in Cyclic epic signifies again what a different outlook the *Iliad* has in its dealings with the fantastic.

Chapter 3
Archers

This third chapter is primarily concerned with the course of the Trojan War and the part played by the various archer figures in the *Iliad* (and, to a lesser degree, their role in the *Odyssey*). The principal aim of the first section is to argue that in the *Iliad* Troy is fundamentally associated with archery at the human and divine levels. The prominence of the archer Apollo as the main divine supporter of Troy corresponds to the practice of archery at the highest levels of Trojan society. Trojan archers on the one hand, and Greek archers on the other, are distinguished by a very different class background. Leading archers on the Trojan side are aristocrats, or at least men of means, whereas the Greek archers in the war are men with a clearly defined secondary rank. The text of the poem signals this difference rather strongly, especially on the Greek side where there is an important connection between archery and illegitimacy of birth.

The fundamental difference in the social class of the bowmen on the two sides helps to inform the poem's attitude both towards archery itself, and, more generally, to Greeks and Trojans as ethnically distinct from one another. Greek aristocrats to a man adhere to a strict value system associated with the spear. They do so verbally (especially in the speech of Diomedes to Paris, 11.385-7), and in practice, by fighting only with weapons of close combat. Indeed the idea of using the bow as a weapon on the field of battle never seems to enter into their minds at all. The aristocrats on the Trojan side, by contrast, make a conscious *choice* of which weapon to use, either the spear or the bow, and this choice then informs their heroic profile and identity. The *Odyssey*, however, evinces an entirely different attitude to archery. This includes reference to the use of the bow and arrow by leading Greek warriors *at Troy* (ie. Philoctetes and Odysseus, 8.215ff.). Our initial task in the first section of this chapter therefore is to explore the implications of the emphatic rejection of archery by aristocratic Greeks in the *Iliad*, and its acceptance and use by them in the *Odyssey*.

It will be argued therefore that Troy in the *Iliad* has a very significant connection with archery, one that helps to inform the identity of the city and its people as quite distinct from the Greeks. The 'exception that proves the rule' in this argument is Philoctetes, the most renowned Greek archer in the story of Troy. He challenges the case put forward in the first section of this chapter by virtue of the fact that he is an *aristocratic* Greek archer, and he is therefore quite different in status from the other Greek archers in the *Iliad*. He is, however, absent from the scene of the fighting, and it will be argued that this is an important signifier of the poem's attitude to archery on the Greek side. Of further importance is the fact that Philoctetes is referred to as an exceptional archer in both the *Iliad* and the *Odyssey*. These references offer very little detail about his life and his martial career. In both poems he really represents the best that there is in the way of archery among the Greeks in the generation of the Trojan war. The second section of this chapter will argue that the reference in the Catalogue of the *Iliad* to the absent Philoctetes (2.716ff.) helps to point to the part played by archery in both defeats of Troy.

The first of these was the sack of the city by Heracles in the previous generation; and the second is Philoctetes' own role in the second defeat of Troy. Heracles was the archer *par excellence* in the previous generation, and Philoctetes takes over that role in his own time. Moreover, in later versions of his life, Philoctetes holds the bow and the special arrows of Heracles which sacked the city once; and he must return to use the same weapons to defeat the city a second time. The case will be put that the dominance of the bow in these two victories over Troy is quite distinct from the period of Achilles' dominance with the spear. The 'world of Achilles', if we can call it that, is 'framed' by periods of Greek heroism where a very different warrior value system is in place. References to victory in war at Troy in the past and in the future are included within the poem to differentiate these periods from the main story. The 'framing' of Achilles by Heracles and Philoctetes helps to highlight his dominance of a special period in the mythic past.

The third section of the chapter is concerned with the part played by a special bow in breaking a siege. It will be argued that the *Odyssey* seems to draw on the story of the siege at Troy to describe the defeat of the suitors in Odysseus' house. The passing down of Eurytus' special bow to Odysseus parallels the gift of Heracles' bow to Philoctetes, which he uses in the defeat of Troy. There is a parallel process of gift-giving in place between the generations in which a special bow resolves a protracted crisis and stalemate. The fourth section then deals with the figure of the archer god Apollo, the principal divine supporter of Troy in the *Iliad*. It will be argued that both epic heroes, Achilles and Odysseus, 'mirror' Apollo in different ways, and the crucial difference between them is in the area of weaponry. Achilles is the Iliadic spearman *par excellence* and he (implicitly) rejects the bow and arrow and all that it stands for in his world. In the *Odyssey* however Odysseus uses the bow very prominently as his weapon of vengeance on Apollo's festal day to defeat and kill the suitors. The rejection of the bow by Achilles is linked thematically to his death by an arrow fired by Paris and guided by Apollo. The *Iliad* anticipates his death by treachery and archery, and this kind of death only enhances his status as the 'best of the Achaeans'.

The dominance of the spear on the Greek side in the *Iliad*, together with the signification that the bow and arrow was supreme in earlier (and later) periods, raise various questions about the part played by the historical context in the poem's treatment of weaponry. Does the warfare presented in the poem represent an attempt to convey an actual change in battle-practice, or perhaps the poet's belief that such a change had occurred?[1] Or is it rather the case that the poem consciously seeks to differentiate the generation with which it is primarily concerned from those who went before (and after)? Kirk considers these sorts of questions in the following way: 'On the whole the evidence is too indefinite for us to say whether the small part played by long-distance and mobile warfare in the *Iliad* reflects a historical stage in the late Bronze Age, or whether it is due to poetical selection and the desire of the singers to concentrate on truly "heroic" encounters in which sheer strength and nerve were best revealed in close fighting'.[2]

It would seem foolish to deny the possibility that historical processes lie in some way behind the apparent transition in fighting across the generations in the *Iliad*. But the poem also seems to have a vested interest in privileging the current breed of warriors, especially Achilles, and in differentiating them from the men of other times. The case is put throughout this book that the incorporation of legendary material dealing with earlier periods is designed precisely to distinguish those men from the current crop. Heracles is none the worse for being an archer in his own time, and none the better for confronting monsters. But he is different. The weaponry that he is described as using in earlier times in the *Iliad* helps to signify his particular heroic context, and the same thing can be said of Achilles.

1. Greek and Trojan Archers in the *Iliad*

'Perhaps the most distinctive feature (*sc.* of the Trojans and their allies in the *Iliad*) actually mentioned is the prominence of the bow as a Trojan weapon. Paris carries a bow (though he has sword and lances as well)...Pandaros also, who leads the Trojans of Zeleia in the foothills of Mt. Ida, is a noted archer: his bow is of horn, and his arrows are tipped with iron. And when Menelaus is struck by an arrow Agamemnon at once assumes that it was shot by a Trojan or a Lycian (4.196ff.)'.[3]

The view expressed here by Thomas and Stubbings singles out archery as an especially Trojan characteristic in the *Iliad*, and part of the reason for this, which the authors deal with immediately afterwards (300-301), is that 'in many respects...the Trojans differ little from the Achaeans'. The essence of their argument is that archery distinguishes the two sides in the war in a very clear and identifiable way, something which cannot be said for many other aspects of Greek and Trojan life and society in the *Iliad*.

It must be said in the first instance, however, that the evidence, as it is presented here, is hardly compelling. It would be difficult to argue with the prominence of Paris and Pandarus as archers on the Trojan side; but archery is not restricted to the Trojans alone. The Greeks too have their prominent archers, and they should really have received a mention in the passage cited. As to the wounding of Menelaus by an anonymous arrow (which is fired, as it happens, by Pandarus), one would hardly expect Agamemnon (4.196ff.) to rush to the conclusion that it had been fired by a Greek. He does come to the obvious conclusion - and the right one, as it turns out - that it was fired by an enemy archer.

So if there is a case that the practice of archery helps to inform Troy and the Trojans in the *Iliad*, which I believe there is, then it needs to be put forward more strenuously and more comprehensively than Thomas and Stubbings do here. This section of the chapter explores the role of archery in the *Iliad* in much greater depth, with particular reference to the relative social class of the archers on both sides of the conflict. The need for a more detailed study of the subject is particularly evident when one bears in mind the important and more recent arguments of Edith Hall and Oliver Taplin (on whom we will make comment later) that archery in the *Iliad* is as much a Greek occupation as a Trojan one. Their view is that the Trojans of the *Iliad* have been the victims of pro-Greek scholarly readings which prefer to see inferior attributes, like the use of the bow as a weapon of war, placed firmly in the hands of the poem's non-Greek characters. They argue that these readings create a sense of ethnic difference between Greeks and Trojans that the contextual determinants of the poem itself do not justify. As we shall see, Hall in particular argues that negative attitudes towards foreigners (ie. the idea of the barbarian) arose in the Greek world with the rise of Persia, *long after* Homer's *Iliad*.

One aspect of this whole question is the prominent role of Greek archery in the *Odyssey*, especially in the figure of Odysseus himself; and so we begin this section with some brief comments on Odyssean archery before moving back to the *Iliad*.

In *Odyssey* Book 8 Odysseus is a guest of the Phaeacians on the island of Scheria, but he is yet to identify himself, and he does not actually do so formally until the beginning of his long narration in the next book (9.19). A reminiscence of the Trojan war on Odysseus' part is precipitated by a tense moment or two between hosts and guest. It begins when Laodamas, son of the king Alcinous, invites Odysseus to take part in the athletic contests that have just begun (8.145-51). Laodamas says that Odysseus can cast away his cares (*kêdea*) from his heart if he will take part in the festivities. The reply of Odysseus however (8.153ff.) is far from positive. He says that he has sorrows (*kêdea*) on his mind, not athletic contests (*aethloi*). His thoughts are much more on his return home, than on the contests.

This negative response in turn precipitates an unfortunate moment when another Phaeacian, the rather more aggressive Euryalus, insults him by calling into question his ability as an athlete (8.159-64). On this occasion Odysseus responds with vigor, rejecting emphatically the idea that he is not a very good athlete (8.166-85). And he proves it immediately by picking up the discus and throwing it much further than anyone of the Phaeacians. Then, in a long speech in which he issues a challenge to the Phaeacians (8.202-33), he makes claims to be similarly strong in other contests, especially in the bow contest:

> *eu men toxon oida eüxoon amphaphaasthai:*
> *prôtos k' andra baloimi oïsteusas en homilôi*
> *andrôn dusmeneôn, ei kai mala polloi hetairoi*
> *agchi parastaien kai toxazoiato phôtôn.*
> *oios dê me Philoktêtês apekainuto toxôi*
> *dêmôi eni Trôôn, hote toxazoimeth' Achaioi.*
> *tôn d' allôn eme phêmi polu propheresteron einai,*
> *hossoi nun brotoi eisin epi chthoni siton edontes.*
> *andrasi de proteroisin erizemen ouk ethelêsô,*
> *outh' Hêraklêï out' Eurutôi Oichaliêï,*
> *hoi rha kai athanatoisin erizeskon peri toxôn.*
> *tôi rha kai aips' ethanen megas Eurutos, oud' epi gêras*
> *hiket' eni megaroisi: cholôsamenos gar Apollôn*
> *ektanen, houneka min prokalizeto toxazesthai.*
> (*Od.* 8.215-228)

I know well how to handle the polished bow
and first I would shoot and hit my man among the throng
of hostile men, even though many companions
stood right beside me and were shooting at men with bows.
Philoctetes alone surpassed me with the bow
in the land of the Trojans, when we Achaeans shot with it.
But of the others, I say that I am better by far,
of all mortals that are now upon the earth and eat bread.
Yet with earlier men I will not seek to contend,
with Heracles or with Eurytus of Oechalia,
who (both) used to strive even with the immortals in archery.
And so great Eurytus died quickly, and old age did not

come upon him in his halls, for Apollo grew angry
and killed him because he had challenged him to an archery
   contest.

We will have a lot to say in this chapter about what Odysseus says here, and the implications that it has for archery, both in the *Odyssey* itself, and in the *Iliad*. The first thing that might be said is that the speech is fundamentally linked to the question of Odysseus' identity, which is yet to be revealed to his Phaeacian hosts. Odysseus by no means tells them who he is, but he does give them a clue or two:[4] he used to fight at Troy, and he has obviously been in the process of returning from there. His reminiscence of Troy is meant to be of great interest to the Phaeacians after the earlier song of Demodocus (8.72ff.; cf. 8.83ff. where the song brings him to tears, giving them a sign of his personal involvement in the story). The war at Troy is clearly a favorite theme with the Phaeacian bard. Two songs dealing with the war are told in reported speech in Book 8; the first (8.72ff.) a story of a dispute between Achilles and Odysseus at Troy, and the second (8.487ff.) an account of the wooden horse. The feats of Odysseus are therefore the stuff of legend only a short time after the war; and we anticipate from all this that the Phaeacians will be delighted when Odysseus does finally reveal his real identity and the story of his adventures.[5]

Odysseus' narration of the fighting at Troy (8.215ff.), therefore, has considerable relevance to his hidden identity on Scheria, and seems to add to the general interest there in the subject of the Trojan war. But the passage does much more work than this. Clearly the reference to his archery anticipates the bow contest that will be set up in Odysseus' house later in the poem, and the fight in the house that immediately follows it.[6] Odysseus is an excellent archer, just as he is a master of disguise and a shrewd strategist. He clearly has many 'weapons' at his disposal in the *Odyssey*, and we hear about most of these in the poem itself prior to their actual use back on Ithaca (such as creeping into Troy in disguise [4.242ff.], shooting many goats with the bow and arrows [9.152ff.], plotting the blinding of Polyphemus and the subsequent escape from the cave [9.318ff.]). Many of the special skills of Odysseus are revealed to us in his various adventures, and they have direct relevance to his return to his house. It is for this reason, presumably, that special emphasis is placed on archery in the speech. Whilst he does mention his special skills in other contests - boxing (8.206), wrestling (8.206), running (8.206, 230ff.), and spear-throwing (8.229) - the greatest emphasis by far is placed on the subject of archery (note esp. *toxon*, 8.215, *toxôn*, 8.225, *toxazomai*, 8.218, 220, 228).

But Odysseus' boast does not just deal in a general sense with firing a bow and arrow and hitting a target, as might occur in a contest (the two Homeric examples of which are *Od*. 21.68ff. and *Il*. 23.850ff.). It specifically describes fighting with the bow in the *war at Troy*, which is a very different matter entirely. His skill is revealed in his capacity to hit *men*, Trojan men (8.216-8). This clearly anticipates the use of his bow against the suitors in his own house after his victory in the contest (Books 21 and 22 *passim*). His expertise as an archer will be called upon in a different kind of siege.

Moreover, the reminiscence has the effect of making the Trojan war sound like a conflict of archers. Indeed, if you shut all other accounts of the war at Troy from your mind, especially the *Iliad*, and if you imagine that this speech of Odysseus is our only early source for the war, then you would probably think of it as a conflict played out by archers on both sides.[7] Clearly Odysseus and Philoctetes are not the only archers there, and he seems to imply the widespread use of the bow (note 'when we Achaeans shot with the bow' [*hote toxazoimeth' Achaioi*, 8.220], although this could mean that they fought with the bow only some of the time). I am not suggesting that the *Odyssey* has any particular interest in promoting the idea that the Trojan war is fought out entirely by archers. In fact, the broad range of Odyssean references to the fighting at Troy convey the idea of mixed spear and bow use (much as the defeat of the suitors themselves combines the use both of the bow and the spear).[8] But the role of the bow at Troy is very emphatic in Odysseus' reminiscence, and this has some important implications.

Perhaps the most important implication is the great difference that the passage reveals in the use of weaponry across the two Homeric epics. An audience steeped in the *Iliad* has a very different perception of the fighting at Troy from what Odysseus presents to us here. This is because aristocratic individuals like Odysseus are never shown fighting with the bow and arrow. The closest references in the *Iliad* to the use of the bow by Greek aristocrats are Odysseus in the night-raid in Book 10, the *Doloneia*, (esp. 10.260-1; 10.498ff.); and the allusion to the aristocratic archer Philoctetes in the Catalogue of Ships (2.716ff.), which we shall examine in more detail later in this chapter. Both of these passages have their importance to the way that archery and heroism are dealt with both in the *Iliad* itself, and in the *Odyssey*.[9]

In Book 10 of the *Iliad* Diomedes and Odysseus are without their usual battle-gear during the impromptu conference among the Greeks that precedes the night-attack on the enemy camp. And so as part of their preparations for it, they take their outfits and accoutrements from those lower down on the social scale. Odysseus takes his from Meriones, the second-in-command to the Cretan leader Idomeneus, and Diomedes takes his from Thrasymedes. The gear that they take is different in each case, and it is significant that part of Odysseus' weaponry on the mission is a bow ('and Meriones gave to Odysseus a bow and a quiver and a sword…', *Mêrionês d' Oduseï didou bion êde pharetrên/ kai xiphos*…10.260-1). The full range of accoutrements which Odysseus takes are a boar's tusk helmet, a shield, a bow, a quiver, and a sword. Diomedes in turn has a spear (apparently his own, 10.178, 369ff.), a sword, a shield, and a bull's hide skull-cap given to him by Thrasymedes (10.254ff.).

When the two of them make their way into the enemy camp they use the various weapons as the need for each arises. The swords of the two men are widely used to kill the enemy as they sleep (10.454ff., 482ff.); and Diomedes uses his spear in the first instance to capture Dolon (10.369ff.). It also seems to be important that Odysseus uses the bow that he carries, but not in the normal way. Rather than shooting arrows with it, he uses the bow as a whip for the horses that they encounter ('smiting [the horses] with his bow, since he did not think to take in his hands the shining whip from the elaborate chariot', *toxôi epiplêssôn, epei ou mastiga phaeinên/ poikilou ek diphroio noêsato chersin helesthai*, 10.500-1). Shortly afterwards he is described again as hitting the horses with his bow (10.513-4). Towards the end of the mission, therefore, Odysseus, in a typical piece of quick-minded improvisation (cf. Diomedes' description of him earlier, at 10.242ff.), takes the bow given to him by Meriones, and proceeds to use it as a replacement whip (10.500-1, 513-4).[10]

This rather strange and very 'Odyssean' episode (and it is worth bearing in mind the significant doubts about the authenticity of the *Doloneia*) is definitely the nearest that we come to the aristocratic use of the bow on the Greek side in the *Iliad*. The really striking thing about weaponry in the *Doloneia* is the fact that Odysseus and the devious Trojan Dolon both take the bow on their respective missions (for the bow of Dolon, 10.333, 458ff.). Given the signifying effect of weaponry in the *Iliad*, this suggests, at least for this episode, a parallel heroic character and temperament among the bow-bearers. Neither of them ever fires an arrow in the course of the encounter, and so the bow (and some of the other gear that they wear) seems largely to inform the treacherous nature of the events taking place. As we shall see, treachery and archery often go together in the *Iliad*. Odysseus outdoes Dolon in the very aspect of trickery and deception which his name signifies.[11] In this particular episode therefore Odysseus acquires his bow from a recognized archer (cf. Meriones in the archery contest, 23.859ff.), a man of secondary rank, and he uses it, but only as a whip and not as a weapon in the normal sense.

The fact that Odysseus takes a bow with him on his night mission with Diomedes might be thought of as 'the exception that proves the rule' that Greek aristocrats, including Odysseus, only carry the spear and associated heavy weaponry in the *Iliad* (and if they lose their spear in the fighting, they may then take up the sword or even a very large rock).[12] In normal battle-combat the warrior confronts his opponent face to face, at close quarters, rather like the hoplite figure of Greek history. He puts his own life on the line in an immediate way, and it is in this context that the spear is a crucial signifier of heroic excellence in the *Iliad*.[13]

It is fitting that the poem's hero should have a special spear which does justice to his power and prominence on the field of battle. This is the spear made by Chiron about which we shall make some comments later (16.141-4=19.388-91). This is the one accoutrement of Achilles' armor which Patroclus does not use in the fighting, because only Achilles himself can wield it in battle. We are told that Chiron gave the spear to Peleus who then passed it on to his son before he went to Troy. This spear, of which the Trojans are very cautious (cf. 5.790; 20.97ff.), might be seen as part of the formidable supernatural assistance that Achilles receives within the course of the poem. This divine support manifests itself in numerous ways too; and other examples of note are his new armor (from Thetis/Hephaestus, 18.369-617), his horses (from the gods or from Poseidon, 16.380-1,

866-7; 17.443ff.; 23.277ff.), the fire of Hephaestus (called upon by Hera) at the river Scamander (21.328ff.), and Athena's assistance to him in his killing of Hector (22.214ff.).

The greatest warrior of the *Iliad* therefore has a special spear befitting his status, and we are reminded of the fact at key points in the narrative. At the other end of the spectrum in the *Iliad* is the archer figure whose weapons seem to be held in low esteem by the leading Greek princes at Troy. The speech of Diomedes to the archer Paris in Book 11 is usually cited as the classic statement of this (11.385ff.). Diomedes has just killed Agastrophus and he is in the process of stripping his armor from him when Paris hits him with an arrow in the right foot. Paris is jubilant at the fact that his arrow hit its mark; and with a merry laugh (*hêdu gelassas*, 11.378), he leapt out from his hiding place (*ek lochou ampêdêse*, 11.379). He says to Diomedes that his one wish is that he had hit him in the belly and taken his life (11.380ff.). In response, Diomedes hurls some abuse at Paris focusing on his mode of fighting and on his reputation as a ladies' man:

> *toxota, lôbêtêr, kerai aglae, parthenopipa,*
> *ei men dê antibion sun teuchesi peirêtheiês,*
> *ouk an toi chraismêisi bios kai tarphees ioi:*
> *nun de m' epigrapsas tarson podos eucheai autôs.*
> *ouk alegô, hôs ei me gunê baloi ê païs aphrôn:*
> *kôphon gar belos andros analkidos outidanoio.*
> *ê t' allôs hup' emeio, kai ei k' oligon per epaurêi,*
> *oxu belos peletai, kai akêrion aipsa tithêsi.*
> *tou de gunaikos men t' amphidruphoi eisi pareiai,*
> *paides d' orphanikoi: ho de th' haimati gaian ereuthôn*
> *puthetai, oiônoi de peri plees êe gunaikes.*
> (*Il.* 11.385-95)

> You, archer, vile man, lovely in your locks, ogler of girls.
> If you were to make trial of me man-to-man in armor
>   then your bow and your close-showered arrows wouldn't help you at all.
> But now having scratched me on the flat of my foot, you give a
>   boast like this.

> I have no concern, any more than if a woman had hit me or a
>   witless child;
> for blunt is the weapon of a weak man and a nobody.
> Differently from my hand is the spear sharp, even if it only
> grazes, and straightaway does it make its man lifeless.
> The two cheeks of his wife are torn in mourning
> and the children are fatherless; while he, making the earth red
>   with his blood,
> rots away, and there are more birds around him than women.

These lines obviously seem a very long way from the reminiscence of the war which Odysseus offers to his Phaeacian hosts in *Odyssey* 8. We will therefore have more to say about both speeches in a moment. The speech of Diomedes is often taken to represent a more general view of the archer, one that is held by the leading figures in the *Iliad*.[14] And it is easy to imagine the same speech, or something like it, coming from the mouth of any of the leading Greeks, especially in response to a painful arrow wound in the foot.[15] There is not much doubt about what Diomedes thinks of archery, and even less doubt about what he thinks of Paris.

But are there implications in the speech for the thornier issue of ethnic identity? It is but a small step to see the conflict between Diomedes and Paris as representative of something much bigger - a clash of cultures and different value systems: the noble Greek spear-warrior against the cowardly Trojan archer and womanizer. The description of the action of Paris (firing the bow from his lair [*lochos*]), and the speech of Diomedes in response, both seem to affirm Greek bravery on the one hand, and Trojan treachery and cowardice on the other (confirming perhaps the impression already gained from Pandarus' breaking of the truce, 4.104ff.).[16] So to what extent should we read the encounter between them as representative of the poem's general attitude towards archery and the Trojans?

The issue of ethnic predisposition to weaponry is complicated by the presence in the poem of brave spearmen on the Trojan side, like Hector and Sarpedon, and prominent archers on the Greek side, like Teucer and Meriones. Their presence can make it hard to justify broad statements about weaponry and ethnic identity in the *Iliad*. The Trojans cannot be stereotyped as cowardly archers any more than the Achaeans are all spearmen of the highest warrior class. And one challenge to the view of Thomas and Stubbings is advanced by Edith Hall in her important book *Inventing the Barbarian*. She takes quite a different position, and writes on Greek and Trojan archery in the following way:

> 'It has also been asserted that archery is a more predominant mode of warfare among the Trojans than among the Greeks. Since in classical times archery was despised and considered suitable only for Cretans and Scythians, this has been taken to imply the cowardice and inferiority of the Trojans. The only cogent evidence for this view is a single line in which Diomedes insults Paris, calling him, amongst other things, 'archer' (*toxota*, 11.385). The word itself is a Homeric *hapax*, which may indicate that it is a late entrant into the language of epic, and what we seem to be dealing with here is two different and historically discrete views of the status of the archer, for elsewhere, of course, the poem does not support Diomedes' opinion. Two of the most conspicuous archers in the poem, Teucer and Meriones are Greeks. Philoctetes, 'well-skilled in archery', who was to become so important at the end of the war, merits a place in the Catalogue despite his absence (2.718). The archery contest at Patroclus' funeral games is emphasized by its position at their culmination (23.850-83). Nor should it be forgotten how essential the hero's bowmanship is to the *Odyssey*; the archery contest for the hand of a woman may even be an Indo-European theme dating back to pre-Greek days'.[17]

Hall makes a number of important points here, which will be taken up in this section, and in the next. The two principal issues that will concern us are her rejection of the idea that the bow and arrow is a fundamentally Trojan weapon; and the related implication (based largely on her rejection of 11.385) that it is not really a weapon of treachery and cowardice at all.[18] It should be said in the first instance that the position Hall adopts here is part of a more expansive argument of cultural history focused largely on classical texts, rather than specifically on early Greek epic. Her aim is to demonstrate that a fundamental shift in Greek attitudes towards foreigners took place in the classical period in response to the Persian threat: 'the idea of the barbarian as the generic opponent to Greek civilization was a result of this heightening in Hellenic self-consciousness caused by the rise of Persia' (9). The treatment of the Trojans in the *Iliad* as a foreign enemy of a Greek army poses a challenge - or could pose a challenge - to the main thrust of Hall's book, in light of the early date of the poem. The use of the bow in the *Iliad* is only one aspect of her very wide-ranging argument; but it is an important one because of the significance of weaponry in the warrior value systems in the poem (to say nothing of the hostile Greek attitude towards the bow as a foreign weapon in the classical period). It clearly strengthens the central argument of Hall's book if the case can be made that the bow is as much a Greek weapon as a Trojan one in the *Iliad*.

And in one sense it is, as Hall herself points out (vis-à-vis her references to the Greek archers, Teucer, Meriones, Philoctetes, *et al.*). Greek archery is certainly as prominent in descriptions of the fighting as it is among the Trojans. But when the analysis extends beyond the basic issue of ethnicity (ie. who is firing a bow, and what side they are on), to explore the related issue of social class, then we get a very different picture. It is significant that the *Iliad* makes a general distinction in the social class of the archers on the two sides: Greek archers are part of a much lower level of the social order within the army; whereas the prominent Trojan archers are high born, and seem to have every opportunity to use other weaponry. The poem reveals that aristocrats on the Greek side opt automatically for the spear in battle, and it is inconceivable that they would contemplate using anything else. Not every spearman on the Greek side at Troy is necessarily a leading aristocrat, but every leading aristocrat is a spearman. And they fight *only* with the spear in battle, even those like Odysseus and Ajax who seem to have no horses with them at Troy (above, Chapter 2). The issue of weaponry, however, is not nearly as straightforward on the Trojan side. The choice of weapons in their ranks tends rather to depend on personal preference, and on the individual natures of the people concerned. There is an element of freedom and individual choice about the Trojan use of weapons at the highest social level, and we do not find this among the aristocratic Greeks.

This means that the most prominent Trojan archers in the *Iliad* (like Paris and Pandarus) are not from a lower social background like the Greek archers. The bow is generally a much more reliable indicator of birth and social class among the Greeks in the war than it is among the Trojans, in so far as it seems to be used by all levels of Trojan society, right up to the royal house itself. One clear indication of the treatment of weaponry in the poem is the way that the two sets of brothers are dealt with, Hector and Paris on the Trojan side, and Ajax and Teucer on the Greek side. Hector is firmly associated with the spear, with which he always fights. He is the great defender of the city and the leading Trojan *promachos* (with a Greek name cognate with *echein*, 'to have' or 'to hold', and thus the 'supporter' or 'prop' of Troy; cf. 5.472 etc.). As we have seen, his brother Paris, by contrast, usually fights with the bow and arrow, although sometimes he uses the spear. Similarly, on the Greek side, Ajax, the son of Telamon, is a spearman of the highest caliber, the second best warrior after Achilles (2.768-9), whereas his brother Teucer is a bowman, although he too uses the spear on some occasions.

We have a parallel pair of siblings on each side of the conflict, therefore, whose favorite weapons are quite different: one brother is a leading spearman with a huge shield (Hector/Ajax), and the other is a renowned archer (Paris/Teucer). The main difference however is that in the case of the Salaminians the adopted weaponry is signified and explained by the birth and background of the brothers, whereas no such explanation is forthcoming with Hector and Paris. Teucer's low birth (8.284) helps to explain his use of the bow to the Greek audience, just as Ajax's high birth does with his spear and shield. Hector and Paris, by contrast, have an identical family background *in the Iliad* (although there was a different and more expansive tradition of Paris's birth in later sources). In the *Iliad* both of them are high-born children of Priam and Hecuba; and so their two different characteristic weapons have to be explained by other means than their parentage. There is a general equation made in the *Iliad* between low-born Greek archers on the one hand, and high-born Trojan archers on the other. The class implications of the bow's use on the two sides of the conflict imply a greater acceptance and use of the bow at all levels of Trojan society.

The other side of all this is that the bow and arrow seem to bring an element of military success to the Trojan side on which they appear very reliant. One might even think of the bow as a more 'natural' weapon for Trojans, who are fundamentally inferior to the Greeks in single combat with the spear. The basic rule of war is to operate from one's strengths, not from one's weaknesses. There is a sense in the *Iliad* that Paris does just this. He does what he does best, by fighting most of the time with the bow, not with the spear. Single combat with the spear does not go well for Paris in the *Iliad* (note esp. 3.369ff.). This is the case even against Menelaus, who is hardly the most formidable of the Greeks (cf. the comparison made by Agamemnon of Menelaus and Hector at 7.109ff.).

The signs of Paris's defeat by Menelaus are already there earlier in Book 3 when the two of them come near to one another in battle. Paris has a panther skin, a bow, a sword and two spears, and he challenges the Greeks to a fight (ie. with the spear, 3.15ff.). The first warrior to appear is Menelaus (3.21ff.), and when Paris catches sight of him he falls back behind his companions in a state of panic (*kateplêgê philon êtor*, 3.31). He is then rebuked by Hector (3.39ff.), and it is this that precipitates the single combat between them (3.59ff.). In this conflict he has to be rescued quickly by Aphrodite who lifts him from the battlefield and places him in his bedroom (3.380ff.). Here he stays with Helen until Hector chivvies him back on to the battlefield much later in Book 6 (312ff.). After Helen and Paris have been re-united, she throws at him the fact that he once boasted that he was 'better (than Menelaus) in the strength of (his) hands and with (his) spear' (*sêi te biêi kai chersi kai egcheï pherteros einai* (3.431). The abuse continues when she concludes that Paris has just been 'defeated by a mighty man, he who was my former husband' (*andri dameis kraterôi, hos emos proteros posis êen*, 3.429).

One might have expected an aristocratic warrior to be devastated by such criticism. The text makes is clear that Hector fears this kind of verbal attack on his heroic excellence. He evinces great concern for his reputation among the Trojan men and women, even before he is stranded outside the gates with Achilles (cf. 6.441ff. and 22.99ff.). But his brother Paris is quite different in this regard. Any grief that Paris feels at the public perception of him is only hinted at in the various passages in Books 3 and 6 (cf. 3.451-4; 6.326, 335-6, 523ff.). His immediate response to Helen in Book 3 shows no contrition or shame at the scorn heaped on him: 'just now Menelaus defeated me with Athena's help, but some day I will defeat him, for there are also gods on our side' (*nun men gar Menelaos enikêsen sun Athênêi, /*

keinon d' autis egô: para gar theoi eisi kai hêmin, 3.439-40). Paris's words have a 'proverbial ring' to them (Kirk compares *Il.* 9.497, 13.72 and 21.264);[19] but, for all that, it is almost as if he is saying here that he will have his day with the bow and arrow, and with the god Apollo to help him.[20] He will return to fight on his own terms, in a favorable situation for him, not for his opponent (cf. Paris to Hector at 6.339, *nikê d' epameibetai andras*, 'victory goes from man to man').

And the fact is that within the course of poem Paris is basically right about this. His worst moment is the humiliating loss to Menelaus in single combat with the spear. But he does return to the field of battle to have a significant impact on the fighting in Book 11. This triumph leads ultimately to the returns and deaths of Patroclus (16.786ff.) and Achilles (cf. 22.359-60, on which see below). The spear is not Paris's weapon, and he seems to be self-aware enough, and self-interested enough, to know it.

His brother Hector could not be more different. Hector is the Trojan spearman *par excellence*, the defender of the city (6.402-3). Paris and Hector represent the highest levels in the use of the bow and the spear at Troy; and *Iliad* 6 in particular brings to the surface the major contrasts between them. They may live right beside one another in the royal quarters in the city (Paris's house is 'near to those of Priam and Hector on the citadel', *egguthi te Priamoio kai Hektoros, en polei akrêi*, 6.317), but they are miles apart in other ways; and it is their weapons (*inter alia*) that help to signify this difference. When Hector turns to go back into the city on the advice of Helenus, attention is paid to his huge shield, the rim of which knocks against his neck and his ankles (6.116-18). Not surprisingly, there is considerable scholarly interest in this shield (and also the more renowned shield of Ajax, 7.219ff.). Much of this interest centers on the historical dimension of the description, and how 'Mycenaean' the shield might be. This question in turn has implications for the poem's date and composition. But it is also important that the two huge shields belong to leading warriors who have renowned archers for brothers.[21] The contrast between the two spearmen and the two archers is all the more emphatic because of the size of the shields that Ajax and Hector both carry.

In the case of Hector and Paris there is also an emphatic contrast in their offensive weapons, the spear and the bow. When Hector reaches the city and meets with his mother he tells her (6.264ff.) to go to the shrine of Athena to perform the rituals suggested earlier by Helenus (6.77ff.). He then tells her that his first destination is the house of Paris (6.280ff.). His task (6.326ff.) is to get Paris out of his house and back on to the field of battle (although it is worth noting that this was never mentioned in the speech of Helenus). In the meeting between the two of them in Paris's chamber, some attention is devoted to the armor that helps to signify their heroic identities.[22] On the one hand Hector's entrance is characterized by the extraordinary size of his spear, eleven cubits in length - about sixteen and a half feet or about 5 meters (*enth' Hectôr eisêlthe Diïphilos, en d' ara cheiri / egchos ech' hendekapêchu*; 'there Hector dear to Zeus went in, and in his hand he held a spear of eleven cubits', 6.318-9 [6.318-20 = 8.493-5]). The spear, gleaming with bronze and gold, seems to herald his arrival into the room (6.319-20). Paris, by contrast, is sitting in his bedroom tending to his beautiful arms, 'and examining his curved bow' (*kai agkula tox' haphoônta*, 6.322). Helen is there in the room too sitting with her handmaidens (6.323-4). The juxtaposition of the weaponry in a non-martial context seems designed to reinforce precisely how different the brothers are in their priorities and in their conduct in war.[23] First Hector's shield (6.116-8), and then his spear (6.318-9), are depicted in the whole episode as a striking contrast to the very different weapons and value system of Paris (6.321ff.).

The problem for Hector is that for all his *aretê* ('manliness', 'valor'), and despite the successes that he has in battle within the poem, he is no match for the leading Greek spearmen. The doom hanging over him, especially in Book 6, is anchored to the unmistakable sense, revealed elsewhere in the poem, that the best men of the Greeks easily surpass him in single combat at close quarters (see in more detail below, Chapter 4). He takes up the fight on his enemy's terms, with a weapon that is more fundamentally associated with the Greek invaders than with the Trojans themselves.[24] The culmination of this is his explicit acceptance of his inferiority to Achilles with the spear: 'I know that you are mighty and that I am much inferior to you. But these things lie in the laps of the gods, whether I, inferior though I am, take your life hitting you with my spear, for my weapon too has been found sharp before now' (*oida d' hoti su men esthlos, egô de sethen polu cheirôn./ all' êtoi men tauta theôn en gounasi keitai,/ ai ke se cheiroteros per eôn apo thumon helômai/ douri balôn, epei ê kai emon belos oxu paroithen*, 20.434-7).

Hector fights the war according to a value system to which only some of the Trojan aristocracy subscribes. The royal house itself seems to be fatally divided, even on an issue as fundamental as the weaponry to be used in the war. And it is the two brothers, the spearman and the archer, who signal the division between them. It is significant that Hector pays the ultimate price for his choice of weapon at the hands of Achilles. Paris, however, succeeds where his brother fails, and kills Achilles with a more 'Trojan' weapon. The poem seems to be saying that Paris's success is due to the fact that he stays true to the essence of being Trojan. As far as we can tell from the *Iliad*, Paris has no interest in a noble victory or a noble death against Achilles in single combat with heavy weaponry. In later sources he aims for, and achieves, victory over him with the bow - no doubt in the knowledge that he would not stand a chance with the spear. Like the individualists on the Greek side in the war (especially Odysseus with his characteristic *mêtis*) Paris is conscious of his own special strength in war, and he is content to operate from it, regardless of what the world thinks of him. His role as a great archer puts him 'at one' with Apollo, the archer god and the great divine supporter of Troy.

These comments on the subject of archery in the *Iliad* obviously contradict what Odysseus has to say to the Phaeacians about Greek archery in the *Odyssey* (8.215ff.). As we have seen, it is explicitly stated there that Greeks of the highest class, represented by Odysseus and Philoctetes, use the bow in the conflict at Troy. The difference in the part played by archery within the two poems is bound up in the very different landscapes and triumphs of the two epic heroes. As Gregory Nagy points out in his *Best of the Achaeans* (41), the *Odyssey* is putting forward a consciously different kind of heroic reputation for its hero: 'the triumph of the *Iliad*, however, is that Achilles becomes explicitly the "best of the Achaeans" without having destroyed Troy. Because of the *Iliad* tradition, it seems that the *kleos* of Odysseus at Troy was preempted by the *kleos* of Achilles'. The *Odyssey* has an investment in connecting Odysseus' reputation from previous victories (the sack of Troy) to new challenges (especially in his confrontation with the suitors). The use of the bow by Odysseus within the *Odyssey* is not only a kind of reversion to the earlier world of Heracles in the *Iliad*, who used the same weapon; but it also re-affirms the bow's part in the defeat of the Trojans (most famously, by Philoctetes, but also by Odysseus himself). The rigid warrior value system of the *Iliad* is appropriate to the *kleos* of Achilles and his 'sack of Troy' (ie. the killing of Hector with his spear), but it is irrelevant to the new world in which Odysseus triumphs in the *Odyssey*. The figure of Odysseus in the two poems therefore - or, more properly, the two Odysseus figures - both operate entirely within the value systems that are appropriate to their heroic tasks and contexts. The problem arises (*pace* Hall) when *Odyssean* Greek archery is used to argue a case for the bow's place in the value system of the *Iliad*. The two texts convey quite different forms of heroic glory, and weaponry is an important signifier of these.[25]

In order to identify the different treatment of Greek and Trojan archers in the *Iliad*, let us explore their roles in a little bit more detail, beginning with those on the Greek side in the war. The first named archer in the whole poem is Philoctetes in the Catalogue of Ships:

Hoi d' ara Mêthônên kai Thaumakiên enemonto
kai Meliboian echon kai Olizôna trêcheian,
tôn de Philoktêtês êrchen toxôn eu eidôs
hepta neôn: eretai d' en hekastêi pentêkonta
embebasan, toxôn eu eidotes iphi machesthai.
all' ho men en nêsôi keito krater' algea paschôn,
Lêmnôi en êgatheêi, hothi min lipon huies Achaiôn
helkeï mochthizonta kakôi oloophronos hudrou:
enth' ho ge keit' acheôn: tacha de mnêsesthai emellon
Argeioi para nêusi Philoktêtao anaktos.
oude men oud' hoi anarchoi esan, potheon ge men archon:
alla Medôn kosmêsen Oïlêos nothos huios,
ton rh' eteken Rhênê hup' Oïlêï ptoliporthôi.
(*Il.* 2.716-28)

And they who dwelt in Methone and Thaumacia,
and that held Meliboea and rugged Olizon,
of their seven ships, the leader was Philoctetes,
well skilled in archery, and on each ship embarked fifty
    oarsmen,
well skilled in the strength of the bow in battle.
But Philoctetes lay on an island suffering strong pains,

Archers   111

in sacred Lemnos, where the sons of the Achaeans had left him
in agony with an evil wound from a deadly water-snake.
There he lay suffering; yet soon the Argives
beside their ships were to remember lord Philoctetes.
Yet these, longing though they were for their leader, were not leaderless,
but Medon marshalled them, bastard son of Oïleus,
he whom Rhene bore to Oïleus sacker of cities.

The theme of the comments so far in this chapter has been that the two Homeric poems present us with very different attitudes to the figure of the Greek archer. Now, by contrast, we find a prominent archer, Philoctetes, whose depiction, minimal though it is in both the *Iliad* and the *Odyssey*, seems to be quite consistent. In the *Odyssey* Odysseus tells us that Philoctetes is the best archer of his time; and the Catalogue of the Greek army in the *Iliad* seems to be telling us much the same sort of thing (although his comparative ability as an archer among the Greeks is not stated as such in the *Iliad*). He brought with him only a small contingent of seven ships to Troy, but each of these had fifty oarsmen who are highly skilled archers. So the whole contingent are archers, and Philoctetes is their high-born leader.

The Catalogues of the Greeks and Trojans in *Iliad* 2 do not usually have much to say about weaponry. They do stipulate ability with the spear in some cases (like Locrian Ajax [2.530], the Abantes [2.543], and Hector and his men [2.816ff.]); but there seems to be a standard assumption running through the entries that the leading individuals fight with the spear, unless otherwise stated. And so there is no specific pattern of emphasis in the Catalogue that the leading Greeks are spearmen, even though almost all of them fall into this category. Archery is quite a different matter, or so it seems in Philoctetes' case, and the text makes it clear that he is a leading archer and commander (note also the Catalogue entries on Pandarus and Pyraechmes on the Trojan side [2.824ff. and 2.848ff.]). [26] The archery of Philoctetes is clearly a major signifier of his identity and renown, hence the attention paid to the subject in the Catalogue. Of particular importance in the passage is the fact that Philoctetes, with whom the epic audience is no doubt familiar, is actually absent from the war, and suffers pains on the island of Lemnos. He was left there on the way to Troy by the Greeks after he was bitten by a deadly water-snake. He now leads a life of suffering on the island, and his men miss his presence at Troy (2.726). Included in the passage is the rather enigmatic statement that the Greeks will have cause to remember Philoctetes in time to come (2.724-5, more on this subject later).

So we have here in Philoctetes an aristocratic archer whose great skill with the bow is worthy of mention in both Homeric poems. Equally significant is the fact that his contingent in the *Iliad* is not leaderless but that a certain Medon organizes them, a bastard son (*nothos huios*) of Oïleus (Medon therefore is half-brother of the lesser Ajax). Medon acts *in loco regis* whilst Philoctetes is still on Lemnos. Later in the poem (13.694-7=15.333-6) we learn that Medon now calls Phylace his home, the capital of Protesilaus, because he once killed a kinsman of his stepmother Eriopis, the wife of Oïleus. He appears in these later passages with Podarces as the leader of the Phthians. The point in the present passage is that the noble Philoctetes is absent from his men, and that the very ignoble Medon is there to take command of the contingent. Kirk points out in his commentary that it is strange that such a figure as Medon should be in command of the contingent of his adopted country.[27] The lowly status of Medon is certainly emphasized in this passage, and is then re-affirmed in the later references (13.694 = 15.333).

The emphasis on Medon's ignoble birth is surely explained by the fact that it is a contingent of *archers* who are being described at this particular point in the Catalogue. Archery plays an important role in the first half of the *Iliad* (especially Paris, Pandarus and Teucer), and it does seem to be important that the first named Greek archer who is actually there at Troy is a bastard. On the one hand the reference to Philoctetes in the Catalogue (2.716ff.) points us to an example of a noble archer, and the fact that an aristocrat among the Greeks can lead a cohort of archers to Troy. This gives a semblance of distant respectability to the practice. The passage seems to be saying that Greek archery at a high social and political level can and does exist - just as long as it does not manifest itself within the confines of the poem. The *Iliad*'s investment in Achilles as the quintessential spearman, and the associated dominance of the spear in the poem as whole, leave no place for a man like Philoctetes. His absence on Lemnos, and his replacement by

Medon, are really different manifestations of the same basic idea. A process takes place in the *Iliad* in which archery among the Greeks is marginalized. Philoctetes, the noble and renowned Greek archer, must give way to an ignoble replacement. To my mind there is no clearer example of the *Iliad*'s attitude towards archery among the Greeks, than the way that the noble Philoctetes is marginalized, and the *nothos* Medon is included.

The slightly earlier description of the contingent of Protesilaus from Phylace gives us further insight into the poem's general attitude towards weaponry. Philoctetes never made it Troy (although he will later, 2.724-5), because he was bitten by the snake on his way to Troy, and was then deserted by the Greeks. Protesilaus, by contrast, made it to the Troad, although he was killed as soon as he arrived (2.701-2). The Catalogue entries on these two leaders are very close to one another, with only the short entry on Eumelus of Pherae, the son of Admetus, lying between them (Protesilaus, 2.695-710; Eumelus, 2.711-715; Philoctetes, 2.716-28).[28] In the earlier case Protesilaus is said to have led forty ships to Troy, but he was killed by a Dardanian man as soon as he leapt ashore. He was by far the first of the Achaeans to be killed at Troy (2.702), and it is for this that he is renowned. In his absence, his cohort of warriors, about whom little is said, is led by Podarces, the son of Iphiclus, the son of Phylacus. Podarces is therefore the younger brother of Protesilaus, the deceased leader of the cohort.

The striking thing about the description of Podarces is the emphasis given to his aristocratic birth (he is the '*full brother* of great-hearted Protesilaus' (*autokasignêtos megathumou Prôtesilaou*, 2.706).[29] The explicit comment on the status of Podarces' birth seems to invite comparison with the similar emphasis given to that of Medon. A contrast is constructed in this part of the Catalogue between Podarces, the full brother of the dead aristocrat (*autokasignêtos*, 2.706), who replaces Protesilaus, and Medon, the bastard (*nothos* 2.727), who replaces Philoctetes.[30] The social status by birth of the two replacement leaders is almost certainly explained by the weaponry involved. A cohort of Greek archers is to be led by someone of low birth; but a cohort of spearmen seems to require an aristocrat, even one who is not as good as his older brother ('but he was older and better [*sc.* than Podarces], the warrior valiant Protesilaus', *ho d' hama proteros kai areiôn/ hêrôs Prôtesilaos arêios*, 2.707-8).[31] The (almost) juxtaposition of the two Catalogue entries (Philoctetes/Protesilaus) helps further to emphasize the very different attitude taken by the poem to the two main weapons of war among the Greeks.

With the absence of Philoctetes from the scene of the conflict the only two named Greek archer figures in the fighting scenes of the *Iliad* are Teucer and Meriones (Medon is not described actually using the bow in the fighting within the poem). These are both secondary figures in the army if one compares them to the principal spear-bearing warriors referred to in the Catalogue. As we have seen, Teucer is the son of Telamon from Salamis and he is easily the most prominent of the Greek archers. Like the other leading archers in the *Iliad* (Paris, Pandarus, Meriones and Helenus) Teucer can also fight at close quarters with the spear. The leading archers in the *Iliad*, whether they be Greek or Trojan, are never archers alone. Idomeneus describes Teucer as 'best of the Achaeans in archery, and a good man too in a close fight', *aristos Achaiôn/ toxosunêi, agathos de kai en stadiêi husminêi*, 13.313-4).[32] In Book 13 Teucer kills Imbrius, a son-in-law of Priam, by a spear throw that catches his victim beneath the ear (13.170ff).[33] He also takes up the spear later in the poem (15.458ff.) after Zeus breaks the string on his bow, forcing him to return to his camp to get other weaponry. Having acquired his heavy weapons he then takes his stand beside Ajax in the line of battle (15.483-4).

But it is really the bow for which Teucer is renowned in battle, and with which he is most effective (cf. 'Teucer…well-skilled with the bow', *Teukros...toxôn eü eidôs*, 12.350 and 363). His most prominent victims are the two Lycians, Glaucus (12.387ff.; cf. 16.508ff.) and Sarpedon (12.400ff.), both of whom he hits with arrows. Teucer's arrow causes Glaucus to withdraw from the fighting, but Sarpedon is protected by his shield, and by the assistance of his father Zeus. Later in the poem (15.437ff.) Ajax, in response to a Trojan advance, asks Teucer where are his arrows and his bow? Teucer then stands beside Ajax in the fight, and fires off his arrows at the Trojans (15.442ff.), rather like he does earlier in the poem (at 8.266ff.). The two brothers, spearman and archer, operate as a team at times, with Ajax deriving benefit in battle from Teucer's proficiency with the bow, and Teucer drawing similar benefit from the protection of Ajax's gigantic shield (8.267ff.;15.442ff; cf. 15.483). In response to Ajax's invocation Teucer strikes Cleitus (15.445ff.), and then even goes after Hector, although without any success.

Teucer's most sustained and successful action in the *Iliad* however is in Book 8 (273ff.), where he is the focus of some considerable attention in the narrative. He is described as killing eight Trojans in battle, one after the other (indeed the activity of the bow-fighting here bears comparison with the reminiscence of Odysseus of the bow fighting at Troy, *Od*. 8. 215ff.). Such is the success of Teucer on the field of battle with the bow that he even catches the eye and the approval of Agamemnon himself (8.281ff.). Agamemnon is moved to offer him a prize, second only to his own, if Zeus and Athena should grant it to him to sack Troy (8.287ff.). Earlier in the same speech, in which he is clearly delighted with Teucer, Agamemnon proceeds to remind him of his lowly status in birth:

Teukre, philê kephalê, Telamônie, koirane laôn,
ball' houtôs, ai ken ti phoôs Danaoisi genêai
patri te sôi Telamôni, ho s' etrephe tutthon eonta,
kai se nothon per eonta komissato hôi eni oikôi.
(8.281-4)

Teucer, dear friend, son of Telamon, captain of hosts,
shoot in this way, in the hope that you may become a light to the Danaans
and to your father Telamon, who brought you up when you were little
and, even though you were a bastard, looked after you in his own house.

The final line here troubled the Alexandrian commentators because 'Teucer's origin is out of place, and is of a nature rather to displease than to encourage' (Leaf).[34] The reference to his birth-status might certainly be said to reveal a rhetorical ineptitude on Agamemnon's part; but this is broadly consistent with the general portrayal of him in the poem.[35] The statement of Teucer's social position as a *nothos* is another oblique allusion to the story of the first sack of Troy. As we have seen, Teucer's mother, the unfortunate Hesione, daughter of Laomedon, is not named in the *Iliad*, but the story of her encounter with the monster, and her subsequent marriage, is probably well known to the poem's audience (the monster is alluded to at 20.147). Hesione is really the first human casualty of the perfidy of Laomedon. As a concubine of Telamon she gives birth to Teucer, who therefore 'returns' to the Troad with the Greeks, his father's people, to attack his mother's city, now ruled by his maternal uncle Priam.

So Teucer is defined in the *Iliad* as a bastard, and as the best archer of the Greeks. The reference to his illegitimacy of birth seems definitely to inform his use of the bow (and vice-versa), as it does with Medon. Moreover, his Trojan connection through his mother seems further to enhance this notion. The poem's audience is presumably aware of Teucer's Trojan connection, once Agamemnon has reminded them of it, and they may even relate his characteristic weapon to this background. Archery, so to speak, runs in the family - on his mother's side, but definitely not on his father's.

As far as the general issue of illegitimacy is concerned, the *Iliad* seems to make a clearer and more significant distinction between wives and mistresses on the Greek side than on the Trojan side. Priam is said to have had fifty sons, nineteen of them from the same womb (ie. presumably Hecuba), and the rest by other women (24.495-7). The sons of Hecuba definitely seem to have a greater prestige in the society of the Trojans than those of other women (as with Gorgythion and Cebriones, on whom see below in the next paragraph; see also n.36). And indeed Edith Hall, who is pushing her argument in a different direction, feels compelled to point out (43) that 'it is not clear whether such sons (as Lycaon and those born from women other than Hecuba) were bastards or not; the ambiguity is probably deliberate. Priam's numerous consorts may have been a traditional feature of the Trojan royal house, reflecting for once clear cultural definition'. What does seem to be clear is that no such uncertainty exists in the cases of the Greek archers Teucer and Medon, whose illegitimacy of birth is clearly designated. It seems to me highly significant that there are only two individuals on the Greek side who are actually called 'bastards' (*nothoi*) in the *Iliad*.[36] One of these is Medon, the replacement leader of Philoctetes' cohort, and the other is Teucer, the best and most prominent of the Greek archers.

Agamemnon's reference to Teucer's low birth is not the only way in which the text manages to undercut his claims to success on the field of battle. Teucer's eight victims are an anonymous group of Trojans, but not content with these, he sets his sights on a bigger fish - on the figure of Hector himself (8.293ff.). He keeps missing him however, and hits another two secondary figures instead, Gorgythion, a son of Priam by a woman called Castianeira (8.300ff.), and Archeptolemus, who is Hector's charioteer (8.309ff.; cf.15.458ff.). Hector himself, however, is beyond Teucer's reach in battle; and it is clear from the text that Teucer is simply no match for Hector in the way that his half-brother Ajax certainly is (on the fundamental inequality in battle between Ajax and Hector, see the following chapter).[37] After his charioteer has been killed, and replaced by his half-brother Cebriones, Hector hits Teucer with a rock beside the shoulder, whereupon he and his bow fall to the ground (8.316-29). Ajax has to come to his brother's rescue (8.330-34), and he does so by covering him (*hoi sakos amphekalupse*, 8.331) with his shield.

Thus Teucer's triumph in Book 8 ends unhappily after he is knocked down by Hector, but he might well have lost his life were it not for his brother and his huge shield. The role of Ajax in Book 8 seems designed partly to undercut the glory that Teucer might claim from his victories with the bow. We see the same sort of thing earlier in the episode when Ajax provides cover for Teucer to fire his bow (8.266ff.). Teucer, who has no heavy weaponry of his own at this point, takes his position beneath his brother's shield, and fires his shots using the shield as protection. After he hits each one of the enemy, Teucer scurries back behind the shield to allow Ajax to give him protection again. This whole process of movement back and forth behind Ajax's great shield (his *sakos*, 8.267, 268, and 272), draws an unhappy simile for Teucer:

autar ho autis iôn païs hôs hupo mêtera dusken
eis Aianth': ho de min sakeï kruptaske phaeinôi.
(8.271-2)

> And (Teucer) would go back again, like a child to his mother's shelter,
> so he to Ajax; and he would hide him with his great shining shield.

Needless to say this description is very unflattering for a Homeric warrior, even for one of secondary rank (although it is worth comparing 4.127ff. where Athena protects Menelaus from the arrow of Pandarus like a mother sweeping away a fly from a child; and 23.782-3 where Ajax complains about Athena as a 'mother' to Odysseus).[38] The simile of Teucer as a child hiding behind his mother should be seen in the context of the slightly later reference to him as a (half-Trojan) bastard (8.284), and the fact that his brother has to rescue him on the field of battle (8.320ff.).[39] Teucer's considerable success on the battlefield in Book 8 (and it is worth remembering that he does kill *ten* Trojans here, for which Agamemnon is genuinely grateful), is consistently undercut within the poem. The text points to the spearman Ajax as easily the greater figure of the two. Throughout the poem we see that it is the major spearmen, Ajax, Diomedes, and Achilles, who have the measure of Hector, but Teucer, the low-born archer, is not included in their league. There is obviously no abuse of the archer anywhere here, as there is by Diomedes to Paris in Book 11; and indeed, on occasions the Greek *promachoi* fight together with archers (8.266ff.), and even depend on them (15.429ff.). But at the same time the text leaves us in no doubt about the archer's place in the warrior hierarchy on the Greek side of the conflict.

The other Greek archer figure who is actually named in the *Iliad* is Meriones from Crete, a man who is good enough with the bow to defeat Teucer in the archery contest at Patroclus' funeral (23.850ff.). His use of the bow in the battle (13.650ff.) and in the contest, is presumably linked to his Cretan provenance. Like the other Greek archers, Meriones is a figure of secondary rank, and his main role is as an attendant and second-in-command to the main Cretan warrior Idomeneus (a good example of the latter relationship is 4.250ff.). He is however high enough in status to merit a place in the Catalogue where he is described as 'the equal of manslaying Enyalius' (*Mêrionês t' atalantos Enualiôi andreiphontêi*, 2.651; cf. 7.166, 8.264, 17.259). As far as his status within his own cohort is concerned, Meriones might be compared with Sthenelus, the second-in-command of Diomedes, who also merits a place in the Catalogue after the main leader (2.564).[40] Secondary figures like Sthenelus and Meriones are sometimes described as either effective in their own right, or as significantly lacking in the resolve shown by their leaders. The latter is certainly the case with Sthenelus in Book 5 when he and Diomedes are the intended victims of a charge by Aeneas and Pandarus in a chariot (5.239ff.). Sthenelus' natural instinct is to give ground, and he gets a rebuke from Diomedes for suggesting that this is precisely what they should do (5.251ff.).

Meriones however is a much more prominent figure in his own right than Sthenelus, and also a more effective and fierce fighter. As with the other main archers, Meriones doubles up as an archer and as a spearman. His versatility is shown not the least by the fact that he wins the archery contest (23.850ff.), and is then keen to compete in the spear contest as well (23.884ff.). Similarly in Book 13, in which Idomeneus and Meriones jointly dominate the battlefield, he is described fighting both with the spear (13.159ff.; 246ff.; 526ff.; 567ff.) and with the bow (13.650ff.).[41] Of these two weapons he definitely favors the spear (note especially 13.246ff. where he has a protracted discussion with Idomeneus about spears, bravery, trophies *etc.*). Indeed it may be significant that he is described as using the bow only towards the end of Book 13 when archery acquires some importance in the description of the general fighting (Helenus, 13.576ff.; Meriones, 13.650ff.; Paris, 13.660ff.; the Locrians, 13.712ff.). Thus Meriones uses his bow to kill Harpalion, son of Pylaemenes at the end of the book (13.650ff.). Harpalion tries to kill Menelaus but his spear has no effect and just hits his enemy's shield. When he is withdrawing from his encounter Harpalion is hit and killed by an arrow fired by Meriones.

The greatest moment for Meriones with the bow in the *Iliad* is the contest at Patroclus' funeral (23.850ff.). It seems appropriate that the prize for archery is contested by him and Teucer, the only two named Greek archers from the battle descriptions earlier in the text (it is worth noting that there are no warriors of the first rank involved in this contest, as there are in most of the other events). Meriones wins the contest by killing the dove, thanks largely to the assistance of Apollo. He vows a hecatomb of lambs to Apollo if he shoots the dove (23.872-73). Teucer, by contrast, had promised nothing in the way of sacrifice to Apollo, and so the god begrudges him victory in the contest. Earlier on in the text we learnt that Teucer had acquired a bow from Apollo (15.440-1), but any support that the god may have offered him in the past certainly disappears in the archery contest. Apollo of course is not just the archer god, but also the principal divine supporter of Troy. It is worth remembering that Teucer is embarked on a quest to help destroy the city of his mother (cf. 8.284). His hostility to Teucer in the bow-contest may be connected in some way with this, but the text says only that he failed to make a vow to him.

Meriones therefore is essentially a Cretan spearman (cf. the epithet *douriklutos*, 'famous for his spear', 16.619), who has a bow (13.650ff.), and knows very well how to use it (13.650ff.; 23.850ff.); whereas Teucer is a specialist archer who sometimes uses the spear (as above). A further distinction between the two of them (and Medon) concerns the matter of Meriones' birth and his family background. As we have seen, Teucer and Medon are named as bastards (*nothoi*, 8.284; 2.727) in two unforgiving references, both of which seem to inform their roles as archers. Meriones by contrast does not suffer such a fate in the text of the poem, and his background and his exact relationship to Idomeneus are left quite unclear in the *Iliad*. His father Molus is mentioned twice in the text, first as an earlier owner of the boar's tusk helmet that Meriones gives to Odysseus in the *Doloneia* (10.261-71). This helmet (originally stolen from the house of Amyntor!) is a part of the gear which Meriones also gives Odysseus for the scouting mission (10.260-1, as above), notably a bow, a quiver, and a sword. Molus was an owner of the helmet, which he then gave to his son Meriones when he came to Troy. Molus is also mentioned at 13.249 as the father of Meriones, but this is not elaborated in any way.

Whereas the *Iliad* tells us very little about Meriones' family background, the mythographer 'Apollodorus' provides us with some details which might have a bearing on how we read his role in the *Iliad*. He points out that Molus is the bastard son of Deucalion, and that Idomeneus is his full-born half brother (*Deukaliôni de egenonto Idomeneus te kai Krêtê kai nothos Molos*, 'to Deucalion were born Idomeneus and Crete, and a bastard Molus' 3.3.1; cf. Diod. 5.79 in which Deucalion and Molus are brothers). If this genealogy lies behind the *Iliad*, which is by no means certain, then Idomeneus is Meriones' uncle on his father's side (or half-uncle as the case may be). The role of Meriones, as the principal attendant and second-in-command to Idomeneus, would seem to be appropriate for somebody with such a background (cf. Teucer/Ajax). More importantly, such a genealogy does reiterate the pattern, albeit very obliquely, in which archery and illegitimacy are fundamentally linked signifiers of social status within the army. But the text certainly says nothing explicitly about the status of Meriones' birth. We may therefore at least come to the following conclusion: that it is explicitly stated that Teucer and Medon are archers and bastards, whereas Meriones is a spearman and archer whose father may be a bastard, and this may inform his use of the bow in the poem.[42]

Notwithstanding the significant individual role of Teucer in the fighting with the bow, and the lesser role of Meriones, Greek archery in battle is often an anonymous and collective activity.[43] One noteworthy example of this is Hector's attempt to arrange a halt in hostilities so that Paris can fight in single combat with Menelaus (3.76ff.). As he is getting the Trojans to cease from the fight, the Achaeans keep directing arrows and stones at him until Agamemnon tells them to desist (*tôi d' epetoxazonto karê komoôntes Achaioi / ioisin te tituskomenoi laessi t' eballon*, 3.79-80). Similarly, much later in the poem (13.712ff.), we are told that the Locrians do not follow their leader Ajax, the son of Oïleus, in battle because of their concern that they do not have the appropriate armor and weaponry - helmets, shields or spears. Ajax had plunged into battle alongside his namesake Ajax, the son of Telamon, but the Locrian men place their faith in the bow, and shoot their arrows from behind cover, 'for their hearts did not hold firm in a close fight' (*ou gar sphi stadiêi husminêi mimne philon kêr*, 13.713). At the same time the *promachoi* fight in the front to try to break the Trojan line (13.719-20), while the archers behind keep firing from their hiding spots (*hoi d' opithen ballontes elanthanon*, 13.721). This is a case of archers and spearmen working together in a somewhat different tactic from elsewhere (cf. Janko's note, *ad loc.*); but, as in most cases, the archers fire from their hiding spots, whilst the spearmen are in the close fighting. It is important that the archers have a considerable impact in the struggle because their arrows confuse the Trojans (13.722).

This episode at least reminds us that whilst Greek archery may not be especially heroic in the *Iliad* (and 13.713 and 13.721 make this clear), it can be very effective.[44] As we have seen, this is certainly the case with Teucer in Book 8 whose tally of ten Trojan victims in one brief episode has no parallel in the poem, and certainly not among the Trojan ranks of individual archers. There is no attempt made in the *Iliad* to resist the notion that archery brings some occasional success to the Greeks. It is equally true, however, that the tide of battle never turns significantly on the basis of Greek archery in the way it does through their use of the spear.

On the Greek side of the conflict, therefore, the archer is a figure of a much lower social rank than the leading spearmen, something which the siblings Ajax and Teucer exemplify best of all in Book 8. Further to this, the text establishes a clear connection between archery and illegitimacy of birth (Medon and Teucer); and this connection may also lie behind the poem's treatment of Meriones. The picture of Trojan archery however is much more mixed. On the one hand the leading warriors on the Trojan side, like Hector and Sarpedon, adopt the spear as their characteristic weapon in much the same way as the leading Greeks; and in this context they are generally held in high regard by their peers. Sarpedon may not be the equal of Patroclus in single combat, nor is Hector of Achilles, but their *modus operandi* in battle makes them worthy opponents. The whole notion of undying fame through military achievement (*kleos aphthiton*) necessitates that the Greeks encounter warriors who are worthy of the name. Individuals on the Trojan side, like Hector and Sarpedon, are certainly in this category. But these two meet their ends within the poem itself, and other spearmen, like Aeneas and Glaucus, are lucky to survive their encounters with leading Greek warriors, especially Aeneas who confronts Achilles after his return to combat and has to be rescued by Poseidon, 20.318ff. The poem reveals to us through the descriptions of the fighting, even if it never states it explicitly, that the Trojan spearmen are simply not good enough to match it with the leading Greeks in the spear-fights. The spear seems to be a kind of 'natural' weapon for the Greeks, and they use it to devastating effect within the course of the poem. The sense of doom that hangs over Hector and Troy in the *Iliad*, especially in Book 6, is anchored to the inferiority of the Trojans with the spear in battle.

This is certainly the case in Book 11 where Hector proves to be completely ineffective in the battle. Moreover, this inferiority with the spear (against Agamemnon, Diomedes, and Telamonian Ajax) is contrasted with the impact of Paris on the field of battle with the bow and arrow. As in Book 6 the two brothers are placed side-by-side, but this time it is in a martial context not a domestic one.

And again it is the signification of their weaponry that is central to the contrast. Hector as spearman is completely dominated in battle, whereas Paris turns the tide of battle with his bow.

In the first instance Hector is advised by Zeus through Iris (11.200ff.) to hold himself back from the fighting until Agamemnon withdraws himself from the battle after being wounded. When he sees all this he should rush back into the fray. Hector does exactly what he is told, although it hardly sheds him in a positive light to do so. After Agamemnon is wounded (11.251ff.), and duly withdraws from battle (11.273ff.), Hector plunges back into battle as the leader of his men (11.284ff.). But even then things do not go well for him. First he is knocked out by Diomedes in the fighting when a spear hits him on top of the helmet (11.349ff.). He falls to the ground and remains there for a time; but he revives and makes his escape on his chariot, back through the ranks of men (11.357ff.). Diomedes then pours scorn on him calling him a 'dog' (*kuon*; note that 11.362-7 [Diomedes to Hector] = 20.449-54 [Achilles to Hector]).

And then, when he is described again in the conflict (11.497ff.), we are told that he is doing great things with his spear and in horsemanship, and that he is 'destroying the cohorts of young men' (*neôn d' alapaze phalaggas*, 11.503). This dominance of his opponents in the fighting, however, does not include Telamonian Ajax whom he carefully avoids in battle (*Aiantos d' aleeine machên Telamôniadao*, 11.542). The duel between the two of them in Book 7 (206-302) confirms Ajax's domination of Hector, and it is this, presumably, that motivates Hector's avoidance of him (on the unequal abilities of Hector and Ajax, see below, Chapter 4). Hector prefers to range among the ranks of men than to have to deal with Ajax again (11.540-2). Despite the poem's very considerable rhetoric about Hector's prominence and impact in battle (as, for instance, at 11.503), his clear inferiority to Agamemnon, Diomedes and Ajax in Book 11 does not augur well for the looming encounter with Achilles. Hector's ability as a spearman in the battle descriptions never really matches some of the rhetorical claims made about him within the poem.

Paris, however, a man with little apparent concern as to what the world thinks of him, is much more effective in the fighting in Book 11 because he uses a weapon to which he is well-suited. He fights here from his strengths, not in a mode of fighting where his weaknesses are revealed. His success with the bow in this episode is juxtaposed with Hector's failure, especially against Diomedes (cf. Hector and Diomedes, 11.349ff.; Paris and Diomedes, 11.375ff.). In the course of Book 11 Paris hits three warriors with the bow and arrow, first Diomedes (11.375ff.), then Machaon (11.504ff.), and then Eurypylus (11.581ff.). Diomedes is hit on the right foot, Machaon on the right shoulder, and Eurypylus in the right thigh. These are only superficial wounds, but they are meant to have a great impact on the wider conflict. Arrows, generally speaking, are much less deadly than spears in battle in the *Iliad*, something which is implicit in Idomeneus' view of a doctor's work ('for a doctor is worth many other men for cutting out arrows and applying soothing medicines', *iêtros gar anêr pollôn antaxios allôn/ ious t' ektamnein epi t' êpia pharmaka passein*, 11.514-5; cf. 12.401 and 13.586-7). Paris's arrows are actually much less effective, in life or death terms, than those of Teucer in Book 8, who has a tremendous success rate in killing ten Trojans.[45]

But the issue here is that these three woundings - Diomedes, Machaon and Eurypylus - are meant to complement the other flesh wounds suffered by the Achaeans in Book 11, those to Agamemnon and Odysseus (by spears, 11.251ff.; 11.434ff.). The point is that Paris, more that any other single individual in Book 11, turns the tide of battle towards his own side with his bow and arrows (cf. 11.497-507); and this is an achievement that no other archer in the *Iliad* - Greek or Trojan - can claim.[46] Moreover, he is never punished in return by being hit himself, as other Trojans tend to be after they have hit leading Greeks (cf. Socus and Odysseus at 11.428ff.).

More importantly, it is Paris whose success at this particular stage of the conflict paves the way for the return of Patroclus and Achilles to the fighting. Machaon's wounding (11.504ff.), and his departure from the field of battle (11.511ff. and 596ff.), stir the curiosity of Achilles who sends out Patroclus to find out what is going on (11.599ff.). When he is on his mission Patroclus sees all the signs of a Greek army under pressure. He then hears the full story from Nestor, who, in a typically long speech, urges him to re-enter battle, even on his own without Achilles (11.656ff.). The pressure on Patroclus is only increased when he then meets Euryplus, also recently wounded by Paris, who prevails upon him to mend his wound (11.823ff.). As a consequence of the work of Paris in wounding Machaon, and then Eurypylus, not to mention Diomedes himself first of all, Nestor's task of convincing Patroclus to re-enter the conflict is very much the easier.

Patroclus' return to battle leads ultimately to his own death and Hector's, and (outside of the poem) to Achilles' death by Paris and Apollo (22.359-60). Thus it is very important to recognize that it is *Paris* in Book 11 whose bow sets up the chain of death, Sarpedon-Patroclus-Hector-Achilles, with which the last part of the *Iliad* is concerned. He begins the process in Book 11, and then he ends it, with his killing of Achilles, the 'best of the Achaeans'. But in the flurry of activity described in Book 11, there is no real understanding, least of all by Patroclus, that it is Paris who has brought such strife to the Greeks. When Patroclus meets up with the wounded Eurypylus he says 'but come, say this to me Eurypylus, warrior nurtured by Zeus, will the Achaeans still be able to hold huge Hector or will they now perish, beaten down by his spear?' (*all' age moi tode eipe, diotrephes Eurupul' hêrôs,/ ê rh' eti pou schêsousi pelôrion Hektor' Achaioi,/ ê êdê phthisontai hup' autou douri damentes*; 11.819-21). Patroclus, as it turns out, is ultimately beaten down finally by the spear of Hector. But Hector's spear is not a problem for the prominent Greeks in Book 11. The irony in the question is that Hector has been completely dominated in the recent fighting, and it is rather his brother, the archer Paris, who has brought things to their current state.

Thus Paris is a noble Trojan archer who brings crisis to the Greeks, and who will ultimately achieve the greatest kill of them all, that of Achilles himself. The *Iliad* does not specify that Paris and Apollo will actually use the bow and arrow to kill Achilles. The nearest that it comes to this is at 21.277-8 where Thetis is described as having told him that he 'will be killed by the swift missiles of Apollo' (*laipsêrois oleesthai Apollônos beleessin*, 21.278).[47] In the *Iliad* itself one gets the clear sense that Apollo will kill him 'at the hands of Paris', just as 'flashing-eyed Athena defeated (Hector) at the hands of Achilles' (*chersin Achillêos damase glaukôpis Athênê*, 22.446; cf. 19.411-4). There is considerable emphasis on the fact that Achilles' life will be cut short; and in the final book itself fate (*moira*) and death (*thanatos*) are close beside him (24.132; cf. also 18.96 and 19.416-17). The poem foreshadows his death a number of times, but there is no need for it to specify how it takes place. Everything that needs to be said is actually said by the dying Hector to Achilles (22.359-60); that Paris and Phoebus Apollo will kill him at the Scaean gates (*êmati tôi hote ken se Paris kai Phoibos Apollôn / esthlon eont' olesôsin eni Skaiêisi puleîsin*).

We naturally assume therefore (especially on the basis of 21.277-8) that the god and the man will use their characteristic bows to bring about the death of Achilles (which of course they do in later post-Homeric sources).[48] The anticipation of the death of Achilles *by archery* in the *Iliad* is crucial as a re-affirmation of his greatness as a warrior (cf. *esthlon eont'*, 22.360). It hardly needs to be said that as the 'best of the Achaeans' Achilles cannot be killed by a spear, because a death by this weapon would inevitably diminish his stature as a warrior. That Paris and Apollo kill him with a bow and arrow only enhances the greatness of the man (and much the same thing could be said about the victims of Paris in Book 11). It will be argued later in this chapter that the *Iliad* associates the death of Achilles, at the personal level, with the defeat and sack of Troy at the monumental level. Both of these 'deaths' are anticipated throughout the *Iliad*, even though they take place outside the scope of the poem. Both Achilles and Troy are simply too great to fall to the kind of spear-conflict taking place outside of the city in the *Iliad*. And so both are undone by treachery and archery, which is itself a sign of their monumental greatness.

Paris therefore has a great victory to come, something which Hector seems to know all about at the point of his own death. But there is the sense in the *Iliad* that the glory arising from the death of Achilles will go to the victim, not to the victor. We have every reason to assume that Paris will be delighted by the death of Achilles, just as he is when he wounds Diomedes (11.380ff.).[49] That would only be a natural response to such a result in battle. But the treatment of the bow and arrow in the *Iliad* is such that the archer is robbed of most of the glory that might normally result from a kill with a spear. And even with the death of Achilles yet to come, Paris is a figure without heroic credibility within the *Iliad* itself, not least because he succeeds with the bow and arrow where he fails with the spear (especially his defeat by Menelaus in the single combat, and his rescue by Aphrodite at 3.369ff.). Helen is even concerned that the Trojan women will laugh at her for serving the bed of such a man (3.410-12; cf. 3.428ff.). Likewise the negative perception of Paris evinced by Hector in earlier books (3.38ff.; 6.280ff.; 6.325ff.; cf.13.769ff.) is consistent with the attitude of Priam in the final book, who upbraids him and some of his brothers for their inferiority as warriors (24.248ff.). Paris is one of the nine 'base children' (*kaka tekna*) who have survived so far in the war, whereas the best of them are dead. It is noteworthy, however, that despite the hostile soundings of Hector, Helen, and Priam (to say nothing of the general feelings of the people of Troy about him, 3.454), at no time in the *Iliad* does anyone on the Trojan side explicitly criticize him for his choice of weapon.

One individual for whom the bow brings disappointment and regret is Pandarus, who is the most prominent archer on the battlefield in the early part of the *Iliad*. The Catalogue of the Trojans and their allies tells us that he has Apollo's bow (2.827), which suggests at least that he has great ability as an archer.[50] There is some doubt about the provenance of Pandarus. He is the son of Lycaon, and in the Catalogue he leads the Troes from Zeleia under Ida (cf. 5.102; 5.200; 5.211), but he is also described as a Lycian (where he is the best archer, 5.105, 171ff.).[51] When he fires the shot against Menelaus that breaks the truce (which is described in some considerable detail, 4.104ff.), the bow twangs and the string sings aloud (*ligxe bios, neurê de meg' iachen*, 4.125).[52] The fact that the truce between the Greeks and Trojans is broken by an arrow fired by Pandarus at Menelaus helps to affirm the notion of Trojan perfidy through archery, even if Athena in disguise helps to initiate the action (4.86ff.). But despite his successful actions in wounding both Menelaus (4.127ff.) and Diomedes (5.95ff.), and his great ability as an archer, Pandarus loses confidence in the bow's effectiveness. He is certainly not able to turn the tide of battle in Books 4 and 5 in the way that Paris does later in Book 11. Aeneas urges him to use his bow and arrows against the enemy (5.171ff.), but Pandarus has become despondent about his ability to inflict real harm to Diomedes (5.188ff.), whom he has just hit with an arrow (5.95ff.). He struck him on the right shoulder and pierced the corselet, but it did not defeat him. Nor did it even force him from the field of battle, as Paris is able to do later.

It is in the face of this despondency about the bow's effectiveness in battle that Pandarus offers us some important insights into his background and to his life at home. He reveals to Aeneas that his father, the old spearman Lycaon, had tried to convince him to take horses and a chariot to the war at Troy, and to lead the Trojans in the great conflicts:

*alla pou en megaroisi Lukaonos hendeka diphroi
kaloi prôtopageis neoteuchees: amphi de peploi
peptantai: para de sphin hekastôi dizuges hippoi
hestasi kri leukon ereptomenoi kai oluras.
ê men moi mala polla gerôn aichmêta Lukaôn
erchomenôi epetelle domois eni poiêtoisin:
hippoisin me keleue kai harmasin embebaôta
archeuein Trôessi kata krateras husminas:
all' egô ou pithomên – ê t' an polu kerdion êen –
hippôn pheidomenos, mê moi deuoiato phorbês
andrôn eilomenôn, eiôthotes edmenai hadên.*
(5.193-203)

But somewhere in the halls of Lycaon are eleven chariots
beautiful, newly made, just finished; and cloths are spread
over them; and beside each stands a pair of horses
feeding on white barley and spelt.
Indeed, as I was leaving, the aged spearman Lycaon
enjoined me forcefully in our well-built house:
he told me to climb on horses and chariots
and to lead the Trojans in the mighty combats.
But I did not listen - surely it would have been much better -
but I spared the horses, lest they should go in want of fodder
among the crowd of men, they who were accustomed to eat
    their fill.

So Lycaon wanted his son to take heavy weaponry to Troy, but Pandarus decided instead to come on foot and fight as an archer, thereby forsaking any claim to a leadership role in the fighting with the spear (5.200; contrast Glaucus and his father Hippolochus, 6.206-11; and cf. below, n. 54). This is a decision that Pandarus comes to regret, and he says that he has every intention of breaking the bow and throwing it in the fire if he makes it home (5.212ff.).[53]

Pandarus' long speech to Aeneas, which precedes his death at the hands of Diomedes (5.180-216), gives us a reasonable insight into his background and his life at home. This brief glimpse of his earlier life operates in a similar way to the picture that we get of Paris at home with Helen in Books 3 and 6. Unlike the treatment of the Greek archers, about whom we learn very little, apart from their lowly status in birth, the *Iliad* provides us with some insights into the lives of Paris and Pandarus. The focus in both cases is on the wealth and privilege of their families. It is made very clear that Pandarus could have fought with the sort of heavy weaponry favored by the leading warriors on both sides of the conflict, the spear and the shield. As he points out himself, his father is an old spearman (*gerôn aichmêta Lukaôn*, 5.197), and he has eleven spanking new chariots, with pairs of horses for each one (5.193ff.).

The picture that we get of his domestic and family background is quite clear: he is a man of means (cf. his 'great high-roofed house', *hupserephes mega dôma*, 5.213). He states unequivocally that the bow and arrow was his own choice of weapon, and there was another option available to him. His chosen mode of fighting is not determined by his place in the hierarchy of the society from which he comes; and in fact pressure was exerted for him to use quite a different weapon. No doubt there are many in the poem, just as there were many in Greek military history, whose choice of weapon is largely determined by what they can afford. Horses, chariots and heavy weaponry do not come cheap in the world of Achilles, any more than they do in Greek history. But these are all available to Pandarus, if only he has the will to use them. However he rejects his father's advice on what to take and to use in the conflict.

It is not usually a good thing in Homer to ignore a wise old man. The rejection of elderly advice tends to make a bad situation worse, as happens with the headstrong Achilles, who rejects the efforts at conciliation of both Nestor (1.283-4) and Phoenix (9.434ff.).[54] Antilochus, ever the respectful young man, seems to speak for the poem itself when he says 'that even to this day the immortals honor older men' (*hôs eti kai nun/ athanatoi timôsi palaioterous anthrôpous*, 23.787-8). Pandarus too finally wishes he had taken his old father's advice (5.201). This blemish is compounded by the fact that when he left home for the war he clearly had no interest in playing a leadership role in battle with heavy weapons (5.200). He tells us that his choice of weapon was made, perhaps rather strangely, for the sake of his horses, not for his own sake. The horses will not have their usual allotment of fodder if they are taken to the war.

Pandarus' great ability as an archer gives him, in any case, the option of fighting with the bow and arrow, and this becomes his weapon of choice. Apollo's gift of the bow to him (2.827) suggests that this is the weapon where he has a real and proven skill (cf. 5.105; 5.171ff.). But his new diffidence in the effectiveness of the bow in Book 5, and his feeling that Aeneas would be a better driver of his own horses, means that he prefers to mount the chariot alongside Aeneas and to use the spear against the Argive (5.230-38; esp. *tonde d' egôn epionta dedexomai oxeï douri*, 'this man's approach will I receive with my sharp spear', 5.238). In response to the approach of the two of them in their chariot against the Greeks, Sthenelus, Diomedes' charioteer, wants immediately to withdraw (5.243-50). But Diomedes holds his ground to face Pandarus in a spear fight (5.290-6).

So Pandarus is an archer who also fights with the spear. His use of both main weapons is typical of the Homeric archer, as we have seen (and in some cases archers have a sword too, as with Paris at 3.17-18, and Helenus at 13.576ff.). But in the case of Pandarus, more than any other archer in the poem, weaponry is something of an issue. As a man of wealth he is caught, as it were, between the two main weapons in the war. His father pushed him to adopt a mode of fighting to which, as far as we can tell, he is not terribly well-suited; and yet he strongly desires a significant role in the fighting. He clearly has his share of regrets about choosing the bow, against his father's advice; but he is at least modestly effective with it against two leading Greek *promachoi*. And he stayed alive while he held and used the bow. The harbinger of death for Pandarus is his decision to mount on to the chariot and take up the spear.

In the first instance when they meet up on the battlefield, Aeneas asks only for Pandarus to use the weapon for which he is renowned. 'Pandarus' he says 'where is your bow and your winged arrows and your renown? In archery there is no man here who can compete with you, nor does anyone in Lycia boast that he is better than you. So, come, hold up your hands in prayer to Zeus and fire a shaft at this man'(*Pandare, pou toi toxon ide pteroentes oïstoi/ kai kleos; hôi ou tis toi erizetai enthade g' anêr,/ oude tis en Lukiêi seo g' euchetai einai ameinôn./ all' age tôid' ephes andri belos, Dii cheiras anaschôn*, 5.171-4). The trouble arises for Pandarus when his ambition for a much greater impact in battle gets the better of him (5.180-216).[55] In response to his new dejection after his decision to bring the bow to the war, Aeneas offers him a choice; either to act in the role of charioteer so that he himself can get down and fight Diomedes; or vice versa (5.218-28). And Pandarus chooses the latter (5.230ff.).[56] He himself will fight with the spear and allow the horses to be guided by their accustomed charioteer, should they need to flee from Diomedes.[57]

Pandarus then confronts Diomedes with the spear rather than with his accustomed bow and arrow. 'Son of illustrious Tydeus' he says 'certainly my swift shaft did not defeat you, my bitter arrow; but now I will try again with my spear, to see if I can hit you' (*agauou Tudeos huie,/ ê mala s' ou belos ôku damassato, pikros oïstos:/ nun aut' egcheiêi peirêsomai, ai ke tuchômi*, 5.277-9). He then hits the shield of Diomedes and the spear actually goes through it; but again it fails to inflict any real harm on him (5.280ff.). Diomedes then quickly hurls his spear and quickly kills Pandarus who tumbles out of the chariot (5.290ff.). The archer Pandarus therefore ultimately pays the price for not recognizing the limits of his ability in war. His initial instinct at home was the right one, for he is a bowman through and through. The implication in the poem is that had he stuck with his accustomed weapon, despite its limitations, and fought from his strengths, as Paris usually does, he might have had an impact in the fighting, and even survived the war.

The final Trojan archer about whom something should be said in this section is Helenus, the son of Priam and Hecuba, and a full brother of Hector and Paris. Helenus has the same sort of background in wealth and privilege as the other named archers on the Trojan side. But he is rather different from them in that his principal role in the fighting is as an augur of the Trojans rather than as an archer (6.73ff.; 7.44ff.).[58] Helenus and his augury are not very prominent in the *Iliad*, especially when compared with the Epic Cycle; but it may be important that Hector is prepared to take his brother's advice and to return to the city to call for prayers and rituals to Athena (6.102ff.).

In the fighting itself Helenus uses a great Thracian sword to kill Deipyrus (13.576ff.), but then he is wounded on the hand by Menelaus (13.593ff.). In this encounter Helenus uses his bow against Menelaus, but the arrow hits his armor and falls away harmlessly. In return, Menelaus throws a spear which hits Helenus on the hand, and it also goes into the bow itself. Agenor then binds Helenus' hand with a strip of woolen fleece (13.598ff.).[59] At the end of the poem (24.249) Helenus is the first named of the 'base children' (*kaka tekna*, 24.253) whom the old man Priam castigates prior to going out of the city for Hector's body. It seems to be significant that archery is not specified as the reason for Priam's hostility towards him. And in fact Polites and Deïphobus are included in the list of those rebuked by Priam, and they are especially involved in the close fighting with the spear. Priam says that the sons who are left to him, including Paris and Helenus, are 'liars' (*pseustai*), 'dancers' (*orchêstai*), 'best at beating the ground in the dance' (*choroitupiêisin aristoi*), 'thieves of lambs and kids in you're own country' (*arnôn êd' eriphôn epidêmioi harpaktêres*) (24.261-2).

It is clear that the freedom of the wealthy elite on the Trojan side to choose the bow as a weapon brings with it no explicit opprobrium of the sort that Diomedes verbalizes against his enemy Paris (11.385-95). The leaders on both sides of the conflict are comfortable with the role that their own archers play in battle. Pandarus, Paris and Helenus all make the bow their principal weapon, and no one on the Trojan side in the text itself ever calls them to account for this in any way. The main issue as far as Hector and Priam are concerned is that they should be active and effective in the fighting, whatever form that takes, not shrinking from it (cf. Hector to Paris at 6.325ff.). And so the high-born archers Paris and Helenus are designated company leaders, just like the major spear warriors, Hector, Aeneas and Sarpedon (12.88ff.).

But implicit within the text, and presumably with the poem's Greek audience very much in mind, it is also apparent that weaponry at Troy does signal much about one's character. It is clear that Hector's choice of a leading role with the spear, despite his inferiority as a warrior in the close fight against the best of the Greeks, earns him a dignity and respect that the Trojan archer can never hope to acquire. Pandarus clearly brings disappointment to his father (and himself) for his choice of weapon; and Paris and Helenus end the poem on the wrong side of a very unfavorable comparison with Hector. The roles of the two principal archers on the Trojan side, Paris and Pandarus, seem to be saying on the one hand that the bow represents the best chance for Trojan survival against a greatly superior attacking force. But at the same time there is an impulse on the part of the leading men to follow a code of heroic conduct based on the spear, even if it is with this particular weapon that the

Greeks are so dominant. The doom of Troy is foreshadowed by the fact that the city's esteemed leaders favor a mode of fighting that is better suited to their opponents than it is to them.[60]

To conclude this part of the chapter, a few final comments on the subject of Greek and Trojan archery. Edith Hall is surely right to insist that archery is not necessarily a more predominant mode of fighting among the Trojans than the Greeks. Indeed it would probably be fair to say that the combined references to Teucer, Meriones and Medon on the Greek side of the conflict represent a fairly similar weighting to the roles of Paris, Helenus and Pandarus on the Trojan side. The three most prominent archers in the battle scenes of the *Iliad* are undoubtedly Paris, Pandarus, and Teucer - two on the Trojan side, and one on the Greek. But on the whole the practice of archery does seem to be spread fairly evenly across both sides. There is no need to 'measure' this in actual line numbers: Teucer is the dominant archer in Book 8 with ten dead Trojans to his credit, and Paris is dominant in Book 11 where he turns the tide of battle the Trojan way. Likewise Pandarus is prominent in Books 4 and 5, but Meriones has his moments in Books 13 and 23. And so it could go on. Thomas and Stubbings were therefore on very shaky ground in making the assumption that archery is a more predominantly Trojan weapon because of the roles of Paris and Pandarus. Hall's comments are a useful corrective to this widely held view.

But, as we have seen, an appraisal of the roles of archers on the two sides in the war needs to go beyond a simple comparison of their prominence in battle. I have argued in this section that a more detailed analysis of Greek and Trojan archery supports the position that Troy has a fundamental association with archery, and that this is particularly the case when the archer-gods who support the city, Apollo and Artemis, are brought into the argument.[61] The parallel use of the bow by aristocratic Trojans and lower class Greeks informs a very different social outlook on the practice by the two sides. This line of argument clearly runs counter to the case put forward in Edith Hall's book, that the Trojans of the *Iliad* are the innocent victims of later Greek attitudes towards foreign archery.[62] My own view is that the Trojans of the *Iliad* are inevitably a manifestation of 'the other' in one sense of the term, in so far as they are a foreign enemy of the Greeks in a world where the monsters and the Amazons have disappeared from the heroic landscape. They are certainly not demonized;[63] and indeed, I have already argued (in Chapter 1) that Hector and his father are pre-eminent heroes in their own right by confronting somebody whose terrifying powers transcend the ordinary human condition. But the Trojans are different from the Greeks in a number of ways, and it is the role of archery, more than any other single characteristic, that helps to signify this.

2. Philoctetes

We saw earlier that the Catalogue entries on the cohorts of Protesilaus (2.695ff.) and Philoctetes (2.716ff.) have distinct structural and linguistic similarities based on the fact that both leaders are absent from the fighting. Protesilaus is dead, whereas Philoctetes is nursing his snake-wound on Lemnos. The character of the two entries, and their proximity within the Catalogue itself, help to reveal very different attitudes within the poem to the spear and the bow on the Greek side of the war. The text makes it clear that Protesilaus is replaced by his high-born full brother Podarces, whereas Philoctetes' company of archers is led by a bastard Medon. The two passages seem to signal, at the very beginning of the poem, the place that the bow has in the social and political hierarchy of the Greek army at Troy. This kind of close contrast in Book 2 bears a resemblance to the way that the two high-born Trojan brothers Paris and Hector are placed side-by-side in the *Iliad*, first in the domestic context within the city itself (in Book 6), and then in the martial context when they are both active in the fighting at the same time (in Book 11). As we have seen, the specific weaponry that informs Paris and Hector is central to the contrast between the two of them in these books. We can identify therefore a process throughout the *Iliad* in which juxtaposition and contrast are used to reveal the different roles of archery on the two sides fighting in the war.

Philoctetes therefore is rather different from the other Greek archers in the poem by virtue of his aristocratic status. And although he plays no part in the action of the poem itself, and is himself replaced by a bastard, the inclusion of his name and his special skill does seem to be significant. The reference to Philoctetes in the Catalogue has the effect of taking us back in time to the period just before the war; and it also looks forward to when the city itself will be defeated. The Catalogue entries to Philoctetes and Protesilaus allude to three separate events in three different periods in the story of the Trojan war (in addition to the present roles of the contingents which they originally led). First there is the actual voyage to the Troad (Philoctetes on Lemnos); then the arrival of the Greek expedition at Troy (the death of Protesilaus); and then there is the oblique allusion to Philoctetes' role in the eventual defeat of Troy (2.724-5). Thus the references to the two absent leaders give us an insight into the way that Greek archery is dealt with in poem, and they also offer a much wider temporal sense of the whole expedition, from the initial sea-voyage to the Troad to the defeat of the city itself.

In order to get a sense of the work being done by the single passage devoted to Philoctetes in the *Iliad*, it is worth making some comparative comment on the role of the Centaur Chiron in the poem. This comparison is instructive of the way that similarly marginal figures are dealt with in the *Iliad*. Neither Philoctetes, as an aristocratic Greek archer, nor Chiron, as a hybrid creature, is an appropriate inclusion in the action of the poem, especially Chiron whose physical form belongs to a bygone era. There are four allusions to Chiron in the *Iliad*, three of which deal with his role in the previous generation. There are two references to the spear of Achilles, which came from Chiron via Peleus (16.141-4 = 19.388-91). This is a special spear that only Achilles can wield, and it is the single object that Patroclus does not take into battle. The spear was given to Peleus, presumably as a wedding present, and was then passed down to Achilles. Chiron is also referred to as the former teacher of Asclepius, the master healer. Asclepius' two sons, Machaon and Podalirius, who are both doctors too, are at Troy with the army, and Machaon still has with him some of the drugs that Chiron gave to his father (4.219). It is these drugs that Machaon uses to heal the wound of Menelaus (4.217-9) after he has been hit by Pandarus.

These three references help to convey the notion that Chiron's presence is still felt on the battlefield at Troy, both through the spear and through the drugs that he passed on. Both of these objects offer special powers to their users. Achilles has an enhanced capacity to kill through the use of Chiron's spear; and Machaon has a greater power to heal by virtue of Chiron's special drugs. The

Centaur himself is at the margins of the *Iliad*, but significant objects associated with him are mentioned at key moments, which ensure that his presence is felt within the action of the poem.[64]

Had the references to Chiron been limited to these three, then we might reasonably have come to the conclusion that the Centaur has been consigned to the earlier period, together with the other monsters and hybrids whom we examined in Chapter 1. In that case he would have been active in Thessaly with Asclepius and Peleus; and his presence would still be felt in the war itself through their sons (Machaon, Podalirius, and Achilles) who use his special objects. The tradition of Chiron as Achilles' teacher, which clearly lies behind the *Iliad*, might not have appeared in any explicit way in the text, especially when one bears in mind the important part given to the old man Phoenix in this role. The story of Achilles' upbringing by Phoenix seems most likely to be one of the 'inventions' of Homer created for the purpose of the poem itself.[65] As has long been recognized, the human figure of Phoenix is able to meet the needs of the poem much better than Chiron; and it is in this context that Phoenix is given an important role in Book 9 in trying to convince Achilles to return to battle.[66]

But, notwithstanding the role of Phoenix in the *Iliad*, a single explicit reference to Chiron, uttered by Eurypylus in Book 11, has the effect of bringing the Centaur into the more recent past, into the earlier life of Achilles himself. Eurypylus has been hit by Paris with an arrow in the right thigh (11.581ff.), and, in need of help, pleads to Patroclus for some medical assistance:

all' eme men su saôson agôn epi vêa melainan,
mêrou d' ektam' oïston, ap' autou d' haima kelainon
niz' hudati liarôi, epi d' êpia pharmaka passen,
esthla, ta se proti phasin Achillêos dedidachthai,
hon Cheirôn edidaxe, dikaiotatos Kentaurôn.
iêtroi men gar Podaleirios êde Machaôn,
ton men eni klisiêisin oïomai helkos echonta,
chrêïzonta kai auton amumonos iêtêros,
keisthai: ho d' en pediôi Trôôn menei oxun Arêa.
(11.828-36)

But save me and lead me to my black ship,
and cut the arrow from my thigh, and wash the black blood from it
with warm water, and put on it soothing drugs,
excellent ones, which they say you learnt about from Achilles
whom Chiron taught, most just of the centaurs.
For the doctors Podalirius and Machaon,
the one I think lies amidst the huts with a wound,
with need himself of a blameless doctor,
and the other on the plain waits for the sharp battle of the
    Trojans.

This brief speech tells us a lot about the way in which the recent pre-war past is evoked in the *Iliad*. When one reads through the poem it first appears to us that a radical poetic process has taken place in which the inclusion of Phoenix (in Book 9) seems to signal the absence of the Chiron/Achilles tradition. There seems little doubt in Book 9 that Phoenix 'replaces' Chiron because he better suits the needs of the poem. But in the midst of the impassioned appeal of Eurypylus to Patroclus in Book 11, a very significant reference is made to the 'traditional' narrative of Chiron's role in Achilles' earlier life. This means in practice that there are allusions within three books to two different versions of Achilles with his two different tutors - Chiron, (11.828ff.), and Phoenix (Book 9 *passim*, esp. 434ff.). Eurypylus states quite clearly that Chiron taught Achilles himself the same sorts of healing skills that Asclepius acquired (cf. 4.217-9).

So Chiron operates in an obscure way in the past across two generations, and Phoenix has a major role to play with Achilles within the present context of the war. The single reference to Chiron as his teacher means, *inter alia*, that Achilles has a unique background with a Centaur, but that he also has an essentially 'normal' background too (with Phoenix). On the one hand he has special skills and powers (like healing from Chiron) because he comes from a different kind of world from the other *promachoi*; but he also has an understanding of the demands and expectations of being part of an organized military expedition (from Phoenix, especially at 9.438ff. and 9.485ff.). Achilles' identity, and the crisis that he goes through within the poem, are informed partly by the two teachers who have played a significant part in his earlier life.

So the single allusion to Chiron as Achilles' teacher has the effect of enhancing our understanding of Achilles as a fundamentally different kind of figure from those around him (as a healer-warrior, as a teacher, and as a student of a Centaur); and in so doing it provides us with an insight into the rather remote world of Thessaly, not long before the war began. In a similar way the Catalogue reference to the life and career of Philoctetes does plenty of work within the poem too, not least because it foreshadows the notion that the current breed of warriors will need to call on an aristocratic archer to win the final victory in the war. Philoctetes will return to Troy and play a great part in the defeat of the city a second time, because the Greeks will have a need of him ('yet soon the Argives beside their ships were to remember lord Philoctetes', *tacha de mnêsesthai emellon / Argeioi para nêusi Philoktêtao anaktos*, 2.724-5).[67] As we have seen in the previous section, archery plays a very secondary role to the spear in the warrior hierarchy on the Greek side within the action of the poem; but there will be a time when its prominence will be restored.

The message is clear in the *Iliad*, and it is signaled as early as the Catalogue, that the dominant spear-culture in the world of Achilles will ultimately prove to be a failure as far as the actual taking of Troy is concerned. As Apollo says to Patroclus before he helps to kill him: 'get back Patroclus, born of Zeus. It is not fated for the city of the lordly Trojans to be sacked by your spear, nor by that of Achilles, who is much better than you' (*chazeo, diogenes Patroklees: ou nu toi aisa/ sôi hupo douri polin perthai Trôôn agerôchôn,/ oud' hup' Achillêos, hos per seo pollon ameinôn*, 16.707-9). What he could have said is that Troy will not fall to the spear at all. The reference to the need for Philoctetes' return to Troy (2.724-5) implies that the predominant mode of fighting among the Greeks will not bring about the sack of the city. Achilles may be the best warrior of his time, but there seems to be an inherent failure in the manner of his fighting, as far as sacking a great and monumental city like Troy is concerned. The spear will bring Achilles undying fame (*kleos aphthiton*), and he will actually 'sack' Troy in the *Iliad* itself, after a fashion, by killing Hector. But neither he nor his principal weapon will bring about the actual destruction of the city. The failure of Achilles to take the city with his spear (16.707-9), and the future need of the Greeks to restore Philoctetes to his principal role (2.724-5), are really different sides of the same coin.

So the oblique allusion in the Catalogue (2.724-5) almost certainly plays on the audience's knowledge of the career of the archer Philoctetes. It anticipates his role in the imminent defeat of the city, rather like the way that various references to the use of fire within the *Iliad* anticipate the eventual torching of the city by the Greeks (see Chapter 4). In the case of Philoctetes, the future (ie. his part in the sack of Troy) is anticipated within the context of the recent past (the story of the snake-bite and his desertion on the island of Lemnos). But there is also a case to be made that the more distant past is alluded to in this passage as well. Philoctetes' renown in the classical period (especially in the Sophoclean play *Philoctetes*, 801ff.) is as the keeper of Heracles' bow and arrows. These special weapons were used to defeat Troy in the previous generation when Laomedon broke his word to give over the special horses that he had promised to Heracles (5.648ff.). In the Sophoclean play the same weapons need to be used again before the city will fall a second time. Odysseus says that 'if the bow of this man is not captured, it is not possible for you to conquer the land of Dardanus' (*ei gar ta toude toxa mê lêphthêsetai,/ ouk esti persai soi to Dardanou pedon*, Phil. 68-9).

The tradition of Philoctetes as the keeper of Heracles' bow is not spelt out in the *Iliad* or the *Odyssey*, although it is probably implied in Proclus' account of the Cyclic epic *Little Iliad*. This says that 'after this (*sc.* the awarding of Achilles' arms to Odysseus, and Ajax's attempt at revenge) Odysseus ambushes Helenus and captures him. Following a prophecy he makes about the taking of the city, <Odysseus with> Diomedes brings Philoctetes back from Lemnos. He is healed by Machaon, and fights alone against Alexander and kills him' (*meta tauta Odusseus lochêsas Helenon lambanei, kai chrêsantos peri tês halôseôs toutou Diomêdês < Odusseus meta Diomêdous* Ap. > *ek Lêmnou Philoktêtên anagei. iatheis de houtos hupo Machaonos kai monomachêsas Alexandrôi kteinei*, M.L.West, Loeb text and trans.).[68] As West points out in his text (n.27), the prophecy referred to was that Troy could only be sacked if Heracles' bow, which was in Philoctetes' possession, was used against it.

These later references to the passing down of Heracles' bow to Philoctetes do not 'prove' anything about what lies behind the *Iliad*.[69] As we have seen, the passage devoted to Philoctetes in the

Catalogue is more concerned to spell out details of his recent past, and his absence from the current fighting; and in this context there is only a strong hint of his role in the defeat of the city. But there is also the possibility that the passage is one further oblique allusion within the *Iliad* to the first sack of Troy, in light of the fact that the bow that destroyed Troy once needs to be used again in a critical way to ensure victory a second time. Thus we are in a position to say that the *Iliad* consciously alludes in some rather oblique ways to the fact that the city falls twice to archers; once to the archer Heracles (5.638ff. etc.), and once to Philoctetes and the Greeks (2.724-5). There is the possibility too, largely depending on what lies behind these references, that the same bow and arrows are used in both cases.

Philoctetes therefore, as a great aristocratic bowman on the Greek side, represents a form of fighting that defeated Troy in past times, and one that will also have a profound effect in time to come. The inclusion of his name, which is clearly well-known to the poem's audience, certainly alludes to one victory at Troy (that is, in the future, after he is brought back from Lemnos), and possibly to two (Heracles' sack of the city), both of which are achieved through the bow and arrow. The *Iliad*'s oblique allusions to the twin defeats of the city by archery have the effect of emphasizing the current period of the spear's dominance. In between the two great moments of Greek archery, both of which result in the sack of Troy, the one performed by Heracles, and the other by Philoctetes, is the world of Achilles and his special spear that Chiron made. The references to Philoctetes in the future, and Heracles in the past, allow the poet to set the middle period apart as a special time and place, when a different kind of ethos prevails, when the bow is absent entirely from the aristocratic Greek military effort. The time of the spearman Achilles in the *Iliad* is 'framed' by periods where the bow wins the day; and the reference to Philoctetes in the Catalogue plays an important part in conveying this.

3. The Generations of Archers

The brief reference to Philoctetes in the *Iliad* therefore seems to do a lot of work in the poem. It certainly looks ahead to the future sack of Troy; and it may well evoke the narrative of the previous sack of

Troy too, especially if later, more expansive, accounts of Philoctetes with Heracles' bow also lie behind the *Iliad*. This section too touches on the subject of Heracles' bow, except we will focus here much more on the *Odyssey* than the *Iliad*. The argument of this short third section is that Odysseus' speech to the Phaeacians, with which we began the chapter (*Od.* 8.215ff.), evokes the notion of two different 'sieges'- the one at Troy, the other in Odysseus' house – both of which are broken by an archer with a special bow. Philoctetes and Odysseus are not just archers of great renown, but they also use their weapons to end the suffering of their peoples after long and painful periods of conflict and stalemate.[70] The two men even seem to have rather similar personal experiences, in that they both endure long periods of misfortune and isolation on a journey (cf. *Il.* 2.716ff.). After their protracted periods of suffering they both take up a special bow with which to break a long stalemate. Odysseus' role as an archer in the *Odyssey* seems to be conscious of the renowned achievement of his more highly skilled contemporary Philoctetes, and his role in the breaking of a siege.[71]

We saw earlier in this chapter that when Odysseus comes to reflect upon Greek archery (*Od.* 8.215ff.) he names four individual bowmen, Heracles and Eurytus from the earlier generation, and Philoctetes and himself from the recent Trojan war. He says that he would not be prepared to compete with the heroes of the earlier period, they who were apparently much better archers than the men of his own time.[72] His assessment of his own relative skill in archery seems to leave him in last place of the four archers whom he mentions. He is quite explicit that Philoctetes is the best archer of his generation, and that he himself is second best.[73] The two of them however do not seem to be a match for the bowmen of earlier times, represented here by Heracles and Eurytus. The text does not state explicitly that Heracles surpasses Eurytus in the earlier generation, but that is probably the best way to read it. It would certainly be in keeping with Heracles' characteristic dominance of the heroic landscape (as well as this, there is a tradition outside of Homer in which Heracles defeated Eurytus for the hand of his daughter Iole).[74] Moreover, Eurytus, for all his skill with the bow and arrow, clearly lost an accurate sense of his own abilities, and made the mistake of challenging Apollo to a bow contest. For this act of arrogance he paid the ultimate price.

Drawing therefore on the assumption that Heracles is meant to be the best archer of his generation, the order of ability in Odysseus' speech is Heracles, Eurytus, Philoctetes, and then Odysseus himself. This appraisal of their relative skill with the bow might evince a certain modesty on Odysseus' part, something for which he is not renowned.[75] But the point being made in the speech is that he is in very esteemed company. There is no disgrace attached to being fourth in this group.

As far as Heracles and his bow are concerned the Homeric poems consistently portray him as an archer (his famous club seems to be a post-Homeric invention [Stesichorus fr. 229 Page]). In the *Iliad* Dione tells her daughter Aphrodite, who has been wounded by Diomedes, that Hera was once hit by Heracles on the right breast with a three-barbed arrow and it caused her unendurable pain (*tlê d' Hêrê, hote min krateros païs Amphitruônos/ dexiteron kata mazon oïstôi triglôchini/ beblêkei*, 5.392-4). And huge Hades too suffered an arrow wound in Pylos among the dead at Heracles' hands, also causing pain to him (*tlê d' Aïdês en toisi pelôrios ôkun oïston,/ eute min ôutos anêr, huios Dios aigiochoio,/ en Pulôi en nekuessi balôn odunêisin edôken*, 5.395-7). Hades is forced to go to Olympus where Paeëon eased the pain and healed him.

There is an important parallel drawn in *Iliad* 5 between the actions of both Heracles and Diomedes in their wounding of gods. Whereas Heracles in the earlier generation wounds Hera and Hades with some element of ferocity and bravado (5.403-5, albeit in circumstances that are by no means certain), Diomedes at Troy wounds Aphrodite and Ares - two gods who are hostile to the Greeks. A major difference in these encounters is the weaponry involved; for Heracles uses the bow and arrow, and Diomedes uses the spear. One central aspect of the comparison is that Heracles uses a weapon for which Diomedes seems to have nothing but contempt (11.385ff.). But, as I have argued throughout this book, no demands or expectations are made in the *Iliad* for warriors of the earlier generation to conform to later attitudes (or vice versa). The point is clear that both Heracles and Diomedes use weapons that are appropriate to their heroic surroundings and contexts.

So Heracles' arrows in the *Iliad* have a real sense of menace associated with them. The text does not actually refer to their magical powers, or to the application of poison on the tips (as we find, for instance, with the death of Nessus in Sophocles' *Trachiniae*, 569ff.); but the effect of the arrows on the two gods is probably in keeping with some kind of special power. Contending with gods on an apparently frequent basis characterizes the Odyssean Heracles too (*erizeskon*, 8.225, 'used to contend'), although there is no specific statement of what form these disputes took (as there is in the case of Eurytus, 8.226-8).[76] There is one other Homeric reference to Heracles as an archer, in the *Nekuia* of Odysseus in the *Odyssey* (11.601ff.). When Odysseus encounters his phantom among the dead it is his bow and arrow that help to characterize him (11.606-8). Heracles' bow is drawn, and he is on the whole a menacing figure, not unlike Apollo himself (cf. the important repetition of the phrase 'similar to night', *nukti eoikôs*, *Il.* 1.47 [Apollo] / *Od.* 11.606 [Heracles]).

Working our way through both Homeric epics therefore, we can say that Heracles' reputation is founded on the bow and arrow. With this as his characteristic weapon he is the great monster-slayer, the destroyer of Troy in the time of Laomedon, and the peer of gods in battle. His deeds are alluded to in speeches of mortals, in speeches made by gods, and within the narrative itself. Odysseus in the *Odyssey* seems to remember him as the best of the human archers, someone whose reputation dominates the later generations.

So everything in both the *Iliad* and the *Odyssey* seems to bear out Odysseus' statement about the supremacy of Heracles as an archer in his generation, and Philoctetes in his (*Od.* 8.219ff.).[77] Moreover in the *Odyssey* their supremacy with the bow runs parallel to the 'second-best' status of Eurytus and Odysseus. It is also very important that the two 'second-best' archers use the same bow. Eurytus gave over his bow to his son Iphitus, who then passed it on as a gift to Odysseus (21.11ff.).[78] Odysseus as a youth had gone to Lacedaemon on business and had met Iphitus in Messene at the house of Ortilochus.[79] At their meeting Iphitus gave to Odysseus the bow which had belonged to Eurytus (21.13ff., 31ff.).[80] It is noteworthy that Iphitus was thereafter killed by Heracles in an atrocious breaking of the rules of guest-friendship (21.22ff., which is connected thematically with the behavior of the suitors in Odysseus' own house). We also learn that Odysseus leaves the bow at home when he goes to the war, and carries it only in his own land (21.38-41). This decision would appear to reflect the value of the bow as a special memorial (21.40-1), rather than Odysseus' aversion to archery. He clearly took a bow with him to Troy (cf. 8.215ff.), but not the special one which he received from Iphitus. In any case, the bow is waiting for him when he returns from Troy, and it is this bow that helps to bring about the suitors' demise.

Thus we have two pairs of archers across the generations who are linked within the *Odyssey* on the basis of their relative skill with the bow - Heracles and Philoctetes on the one hand, and Eurytus and Odysseus on the other. The latter two are connected by a special bow in the *Odyssey*, and the former are connected by a special bow in post-Homeric sources. So we are left wondering again whether the handing down of Heracles' bow to Philoctetes lies behind the *Odyssey*. The evidence of the text seems to suggest that it does (together with *Il.* 2.724-5, and the later evidence of the *Little Iliad* as described by Proclus). The *Odyssey* does seem to draw on the Heracles/Philoctetes-at-Troy tradition to evoke the idea of the breaking of a siege in Odysseus' house on Ithaca. Odysseus, the archer, seems to take on the role of siege-breaker that Philoctetes had at Troy, and he also uses a special bow to do it.[81] The *Odyssey* tells of a hero who moves from one long siege to another. Having helped to break the long stalemate at Troy (especially in the wooden horse), Odysseus claims again his special bow to resolve the protracted crisis in his own house. Archery (Philoctetes) and cunning intelligence (Odysseus) brought about the defeat of Troy, and it is important that these same two weapons also defeat the suitors back on Ithaca.

Odysseus' speech to the Phaeacians therefore (8.215ff.) not only anticipates the bow contest in his own house on Ithaca, the fact that he has great ability with the bow, and will certainly be a match for any of the suitors who challenge him. It also foreshadows the later reference (21.11ff.) to the fact that a special bow, passed down through the generations, will play the key role in ending the long suffering of those involved, as happened at Troy.[82] As with Chiron's spear (used only by Achilles), and Heracles' bow (used only by Philoctetes in later accounts), the bow of Eurytus demands use by a special individual who is uniquely equipped to handle it.[83]

4. Apollo, Achilles and Odysseus

As we have seen, the principal divine supporter of Troy is Apollo, the archer god. It was suggested in the first section that Apollo's presence (together with the less significant support of his sister Artemis) helps to convey the notion that Troy is associated with archery at the divine level. There are no divine archers on the Greek side, but there are two Olympian archers on the Trojan side. In a graphic image of this, Apollo even takes his stand with his winged arrows (*echôn ia pteroenta*) against Poseidon in the *Theomachy* (20.67-8), just as Artemis does against Hera (20.70-71). As it turns out there is no actual conflict between Poseidon and Apollo, but the divine archer's support for Troy is graphically represented nonetheless. Indeed the presence of the two divine archers, together with the aristocratic nature of Trojan archery, means that Troy is fundamentally associated with archery at both the human and divine levels.

This final section of the chapter however is not really concerned with Apollo and his association with the Trojans, but rather with Apollo and the Greeks. The central argument of the section is that the principal heroes of both Homeric epics, Achilles and Odysseus, are made to resemble Apollo, but that each poem identifies different characteristics of the god. It will argue that whilst both heroes can be said to resemble Apollo, there is a major distinction in the weaponry that they take up and use. Achilles implicitly, though emphatically, rejects the weapon of the god and all that it stands for in his world. As the 'best of the Achaeans', the bow is no concern of his, and much is made instead of the special spear that he uses. Odysseus however takes up the special bow and uses it to secure vengeance against the suitors. The bow contest, which helps to decide the issue with the suitors, is held in the social and religious context of a festival of Apollo, a fact which has its own symbolic implications for the role and conduct of Odysseus.[84]

The choice of weapons made by the main heroes in the two poems inevitably affects the character of their associations with Apollo. The hatred of Apollo for Achilles is linked, not to a similarity of weaponry between the god and the man, as is sometimes the case (cf. Eurytus and Apollo at *Od.* 8.223ff.), but to entirely different weapons. It will be argued finally that the anticipated death of Achilles by the bow and arrow in the *Iliad* is the end of an era of the spear's dominance, and the harbinger of another era dominated by archery and cunning intelligence.

But first a few brief comments on the archery of Apollo and Artemis in the two poems.[85] Fundamental to the role and identity of Apollo in Homer are the associated notions of archery and healing. The archer god is the plague god, and it is important that the principal action at the outset of the *Iliad* deals with the effect of Apollo's arrows on the Greeks. The *Iliad* is 'framed' by descriptions of Apollo's archery (1.8ff./ 24.602ff.), and in both cases the effect is deadly. After Agamemnon's arrogant rejection of Chryses' plea for the return of his daughter, the Greek army bears the full brunt of the plague sent by Apollo (1.8ff.). This is depicted graphically in the form of arrows which go through the Greek camp (1.43ff.; 380ff.) hitting first the animals, and then the men themselves; and it is only when the Greeks make due recompense at Chryse that Apollo is appeased and sends a favoring wind for their return journey by ship (1.430-87). The deadly effect of Apollo's archery quickly resolves the impasse over the detention of Chryseis, even if it precipitates a new set of problems for the Greek leadership.

In the final book there is reference to the fact that the arrows of Apollo and Artemis killed the children of Niobe, who had boasted that she had produced many children, whereas Leto had only two (24.602ff.). Vengeance is ruthless, and Apollo kills the boys, and Artemis the girls. [86] Achilles' narration of the fate of Niobe is one of the major paradigm stories of the *Iliad*. She is described as enduring the ultimate in suffering - a mother who loses all her twelve children. But even she, despite the magnitude of her loss, took food after the gods had buried them on the tenth day. And so Niobe is a mythical *exemplum* for Priam (and Achilles) in coming to terms with the death of loved ones.

Artemis herself, despite her nominal stance as a defender of Troy, has a minimal role in the *Iliad*, and the only scene in which she appears sees her humiliated at Hera's hands (*Il.* 21.470-513). She exhorts Apollo to get in and fight, because his bow seems to be as useless as the wind (*anemôlion*, 21.474; cf. Pandarus at 5.216, *anemôlia* [sc. *toxa*] *gar moi opêdei*). Hera upbraids her and then snatches her bow from her shoulders, and beats her over the ears with it, whereupon the arrows fall from her quiver. Artemis disappears to Olympus in tears leaving her mother Leto to pick up her bow and arrows. It is clear in the *Iliad* that the wild (cf. *potnia thêrôn*, 'queen of the wild animals', 21.470), not the battlefield, is the place for the arrows of Artemis (cf. 5.51-4; 21.481ff.).[87]

Neither Apollo nor Artemis appears at all in the *Odyssey* but their presence is referred to in many different ways. Their arrows are as deadly in the *Odyssey* as they are in the *Iliad* (Artemis, 5.121ff. [Orion]; 11.171ff., 198-9 [Odysseus' mother, Anticleia]; 11.324f. [Ariadne]; 15.476ff. [Eumaeus' Phoenecian nurse]; and Apollo, 3.278ff. [Menelaus' helmsman]; 7.64ff. [Rhexenor]; 8.226ff. [Eurytus]). But in the *Odyssey* there is a much greater emphasis on the notion of painless arrows, and a kindly death.[88] For instance, Eumaeus tells Odysseus about the island called Syria, which is a thoroughly fine place to live, plentiful in food and drink, and with no sickness for mortals to confront (15.403ff.). Death is pleasant too, for it comes, when people have grown old, in the form of painless arrows (*aganois beleessin*, 15.411) fired by Apollo and Artemis. The same notion of euthanasia (*malakos thanatos*) runs throughout the poem, especially in the case of Penelope who wishes that Artemis would end her suffering (18.201ff.; 20.61ff.).[89] The avoidance of pain is a crucial theme in the *Odyssey*; and it is appropriate therefore that Helen, who has acquired some expertise in the healing of suffering by means of drugs (4.219ff.), should be likened earlier to Artemis (4.120ff.). The arrows of Artemis can bring a sudden and gentle death to women, just as Helen's drugs can ease the most acute human suffering.[90] The archery of Apollo and Artemis in Homer therefore is associated both with divine retribution for arrogant conduct (as with Agamemnon, *Il*.1.8ff.; Niobe, *Il*. 24.602ff.; Eurytus, *Od*. 8.226ff. etc.); and with the cessation of suffering (the pain associated with old age, grief at the loss of a loved one, death by natural causes).[91] The twin elements of destruction and healing are clearly seen in the use of their characteristic weapon.

It has long been recognized that the Iliadic Achilles 'mirrors' the figure of Apollo in various ways.[92] This resemblance between the god and the man manifests itself in a number of ways. There is a suggestion of a physical resemblance between the two;[93] they also have a similar level of emotional intensity in the conduct of their vengeance; and they both have a clearly specified association with destruction, healing and music. They are both austere and remote, and rather isolated in some ways from those around them. And indeed, as Gregory Nagy points out in a formative study (see n.

92), their association is signified in a major way through the epic diction itself. The *mênis* ('anger') of Achilles' response to the taking of Briseis is the consequence of the *mênis* of Apollo's response to the treatment of Chryses. This characteristic *mênis* on the part of both of them has the effect of bringing *loigos* ('destruction') to the Greeks (the plague in Book 1 / Hector's victory at the ships) both of which bring further pains (*algea*) to the Greeks.

Achilles therefore shares with Apollo the capacity to inflict or to ward off grief and devastation from the Greeks: or, as Laura Slatkin puts it, 'the successful capacity to *loigon amunein* (or *amunai*) *within the framework* (her italics) of the *Iliad* is restricted to two figures of *menis* - Apollo and Achilles - who, like the third, Zeus, can both ward off devastation for the Greeks and bring it on them as well'.[94] Apollo and Achilles are destroyers and healers, and we see these roles within the *Iliad* itself. Achilles' capacity to perpetrate physical torment and mutilation of a body is the other side of his ability to heal physical wounds.[95] Similarly, his role in inflicting the most acute levels of human suffering on other people (as he does to Priam by his treatment of Hector's body, 22.395ff.) parallels his ability to end it through acts of compassion (as he does also with Priam in Book 24.518ff. and esp. 24.656ff.). This ability to heal suffering is also borne out by the joy that he takes, at a difficult time, in playing the lyre (9.186ff.).[96] This reiterates his similarity to the figure of Apollo whose own lyre-playing among the gods is referred to in the first and last books of the *Iliad* (1.603; 24.63).[97]

These clear resemblances in the figures of Achilles and Apollo in the *Iliad* run parallel to the hostility that they have for one another within the course of the poem itself (as, for instance, in their encounter at 22.7ff.). They may have a physical resemblance, and they may conduct themselves in similar ways with similar effects, but their relationship is characterized by a strong and mutual hostility.[98] The antipathy of the god for the hero is explicit in the text after his return to the fighting, especially when Achilles mutilates the body of Hector (note especially 24.33ff.).

It is often pointed out that the motif of a particular god's hostility to a mortal with similar attributes is seen elsewhere in the *Iliad* (Thamyris and the Muses, 2.594-600; Helen and Aphrodite, 3.413ff., Teucer and Apollo, 23.862ff.); and also in the *Odyssey* (Orion and Artemis, 5.121-4; Eurytus and Apollo, 8.225ff.).[99] In these cases the resemblance of the mortal and the immortal is constructed around *the* (or at least *a*) principal attribute of the pair. So Thamyris is a Thracian singer of special power (cf. the Muses); Helen is an awesomely beautiful woman who almost earns the wrath of Aphrodite with whom she is associated; Orion is a hunter (cf. Artemis), and so forth. In the case of Apollo and Eurytus in the *Odyssey*, and, to a lesser degree, Apollo and Teucer in the bow contest in the *Iliad*, divine resentment is built upon the use of the god's characteristic weapon. Eurytus thinks he is so good an archer that he can contend with Apollo; and Teucer thinks that he can defeat Meriones in the bow contest without any need to provide an offering to the god of archery. And so they both pay the price in very different ways for crossing Apollo.

The resemblance of Achilles and Apollo in the *Iliad* operates in quite a different way. It exists *in spite of* the weaponry that the two of them use, not because of it. Achilles is no Eurytus and no Teucer. The hatred of Apollo for him is not based on the use of the same kind of weapon. Indeed, if Achilles' devotion to his special spear is anything to go by, and if we can take Diomedes' resentment of archery (11.385ff.) as a view shared by all the best princes, then Achilles and Apollo are completely at odds in the area of weaponry. To put it another way, Achilles is the pre-eminent representative of a spear-bearing elite who reject the bow and everything that it stands for in their heroic landscape.[100] The similarities in the roles and identities of Achilles and Apollo must therefore be set alongside the fundamental opposition in their characteristic weapons. In the *Iliad* Achilles and Apollo are informed, not just by the conditions of their existences (mortal/immortal), and by their respective sides in the war (Greek/Trojan), but also by the weapons with which they strike their enemies (spear/bow and arrow). Achilles is as much the (mortal) spearman as Apollo is the (divine) archer, and the eventual conflict between them is settled largely on these terms. Achilles' pre-eminent use of the spear as his weapon, and his death by the bow and arrow, are really different sides of the same coin.

If the different weapons of Apollo and Achilles in the *Iliad* play some part in defining the relationship between them in the *Iliad*, then one could make the contrary statement about Odysseus' use of the bow in the *Odyssey*. As we have seen, Odysseus is easily the best archer in the action of the *Odyssey*, even if he is able to identify more highly skilled bowmen in his past. And the fact that Odysseus' bow comes ultimately from Eurytus (and before this from Apollo himself?),[101] seems to signal that Apollo deals out harsh retribution to those who indulge in acts of great arrogance (like Eurytus himself, and, by extension, the suitors in Odysseus' own house). Odysseus' use of the bow to destroy the suitors is quite clearly linked to Apollo's role as the avenger of reckless arrogance.[102] Apollo is not even present in the poem, let alone an important divine player in the strategy to destroy the suitors (we can obviously contrast the crucial role of Athena in this regard).

But his presence is evoked in some important ways.[103] The role of Theoclymenus, who is skilled in reading the signs of the suitors' demise, helps to anticipate Apollo's distant role in the retribution inflicted upon the suitors (esp. 15.525ff. [the omen of a hawk, Apollo's messenger]; and 20.345ff.).[104] Moreover the archery contest itself takes place at the festival of Apollo (20.156; 20.276-8; 21.257ff.). Accordingly, it seems appropriate that Odysseus succeeds in stringing the bow like a well-skilled singer strings his lyre (21.404-9). He even tries out the string before he uses it, and it gives out a lovely sound, like a swallow (21.410-11). Odysseus' victory in the bow-contest, and the subsequent slaying of all the suitors with both the bow and the spear, really represent the brilliant use of the characteristic weapons of the two gods who support his actions - Apollo (in his use of the bow, 22.8ff., 75ff., 106ff., 116ff., 246), and Athena (in his use of the spear, 22.122ff., 265ff., 281ff.).[105] As far as weaponry is concerned, the victory of Odysseus over the suitors is achieved through his expertise in both of the main weapons of war, the bow (until he runs out of arrows), and then the spear.[106]

The role of Odysseus therefore is essentially that of an avenger who comes from afar, one who destroys the arrogant suitors with his bow, and then the spear, during a festival in Apollo's honor.[107] Prior to the commencement of the bow-contest Odysseus enunciates an ardent desire for the punishment of the suitors: 'how I wish, Eumaeus, that the gods may avenge the outrage which these men in their arrogance devise, wicked deeds in another's house, and have no place for modesty' (*ai gar dê, Eumaie, theoi tisaiato lôbên,/ hên hoid' hubrizontes atasthala mêchanoôntai/ oikôi en allotriôi, oud' aidous moiran echousin*, 20.169-71). Whereas in the *Iliad* Achilles' implicit rejection of archery, and his death by it, help to inform his relationship to

Apollo, Odysseus' association with Apollo in the *Odyssey* is built fundamentally on his triumph over reckless arrogance using the weapons of the god himself. His taking of Apollo's weapons to destroy the suitors amounts to the adoption of Apollo's role in rooting out outrageous behavior. Having rid the house of the suitors he then has it cleaned with water, sulphur and fire (22.437ff., 478ff.). But Achilles in the *Iliad*, despite his similarities to Apollo, has absolutely no inclination to use the bow and arrow as a weapon of war.

So to conclude this chapter a few brief points. The rather rigid warrior ethos of the world of Achilles at Troy in the *Iliad*, based around the spear, is quite distinct from the world of Odysseus in the *Odyssey*. There is nothing terribly remarkable about this because Odysseus travels through a world where survival depends on his flexibility in the use of weaponry, and his ability to negotiate a wide range of unusual and very dangerous hazards. But by insisting that Achilles' generation of princes uses the spear in battle, and not the bow and arrow, Homer in the *Iliad* seems to set them apart from the previous generation (of Heracles) and the later period (of Philoctetes, Odysseus *et al.*). Heracles was a bowman when he sacked Troy for the first time (*Il.* 5.638ff. etc.), and Philoctetes, the aristocratic Greek archer, will return to Troy after Achilles' death and help to sack it for the second time by killing Paris (*Il.*2.724-5). And when me move our focus to the *Odyssey* we see that Odysseus proves himself to be very adept in the use of the bow to break the 'siege' in his own house. The bow therefore plays a major part in the final victories in these three conflicts (as does *mêtis* in the case of the latter two).

But the period in which Achilles is pre-eminent is set apart in the *Iliad* from what precedes it and what follows it. As far as the *Iliad* is concerned Achilles wins his Trojan war by killing Hector. The fall of Troy itself is not something that Achilles will see, nor is his chosen weapon destined to provide such a victory.[108] The *Iliad* hints at the notion that the period of the spear's dominance comes to an end with Achilles' death by the bow and arrow. Achilles will be killed by two archers, a mortal and an immortal (22.359-60), and the city will fall only when a specialist archer takes up the fight (suggested at 2.724-5). The manner of Achilles' death is the final testimony to his greatness as a warrior in that he can be killed only by devious means, not by the spear itself. But there is also the sense within the poem that Achilles' kind of heroism, great as it is, will not achieve the stated aims of the Greek expedition.[109] Just as the bow and arrow will triumph over Achilles, the greatest of the spearmen, so Troy will not be taken with the spear, but with the arrows of Philoctetes, and through the cunning intelligence and the deceit of Odysseus.

Chapter 4
Fire

Throughout much of this book we have been examining the way that the *Iliad* looks back on the previous generations of heroes to set the main war at Troy in a wider temporal context. The people of earlier times, and the actions that they performed, are alluded to in many different ways; and these range from the long and detailed accounts by people like Nestor and Glaucus and Phoenix, to the more obscure kinds of allusions presented within the narrative itself. Collectively, these reminiscences and allusions provide us with an insight into the way that the past is constructed in the poem, and the way that it is used to influence various situations which the characters have to confront. The *Iliad* conveys the notion that the storytellers either had personal experience of events in the past (as with Nestor's various deeds, or Priam's reminiscence of the Amazons [3.184ff.]); or they know of them in a general kind of way (as with Phoenix's knowledge of Meleager, or Achilles' account of Niobe). Sometimes the narrators tell of their own family backgrounds, as Glaucus does to Diomedes (6.145ff.), and Aeneas to Achilles (20.200ff.), and Tlepolemus to Sarpedon (5.633ff.). But even family reminiscences of particular deeds are sometimes shown to be known far and wide (cf. the Lycian Sarpedon's reply to Tlepolemus, 5.648ff.).

There is no attempt in the *Iliad* to convey the notion that the speakers themselves, or those listening to them, acquired the knowledge of these stories through formal poetic performance. The people of the past certainly seem very real to the characters, not mere figures of song (although these two ideas are by no means mutually exclusive). But it is worth remembering that the Odyssean interest in the figure of the bard and his songs (notably Phemius and Demodocus) has no parallel in the *Iliad*.[1] Indeed among those at

Troy who have a stake in the outcome of the war, it is only Achilles, of all people, who picks up the lyre and sings with it (9.185ff.). In this particular episode he sings of the 'glorious deeds of men' (*klea andrôn*), and this may imply that the subject of his song is Heracles or Bellerophon or Meleager (cf. Phoenix at 9.524). He may even sing about the first sack of Troy! But unfortunately the passage is not concerned to provide us with any kind of detail about the song of Achilles. So within the *Iliad* itself general storytelling and mythical allusion are given preference over formal bardic performance with the lyre.

In previous chapters we have been visiting with considerable regularity the allusions within the *Iliad* to the sack of Laomedon's Troy by Heracles. These chapters have highlighted major differences and distinctions within the poem between the earlier war and the present siege dealt with in the poem itself. Three significant differences in the two wars have been argued for so far, and these correspond to the first three chapters: first, that the 'heroic landscape' of early Troy is fundamentally different from the world in which Achilles operates (especially monsters); second, that the earlier war commences in very different circumstances, and is fought over different objects of possession; and third, that the major heroic weaponry used to fight it has undergone a fundamental transition, from the bow in the previous generation (ie. of Heracles) to the more emphatic use of the spear and heavy armor in the second war (esp. Achilles).

The combined effect of these three aspects is to convey the notion of significant generational change. The case has been argued that legendary material of earlier heroic periods is incorporated within the text of the *Iliad* to make the present period of Achilles quite distinct. This final chapter is concerned to explore the notion of generational change from a different perspective, and its particular focus is the sack of Troy in the two generations. As with the earlier chapters, we will be especially concerned with the destruction of the city as it is dealt with and foreshadowed *in the Iliad itself*, not so much the treatment of it in the ancient sources more generally (such as in the lost Cyclic epic *Iliu Persis*, or in the detailed account in Vergil's *Aeneid* Book 2).

In the case of the Heraclean defeat of the city the evidence is quite bare, with very little detail provided of precisely what is supposed to have happened. It is clear that the Trojans were able to move on after the disaster that afflicted them. The Troy of Priam in the *Iliad*, even after the long years of siege, is still a place of great beauty, wealth and prosperity; and so it is a real prize for the Greeks if they can sack it. Whatever happened when Heracles came, there does seem to have been a quick and successful recovery by Priam and his people (cf. 24.543ff.). Troy was able to renew itself with considerable vigor and success, and the earlier defeat receives no mention at all from the Trojans themselves. It is almost as if the event has dropped out of the collective consciousness of the inhabitants of the place. The city was definitely sacked in very remarkable circumstances (note the part played by the monster!), but the Trojans, for whatever reason, are not inclined to indulge in reminiscences about it. The second invading force of Greek warriors have a very different outlook on war from their fathers; and the foreshadowed sack of the city is very much more grim. The imminent obliteration of the city seems to be on everyone's mind. And it is especially the use of fire as a weapon of attack that helps to signify the differences in the outcomes of the two invasions.

The central argument of the first part of this chapter is that fire in the *Iliad* helps to identify the ruthless force of destruction that will be brought to bear upon Troy when it is eventually defeated.[2] The use of fire is both a harbinger of the imminent burning of Troy, and a signifier of generational change in the conduct of war. By way of a comparison in the divine sphere, it is worth noting that in the *Theogony* fire marks the transition from one cosmic era to the next (cf. 687-735 [Zeus against the Titans]; and 820-69 [Zeus against Typhoeus]). The ultimate hegemony of Zeus and the Olympians is won by the force of fire, an element which then helps to symbolize the transition from one phase in the development of the cosmos to the next. The victory of the Olympians is a triumph of the immortal force of fire that Zeus possesses in abundance. In the *Iliad* too there is plenty of emphasis given to the fact that the victory of the Greeks will be achieved by means of fire (including the Olympian fire of Hephaestus within the poem itself). And thus, by implication, a new phase for Greeks and Trojans begins with the burning of the city (something which we see significantly in Vergil's account in *Aeneid* Book 2).

Most importantly, fire has a crucial role to play in distinguishing the two generations of Greek heroes in the *Iliad* (although it is worth contrasting Euripides' *Trojan Women*, 819ff., where fire destroys the city in both generations). The lack of detail about the first sack of the city, and the emphasis given to the burning of it the second time around, are really different sides of the same coin. And even the use of fire by the Trojans themselves in the *Iliad* seems to foreshadow the burning of their own city. Their achievement in reaching the Greek ships to burn them is a physical manifestation of their success in this phase of the fighting; but it is also a signal for Zeus to turn his support to the Greeks (15.599-602). The one victory (that is, of the Trojans at the ships of the Greeks) leads directly to the other (the sack of Troy). And it is very significant that the actions of Patroclus, and then Achilles, not to mention the role of Zeus, turn the tide of the conflict back towards the Greeks.

The second part of the chapter focuses more specifically on Achilles and his associations with fire. Particular attention is paid to the fire at the river Scamander in *Iliad* 21, and also to Pyriphlegethon, the burning river of Hades (referred to in the *Odyssey* at 10.513). The central argument is that the immersion of Achilles in the burning river is the Iliadic antecedent to his other immersions in fire (and water) in later sources. The description of Achilles in Scamander not only anticipates the destruction of the city, which is explicitly stated by the river god (21.373-6); but it also foreshadows the imminent death and cremation of Achilles himself. The immersion of Achilles in the *Iliad* seems to have an important influence on later descriptions of his life and death; and we will briefly consider some of the relevant passages in post-Iliadic literature. There is also the question of what kind of earlier, pre-Iliadic narrative, or narratives, might lie behind the description of the burning Scamander. In Chapter 1 the argument was put that the *Iliad* has adapted 'traditional' quest-myths of men against monsters to the needs of a very different heroic context (ie. in the encounters of Hector and Priam with Achilles). This chapter too will conclude with a brief speculation that a similar process of adaptation has taken place in the description of the river of fire in the *Iliad*.

1. 'Bring fire!'

The *Iliad* provides us with no clear sense of how to imagine the earlier sack of Troy inflicted on the city by Heracles. Early in the poem we learn from his proud son Tlepolemus that Heracles 'destroyed the city of Ilios and made the streets desolate' (*Iliou exalapaxe polin, chêrôse d' aguias*, 5.642). Tlepolemus gives us no details of what precisely this is supposed to mean, but the two verbs clearly suggest physical destruction of the city, and the slaughter of the people. In the case of the latter this would usually mean the killing of the men, seeing that the verb *chêroô* is also used to describe a wife being turned into a widow (as at 17.36). The fact that he enunciates this in a hostile battlefield context to an enemy warrior presumably influences the nature of his reminiscence. Tlepolemus, grandson of Zeus, confronts Sarpedon, the son of Zeus in battle (5.631), so lineage is something of an issue between them (cf. Glaucus and his favorable reminiscence of Bellerophon, or indeed Aeneas's account of the 'history' of Troy). He is in the business of trying to ridicule Sarpedon's claim to be a son of Zeus; and so he is keen to magnify the deeds of earlier sons of Zeus like his own father. A key part of this is the claim that Heracles came to the Troad for the horses 'with only six ships and fewer men' (*hex oiêis sun nêusi kai andrasi pauroteroisin*, 5.641); but he was still able to sack the place. Thus the speaker has an interest in indulging in a rhetorical boast about the capacity of his father to destroy the city with such a minimal army to support him. The idea is that Heracles was a virtual army in himself, quite different from the likes of Sarpedon. One might also say that the comment hardly presents Tlepolemus himself in a positive light either, seeing that he is part of a huge army and still cannot sack the place after a very long time.

The speech of Tlepolemus clearly bears comparison with statements elsewhere in the two Homeric poems about the superiority of earlier generations of heroes (see Chapter 1). In light of his father's renown Tlepolemus clearly has an interest in privileging the earlier generation of warriors. Sarpedon's reply to all the proud and hostile rhetoric thrown at him by Tlepolemus shows no inclination to argue about the details of what happened when Heracles came on his mission. He seems to have no problem agreeing with his enemy that 'that man (ie. Heracles) destroyed holy Ilios' (*keinos apôlesen Ilion hirên*, 5.648) through the folly of Laomedon's broken promise. Laomedon, it seems, got what he deserved, seeing that he failed to keep his word. The fact that Heracles 'destroyed' (*apôlesen*) the place seems to speak for itself too (cf. *Iliou exalapaxe polin* of Tlepolemus, 5.642).

Somewhat later in the poem we get another brief glimpse, but no more than that, of the earlier sack of Troy. In response to a request from Hera to put Zeus to sleep (14.233ff.), the god Sleep (Hypnos) tells the story that he distracted the mind of Zeus once beforehand. He did so on that occasion so that Hera could have an opportunity to persecute Heracles (14.249ff.). Hypnos paid a price then from Zeus, and he is not keen to go through it all again. The previous episode occurred 'on the day when that man, the great-hearted son of Zeus, sailed from Ilios, after he had sacked the city of the Trojans' (*êmati tôi hote keinos huperthumos Dios huios/ epleen Iliothen, Trôôn polin exalapaxas*, 14.250-1).

Thus the picture that we get from the relevant references is that Heracles came to Troy to do a job, did what was asked of him by the king of the day, and was then cheated of his promised prize. He then destroyed the place, and went away again, presumably with the horses that had been promised. The first sack of Troy therefore is very much a *personal* victory of one man who gathers together a small force to help him get his revenge. The support of the Salaminian Telamon seems to have been important, judging from his role in later sources and from the reference to Teucer as his illegitimate son (8.284, see below).

Despite these recollections of the earlier war by the various characters in the poem, there is no textual reference to any physical damage to the city, nor indeed to any specific human casualties. The walls of the city are still standing, and the memory of them in time to come is a matter of great concern to Poseidon (7.446ff.). It was he who built them (21.446ff.; although at 7.446ff. Apollo is also involved in the building process), and he is not impressed that the Greeks build another wall with which to defend their ships.[3] His concern is based on the fact that they have built it without offering due recompense to the gods (7.446-50; cf.12.3-33). The renown (*kleos*) of the new wall will spread as far as the dawn spreads, and people will forget about the wall built by the two gods when they were in the service of Laomedon (*tou d' êtoi kleos estai hoson t' epikidnatai êôs:/ tou d' epilêsontai to egô kai Phoibos Apollôn/ hêrôi*

Laomedonti polissamen athlêsante, 7.451-3). Likewise, the other early wall referred to, the one built by the Trojans and Pallas Athena for Heracles, is still standing (20.145ff.). This is the wall that they built for him to escape from the monster whenever it drove him from the shore to the plain. It is to this wall that Poseidon leads some of the gods after Zeus has allowed them greater freedom to play a part in the fighting (20.144ff.).

The absence of any apparent physical damage to the city from the earlier sack of the place has its parallel in the fact that there is no specific reference to the killing or enslavement of any individual Trojans, including Laomedon himself. Reference to the sea-monster which Heracles killed (20.147) may be taken as an oblique reference to Hesione who was given over to the creature as an offering. Similarly, the description of Teucer as a 'bastard' (*nothos*, 8.284), seems certainly to assume that Hesione was taken away to Salamis at the end of the war to become the concubine of Telamon, as in later accounts. But Hesione herself is not actually named in the poem, so there is certainly no explicit statement of her unhappy fate. Her brother Priam and his wife Hecuba seem to have survived the earlier defeat of the city completely unscathed. And Priam's brothers, the other sons of Laomedon, Clytius, Hicetaon, and Lampus, are all still alive with Priam on the walls of Troy (3.146ff.; cf. 20.237ff.; contrast pseudo-Apollodorus' account, *Bibl.* 2.6.4, in which the brothers are all killed with their father).

At no point do the Trojans themselves make any reference to the time that Heracles came with his armed force of men. Priam recalls other conflicts, including the time that the Amazons came to Troy (3.189), but he makes no reference at all to Heracles. Likewise Aeneas makes no mention of the earlier war when he recalls the long 'history' of Troy from the days of Dardanus on Mount Ida (20.215ff.). He does refer to 'illustrious' (*amumôn*) Laomedon (20.236), but there is no comment on his period as king. And he certainly refers to the snatching of Ganymede by Zeus from Tros (20.231ff.), an act which proves to be an important antecedent to the war, because Zeus gave the horses to Tros in recompense for the loss of his son (cf. 5.265ff., 648ff.). But it is noteworthy that there is no specific reminiscence of the earlier war by any of the Trojans themselves within the entire *Iliad* (bearing in mind that Sarpedon is a Lycian ally of the Trojans).

The point is clear that the poem seeks throughout to allude to the first sack of Troy in various ways; but, equally, it has no interest in providing any kind of graphic detail of the suffering endured by the Trojans. Presumably the stories were there to be told, especially from the mouths of the Trojans, should the poet have had an inclination to do so. Amplification of the reminiscences of Tlepolemus and Sarpedon is all that would have been required. Later sources refer in much greater detail to the defeat of Troy, including the death of Laomedon by Telamon (Pindar, *Nem*.3.36-7; cf. *Isth*. 6.27-30) or by Heracles himself (Diodorus, 4.32. and 4.49; Apollodorus, 2.6.4). But the *Iliad* is concerned only with some of the bare details. In view of the recollections of Tlepolemus and Sarpedon, one can hardly say that the sack of the city by Heracles and his force of Greeks counted for nothing; but there is no sense in the *Iliad* of any residual collective trauma among the Trojans from that particular campaign (it is worth contrasting Heracles and the Pylians, 11.690ff.). And indeed the continuity in the kingly government of the city implies that it moved on after the upheaval. Priam was somehow able to replace his father, the perfidious king Laomedon, as he might have done in a time of peace (cf. 24.543ff.).[4] Thus we can say that if the earlier war is supposed to have caused a general level of suffering for the defenders of the city, as we might expect, then nothing very much is made of it in the *Iliad* itself.

One aspect of all this is the figure of Heracles himself in the *Iliad* and the *Odyssey*. He is a figure of ferocity and violence in most Greek literature, and this is equally true of the Homeric Heracles.[5] In the *Odyssey* we learn that he murdered Eurytus' son Iphitus, and then stole his horses (21.11ff.). The murder seems to be a rather bizarre episode, not the least because at the time Iphitus is a guest in Heracles' house (21.22ff.). No particular rationale is given for the murder, but it may again be a consequence of Heracles' great love of horses. It is pointed out that he keeps Iphitus' horses after he kills him (*epeita de pephne kai auton,/ hippous d' autos eche kraterônuchas en megaroisi*, 21.29-30). Likewise the figure of Heracles in the *nekuia* in *Odyssey* 11 (601-26), with his bow out of its case and an arrow on the string, is a figure of awesome violence and power; so much so that he raises a din among the dead (11.605-6). In the *Iliad* Heracles is an individual whose violence is directed against all parts of the world, not just against the one unfortunate city and its environs with which we have been concerned.[6] He is a kind of solitary wanderer, a questing hero, whose adventures put him into conflict with many different kinds of enemies. And so he fights and wounds gods with his special arrows (Hera and Hades, 5.392ff.); he has to go to the Underworld to snatch the dog Cerberus (8.362ff.); he confronts monsters like the one at Troy (20.147); and he fights against whole cities or peoples (like the Trojans, 5.633ff. etc., or the Pylians, 11.690ff., upon whom he deals a severe defeat from which they scarcely recover). He is in turn the victim of the hostility of Hera (14.249ff.; 15.25ff.; 18.117-19), and he has to endure being servile to a weaker man (8.362ff.; 15.639-40; 19.91ff.).

All of this seems to point to the fact that the Heracles of the *Iliad* is a man whose energies are put forth in a great many directions against a range of different enemies. Laomedon's Troy is just one enemy among very many. It seems that Heracles had too much on his plate to concern himself with the systematic razing of a city and the complete obliteration of its identity. He seems to have no inclination for genocide. His interest at Troy is to get his hands on the promised horses; and the sacking of the city, whatever that may mean, was the process by which he acquired them. He thus avenges the wrong done to him, and moves on. The generation of warriors with whom the *Iliad* is principally concerned, however, prove to be much more single-minded in their execution of the war, and in their treatment of the people in the city. Within the poem itself Achilles in particular wreaks havoc on the Trojans, and it is made very clear that a more terrible level of destruction will be inflicted on the city itself in a short time to come.

The missing weapon in the earlier sack of Troy is fire (that is, in the Homeric account, but not the Euripidean, *TW*, 819ff.). The apparent absence of fire seems to emphasize the comparative leniency with which the Trojans were treated by Heracles. It is clear that he could have burnt the place down if he had such an inclination, but this is not the way things worked out. The *Iliad* makes the point repeatedly that the same leniency is not going to be forthcoming the second time around (and there is certainly no mercy shown in the vivid account in Vergil's *Aeneid* Book 2. 298-804).[7]

One graphic narrative of what a defeated city can expect from an invading force is told by the old man Phoenix in *Iliad* 9 to the intransigent Achilles. This is the story of the war around the city of Calydon (9.529ff.). The Aetolians were defending the city from the Curetes, and things went well for the defenders whilst the prince Meleager was taking up the fight on their side. But when he withdraws from the fighting in the wake of a dispute with his mother, things start to go very wrong for the Aetolians. The shouting of the enemy rises up as they start to batter the walls of the city, but Meleager shows no signs of relenting, despite the pleas of all those around him (9.573ff.). The Curetes then begin to climb on to the walls and start burning the city (9.588ff.). At this point Meleager's wife Cleopatra tells him all of the awful things that happen to a defeated city: 'they kill the men, and fire levels the city, and strangers lead into slavery the children and the deep-girdled women' (*andras men kteinousi, polin de te pur amathunei, / tekna de t' alloi agousi bathuzônous te gunaikas*, 9.593-4). The fate of the innocents referred to in the speech has the desired effect on Meleager and he duly wards off defeat from the Aetolians just in time (9.595ff.).

The story of Meleager's timely rescue of the Aetolian cause is meant to have a specific relationship to the threat posed by the Trojan use of fire against the Greek ships (9.600ff.). The point that Phoenix is trying to get across is that Achilles, like Meleager, can come to terms with his own anger at Agamemnon by accepting the gifts being offered to him.[8] He can then come to the rescue of the Greeks before it is too late. This will ensure that the Greek ships, like Calydon, are not burnt by the Trojans, who are attacking them with their firebrands (cf. Agamemnon's question to Odysseus on his return from the embassy; whether Achilles 'is willing to ward off consuming fire from the ships?', *ê rh' ethelei nêessin alexemenai dêion pur;'*, 9.674). And indeed it is eventually with this instruction in mind, to avoid the burning of the ships, that Achilles sends Patroclus back out on to the field of battle: 'Up now Zeus-born horseman Patroclus. I see the sweep of consuming fire beside the ships. Let them not take the ships and there no longer be a means of escape' (*orseo, diogenes Patroklees, hippokeleuthe:/ leussô dê para nêusi puros dêioio iôên:/ mê dê nêas hêlôsi kai ouketi phukta pelôntai*, 16.126-8; cf. Achilles at 9.650ff.; 16.80ff.; 18.13-14).

Whilst Phoenix clearly tells his story of Meleager's defence of Calydon precisely to convince Achilles to return to the fighting, the description of what happens to a city when it is sacked has a much more profound resonance for the Trojans than for the Greeks (even though the Trojans are not hearing the story).⁹ And likewise there are important parallels between the role of Meleager's wife Cleopatra in the passage and that of Andromache in Book 6 (407ff.). Both of the wives appeal to their husbands to stave off defeat from the city by defending its walls, although the two situations and the attitudes of the two warriors are very different. One important parallel is the emphasis placed on what happens to a city when it is sacked. Troy's fate will be the same as Calydon's - the killing of the men, the burning of the city, and the enslaving of the women and children (cf. Priam's gloomy anticipation of what will happen to Troy, 22.59-71). Meleager at least was able to do something about this by returning to battle, but Hector is locked into a value-system and a mode of fighting in which his enemies are superior, and he is not the man to stave off defeat. The principal concern of Phoenix, as the teller of the story of Meleager, is with the imminent destruction of Calydon as it relates specifically to the battle at the Greek ships; but everyone among the Greeks and Trojans expects exactly the same fate for Troy when it is eventually defeated.

It is clear therefore that there will be no continuity of kingly government and Trojan identity when the city falls this second time around. A new generation conducts its wars in its own way, according to its own value system; and the present breed of warriors outside Troy are certainly ruthless and single-minded craftsmen of war. Trojan anxieties about the fate of the city and its people are clear from early in the poem. Andromache in particular knows first hand what happens when a city gets sacked. In recent times she lost her family to an earlier attack by the Greeks. Her father Eëtion was killed by Achilles, who at least disposed properly of the body by cremating him with his armor (6.416ff.). Her seven brothers were also killed by Achilles, all on the same day (6.421ff.). Her mother was then enslaved and then brought away with the rest of Achilles' booty before he accepted ransom for her (6.425ff.). But since being ransomed she too has died. So Hector is her father, her mother, her brother and husband (6.429ff.), and Troy is her sanctuary. To make matters worse, the conversation between husband and wife seems to convey the doom of an early death for Hector if he stays outside of the walls. Hector himself does nothing to disperse the gloom hanging over them. He seems to be as confident of the defeat and death of the people of Troy as Agamemnon is of a Greek victory:

'for I know this well in my mind and in my heart: the day will come when holy Ilios will fall, and Priam and the people of Priam of the good ashen spear' (*eu gar egô tode oida kata phrena kai kata thumon:/ essetai êmar hot' an pot' olôlêi Ilios hirê/ kai Priamos kai laos eümmeliô Priamoio*, 6.447-9 [Hector] = 4.163-5 [Agamemnon]).

Moreover it is Hector who raises the spectre of the enslavement of his family. He visualizes Andromache doing menial tasks against her will (6.450ff.), like working at the loom at another's command, or carrying water.[10] These fears come much closer to reality with the death of Hector. Andromache's immediate response to his death is to visualize what the fate of her son Astyanax will be. Even if Troy survives the war with the Achaeans he will be a social outcast because of the fact that he has no father (22.487ff.). He will beg for food from those at the dinner table until he is then pushed aside by one whose parents are still alive (22.484ff.; 22.496ff.). Andromache's fear is that Astyanax might be on the receiving end of rough treatment from members of his own family within the ruling elite. The subtext of this vision is that it will be very much worse for her son when the city actually falls (cf. her gloomier expectations for the city and for Astyanax at 24.725ff.).

The victims of recent Greek rapacity seem to be ubiquitous in the poem; they include the women prizes of recent conquests, like Briseis and Chryseis, over whom the leading princes squabble; and those on the Trojan side who have their own personal losses to narrate. Achilles claims to have sacked twelve cities with his ships, and a further eleven by land throughout the vicinity of Troy (9.328ff.; cf. 9.128ff.). These seem to be secondary places (six of those sacked by Achilles are named within the poem),[11] and they are very different from the great city of Troy that dominates the whole region. The monumental nature of Troy's defenses, and its tremendous capacity to defend itself, make the conquest of this city a far more difficult task than is the case with the earlier victories. But no one has any illusions, least of all the Trojans themselves, about what will happen to them when it does fall.[12]

The fear of the inhabitants of the city for their loved ones outside of the gates, together with the prospect of the enslavement of its remaining people, are linked to the anticipation that the city itself will cease to exist when the Trojans are defeated. This is not a contest for victory or defeat, after which a trophy is put up to claim the day. We read often enough about these sorts of military encounters during the Peloponnesian war in the pages of Thucydides: but Homer's Trojan war is fought for much greater stakes. This war is for the life of the city. When Achilles is pursuing Hector around the walls so that he can kill him in single combat, the poet reminds us that this is no innocuous running contest. The two of them are not running for a prize, 'but they ran for the life of Hector, breaker of horses' (*alla peri psuchês theon Hectoros hippodamoio*, 22.161). In one sense this seems like a statement of the obvious. Given the inequality of the contest (cf. 22.40-1,157ff.), and the terrible predicament in which Hector finds himself, in a fight against Achilles at a time when he is showing no mercy, what else would they be running for? But it is also a poignant comment at a crucial moment on the gravity of this war. For Hector's fate is not his alone, but one that is inextricably linked to the fate of the city itself (cf. the description of the veil [*krêdemnon*] of Andromache that falls from her head (22.468ff.) after she hears of Hector's death).[13] When the Greeks and the Trojans go to war each day, it is for the very life of the city that they fight, and sometimes when we are reading the lengthy battle descriptions we may be inclined to forget this.

By linking together the fates of Hector and Troy (partly through the name Astyanax = 'Lord of the city', esp. 6.403; cf. 22.506-7) the *Iliad* anticipates the death and cremation of Troy itself (cf. 22.410ff.). The city's existence is just like a human life writ large, and at its defeat it will be subjected to fire, albeit it in a very different kind of ritual burning from that which Hector undergoes. Hector's death and the cremation of his body clearly foreshadow the fate of Troy itself (note especially the lament of Andromache, 24.725ff., who anticipates the fall of the city 'from the top down' [*kat' akrês*, 728], and the enslavement of its people [cf.15.557-8]).[14] It is often pointed out that the *Iliad* does not narrate the fall of Troy, even if the gods on the Greek side wait for their moment to destroy the place (esp. 20.313ff.). But in its own way it does describe the fall of Troy through the death and cremation of Hector. Just as Patroclus' death (16.786ff.) and funeral (Book 23) anticipate the death and funeral of Achilles, so Hector's death (Book 22) and his funeral (24.707ff.) foreshadow the sacking and the burning of the city. Both Achilles and Troy await a similar doom at the end of the *Iliad*, and fire plays an important part in the anticipation of this.

Thus the fire of human cremation, and the fire to which a defeated city is subjected, operate at the same symbolic level. Fire is a fundamental symbolic theme, not least because the poem has the notion of destruction and death as a central concern.[15] Fire is used by the characters in the poem in a number of different ways. The Trojans try to burn the Greek ships, Hephaestus inflicts severe violence against Scamander and the Trojans, and the bodies of Patroclus and Hector are given to the flames after their deaths. Fire is never used against Troy itself within the poem, but the characters certainly anticipate its use. In Book 6 Hector tells Paris to get back to the fighting 'so that the city is not soon burnt in consuming fire' (*me tacha astu puros dēïoio therētai*, 6.331). And Hector has good reason to fear Greek fire, for Agamemnon's intentions are clear from very early in the poem. At 2.412ff., in a prayer to Zeus, Agamemnon expresses his fervent desire to kill Hector and to burn the city: 'Zeus, most glorious and greatest, lord of the dark clouds, dwelling in heaven, may the sun not go down and darkness come upon us, until I have torn down headlong the hall of Priam, black with smoke, and burnt the gates with destructive fire, and split Hector's tunic at his breast, torn with bronze…(*Zeu kudiste megiste, kelainephes, aitheri naiōn, / mē prin ep' ēelion dunai kai epi knephas elthein, / prin me kata prēnes baleein Priamoio melathron/ aithaloen, prēsai de puros dēïoio thuretra, / Hektoreon de chitōna peri stēthessi daïxai/ chalchōi rhōgaleon*, 2.412-17).

The anticipation of Troy's fiery destruction by the human players in the war is given further certainty by Hera, the great divine enemy of Troy, who is even more determined that the city will succumb to fire. She tells Poseidon that 'we two, Pallas Athena and I, have sworn many oaths among all the immortals never to ward off the evil day from the Trojans, not even when all Troy is ablaze, burning in consuming fire, and the warlike sons of the Achaeans do the burning', *ētoi men gar nōï poleas ōmossamen horkous / pasi met' athanatoisin, egō kai Pallas Athēnē, / mē pot' epi Trōessin alexēsein kakon ēmar,/ mēd' hopot' an Troïē malerōi puri pasa daētai/ kaiomenē, kaiōsi d' arēïoi huies Achaiōn* (20.313-7). Likewise Scamander, who has seen his beautiful streams reduced to a fiery inferno, promises to Hera 'never to ward off the evil day for the Trojans, not even when all Troy is ablaze…' etc. (20.315-7 [Hera] = 21.374-6 [Scamander]).[16] The sacking and burning of Troy are emphatically anticipated by gods and humans, especially in the later books of the poem (cf. esp. Andromache at 24.728ff. after the death of Hector; and

Priam at 22.59-71 just before it). Verbal repetition has the effect of foreshadowing emphatically the end of the city to come; especially when such graphic anticipations of the city's demise are enunciated by those on different sides in the war (cf. 20.315-7 [Hera] = 21.374-6 [Xanthus/Scamander]; and 4.163-5 [Agamemnon]= 6.447-9 [Hector]).

The change in the heroic landscape across the generations in the *Iliad* seems to bring with it a hardening in the attitude towards the execution of war. This seems to be the principal reason for the inclusion of references to the first sack of Troy in the *Iliad*: the fact that it helps to set the current conflict in a wider temporal context, and identifies some of the distinctive characteristics of the later campaign. The *Iliad* seems to speak to us about a new breed of single-minded professionals, like Achilles and Odysseus and Agamemnon, whose opportunities for acquiring renown are limited to the conquest of human societies. As we have seen repeatedly, the heroic career of Heracles, as it is referred to in the *Iliad*, is not really something that Achilles can emulate, save only for the part that he can play in the violence of organized martial conflict against other cities.

The apparent transformation in the heroic landscape across the generations means that the new breed of young warriors in the *Iliad* acquire their status from war, and from war alone. Heracles moved and operated in a world that offered him a far greater diversity of opportunity than just attacking cities as part of large army. The price for all the changes in the world of heroes seems to be paid by human society, who are now the only targets of heroic violence. As we have seen, there is nothing new about the sacking of cities, but, because of the changes in heroic conduct, the Trojans have to expect very different treatment at the hands of Agamemnon's army from what they received from Heracles. Despite all his old-fashioned violence, and the rawness of his power, there is an implicit humanity in Heracles' dealings with the Trojans in the *Iliad* that is singularly lacking in Agamemnon as the new destroyer of Troy (cf. 6.55-60 etc.). One of the grim messages of the *Iliad* is that the new generation of warriors is a lot more ruthless in the waging of war than the one that preceded it.

So one of the roles of fire in the *Iliad* is to help to identify the level of destruction that this new world of heroes inflicts upon itself. Fire itself is hardly 'new technology' specific to the world of Achilles (as we saw with the story of Meleager), but its widespread use in the poem is meant to reveal something about the kind of war that is being fought out. It is sometimes a matter of puzzlement for readers of the poem that the Greeks bother to build a wall, complete with ramparts, gates, a trench, and stakes (7.433ff.) to defend themselves and their ships against the Trojans. Nestor first advises the building of the wall (at 7.337ff.), shortly after the single combat between Ajax and Hector. One of the many curiosities about it (most of which are dealt with by Kirk, ad 7.327-43) is that it is a plan devised by Nestor at a time when the Greeks are quite dominant in the fighting. The first part of the *Iliad* (up until Book 16) is meant to describe a temporary reversal in the fortunes of the Greek side in the war, whom Zeus drives into defeat as a favor to Thetis (1.393ff.). Achilles' aim in requesting divine support for the enemy is to get retribution for the fact that Agamemnon gave him no honor when he took away Briseis (1.411-2). And so Zeus responds by having the Greeks driven back against their own ships, a situation which ultimately draws Patroclus, and then Achilles, back into the fighting. The main problem in all of this is that the Greeks never seem to lose their natural dominance over the Trojans, especially with the spear. The poet's audience, presumably, want to hear accounts of Greek victories, which they do, more often than not. But they have to do so within a broader context of Greek defeat in the absence of Achilles from the fighting.

It is especially the roles of Hector and Ajax in battle that tend to bear out much of the inequality between the sides. The Greek wall is built almost immediately after the defeat of Hector by Ajax in the single combat of Book 7 (206-322). Hector is left stretched out on his back before the timely intervention of Apollo and two heralds from both sides who call an end to the fight because darkness has fallen (7.268ff). The dominance of Ajax over Hector revealed in the single combat is no isolated occurrence. Before he is defeated and killed by Achilles in the twenty-second book, Hector spends much of the poem either being defeated by Ajax, or else avoiding him in battle (for some of the main contact between them, cf. 7.206-322; 11.542; 13.809ff.; 14.402ff.; 15.9ff.; 15.414ff.; 16.114ff. [Hector gets the better of him here when he casts fire at the ship]; 16.358ff.; 17.125ff.; 17.166ff.; 17.170ff.; note too Hector's defeat by Diomedes at 11.349ff.).

And yet during the same period in which Hector is consistently dominated by Ajax, the poem calls on us to witness the Greeks in crisis, pushed back to their own ships, and on the brink of seeing them burnt. And of the Trojans it is Hector first and foremost whose fiery powers bring about this rout (cf., *inter alia*, 12.466; 13.688; 17.565; 18.154).[17] It is sometimes difficult for readers of the *Iliad*, in the midst of complex descriptions of battle, to get a clear sense of who is winning the conflict as a whole, and who is losing. We are obliged to accept, however, what the rhetoric of the poem tells us to accept, that the Trojans are winning the war, even if our best sense of it is that the leading Greeks are vastly superior to the best men on the Trojan side. Suspension of disbelief is demanded of every reader of Homer's *Iliad*.

The building of the defensive wall by the Greeks, and the intense effort on the part of the Trojans to burn the ships, are of course the principal physical manifestations of Trojan supremacy. It is presumably a more effective poetic device for the Trojans to have a specific physical end to reach (which they do finally reach in Book 16.112ff.), than just to 'win the day' on the rather amorphous Homeric battlefield. Thus burning the ships becomes the great quest of Hector and his forces. It is the measure of their success in battle in the middle section of the poem (cf. 8.180ff.; 8.217ff.; 8.235; 8.498; 8. 554ff.; 9.240ff.; 9.346ff.; 9.601-2; 11.557; 12.175ff. (with Hainsworth's note to 12.177-8); 12.195ff.; 12.440ff.; 13.319; 13.628-9; 14.44ff.; 15.718-46). The ships are to Hector what Troy is to Agamemnon and Menelaus, and to see them burning is his greatest desire. The culmination of this is his cry to 'bring fire' (*oisete pur*, 15.718, cf.15.744) in a struggle which immediately precedes the return of Patroclus to the combat. The Greeks therefore are meant to be 'under siege' within their own wider siege of the city. The ships in turn represent the physical means of a return home for the Greeks, and so to lose them is unthinkable; and even Achilles seems to dread this prospect (16.126ff.).

The Trojan goal of getting to the ships to burn them has other aspects to it too. Zeus uses the fire being employed against the Greek ships as a kind of physical marker of when to end his support for the Trojans: 'for Zeus the counselor was waiting for this, to see with his eyes the glow of a burning ship. For from that time he would make a withdrawal of the Trojans from the ships, and he would give glory to the Danaans' (*to gar mene mêtieta Zeus,/ nêos kaiomenês selas ophthalmoisin idesthai. / ek gar dê tou melle palliôxin para veôn/ thêsemenai Trôôn, Danaoisi de kudos orexein*, 15.599-602). Fire at the ships therefore (esp.16.112-29; 16.293ff.) is the measure of Trojan supremacy on the field of battle until the arrival of Patroclus (16.284ff.). It is the signal that they have reached their goal. But it is also the harbinger of Trojan defeat. Their greatest moment in battle is a sign of their doom to come. The fire at the ships is meant to lead directly to the burning of the city.

The use of fire to burn the ships therefore has many different aspects to it, and most especially it is an important symbolic representation of Trojan success. Its importance in the narrative of the poem is highlighted by the fact that the poet evokes the muses to help him show how fire was first flung upon the Greek ships (16.112-3.). The Trojans get a taste of success and no more; just one ship (appropriately, that of Protesilaus, who was the first Greek to be killed at Troy, 2.701-2) is half-burnt out by the time that Patroclus arrives to drive away the attackers (16.122-3, 293ff.).[18] The firing of this ship seems to represent about the same level of success that the Greeks have had in taking Troy during their time outside of the city. At their meeting on the walls of Troy Andromache points out to Hector that his best course of action is to adopt a defensive strategy, rather than one based on attack: 'come now' she says 'have pity, and stay here on the wall, lest you make your son an orphan and your wife a widow. Place your army beside the wild fig tree where the city is most easily scaled and the wall is open to attack. For here three times the best men came in attack, companions of the two Ajaxes and glorious Idomeneus, and those with the sons of Atreus and the valiant son of Tydeus: either someone well-skilled in prophecy spoke to them, or their own heart urges and bids them', *all' age nun eleaire kai autou mimn' epi purgôi,/ mê paid' orphanikon thêêis chêrên te gunaika:/ laon de stêson par' erineon, entha malista/ ambatos esti polis kai epidromon epleto teichos./ tris gar têi g' elthontes epeirêsanth' hoi aristoi/ amph' Aiante duô kai agakluton Idomenêa/ êd' amph' Atreïdas kai Tudeos alkimon huion:/ ê pou tis sphin enispe theopropiôn eü eidôs,/ ê nu kai autôn thumos epotrunei kai anôgei* (6.431-9; cf. Polydamas at 18.272ff.).

In earlier fighting therefore the Greeks have had a taste of success in reaching their goal of scaling the walls, rather like the Trojans do with their attempt to burn the ships (cf. Patroclus' brief prospect of taking the city, standing three times on the corner of the high wall before being thrust back by Apollo, 16.698ff.). The attempt of the Trojans to fire the ships therefore represents the same basic aim that the Greeks have to burn the city. The former is achieved, albeit only symbolically, within the poem itself. The latter is foreshadowed to occur in time to come, outside the framework of the poem, as a complete destruction of the city. In the *Iliad* the ground is being laid for the city's demise. Zeus and the gods make sure that after the symbolic victory of the Trojans comes the real victory of the Greeks.

2. Rivers of Fire

One of the major distinctions between the two Homeric poems is the part played by fire. Whilst images of fire and Olympian brilliance seem to dominate the *Iliad*, especially the last part of the poem when the rampant and fiery Achilles transforms the whole field of battle, only occasional reference is made to fire in the *Odyssey*.[19] In many cases too the context in which fire is mentioned in the *Odyssey* is a fairly basic one - fire for the domestic needs of cooking, or heating or lighting (eg. 5.59; 7.7; 10.30). It is worthy of note, however, that even in some of the rather bare references to its use by the characters in the *Odyssey*, fire still has an important role to play. The great fire at Calypso's hearth, made of cedar and citron-wood, gives out a scent that spreads right across the island (*pur men ep' escharophin mega kaieto, têlothi d' odmê/ kedrou t' eukeatoio thuou t' ana nêson odôdei/ daiomenôn*, 5.59-61). Fire gives the whole island a special fragrance; and this is just one aspect of the general luxuriance of the setting in which Calypso and Odysseus reside when Hermes comes to set him free.

Similarly, Odysseus and his companions on their return in their ships catch sight of the fires on their home island of Ithaca (10.28ff.). They can see the men of the island tending their fires (*kai dê purpoleontas eleussomen eggus eontas*, 10.30), but just at this point, when they are so very close to completing their return, Odysseus falls asleep, and his men then conspire to open the bag of winds (given to Odysseus by Aeolus). As a consequence of this recklessness they are cast back to the Aeolian island (10.54ff.) and have to endure further hardship (and death in the case of all the companions). The sight of the men on Ithaca, within reach of the light generated by their fires, is a graphic image of just how close they actually come to getting home at this point (cf. the Trojans burning a Greek ship in the *Iliad*, as above).

Later in the poem the suitors even use fire and fat to warm the bow so that it will be easier for them to string (21.175ff.). Antinous calls upon Melanthius to light a fire and bring a cake of fat so that they can then go through with the contest; but they are still unable to string it. In this case fire helps to reveal the weakness of the suitors, the fact that they cannot achieve their goal even with the added strength of fire ('but they could not string it, for they were much lacking in strength', *oud' edunanto/ entanusai, pollon de biês epideuees êsan*, 21.184-5).

One episode where much attention is paid to fire is the incursion of Odysseus and his men into the cave of Polyphemus in *Odyssey* Book 9. Fire in the cave is mentioned several times early in the episode (9.231 [fire for sacrifice], 9.251, 9.307ff.). These references seem designed largely to anticipate the use of fire as a weapon against the Cyclops, 9.328, 9.375ff.). Fire (ie. the burning stake that is thrust into his eye) is joined with the *metis* of Odysseus (9.410 etc.) and the wine from Apollo's priest Maron (9.196ff., 9.345ff.) to make a trio of formidable weapons to use against Polyphemus. These weapons are employed with the same sort of ruthless efficiency with which the Olympians Hera and Hephaestus blast Scamander with blazing fire in *Iliad* Book 21. Fire's use against Polyphemus helps to inform Odysseus' ingenuity, and his violence, in defeating his monstrous enemy and in getting his men safely back to their ship.

In the *Odyssey*, therefore, fire seems to have no single, coherent significance. It is certainly a less prominent element than in the *Iliad* where the force of fire helps to convey the Olympian brilliance and violence that are engulfing Troy. Similarly, the cremations referred to in the *Odyssey* are more isolated reflections on the treatment of an individual after death (especially Achilles). They are not really central to the symbolism and structure of the poem, like the funerals of Patroclus and Hector.[20] In Book 11, the first *nekuia*, reference is made to fire as a means of disposing of the dead (burning the sacrificed sheep to accompany prayers to Hades and Persephone, 11.44ff.; and the body of Elpenor, 11.72ff.). Elpenor had died after falling from the roof of Circe's house (10.550ff.), but he had not received burial because he had managed to separate himself from the rest of his men. His is the first shade that Odysseus encounters in Hades (11.51ff.), and he asks Odysseus (11.72ff.) to burn him with his armor and build up a mound for him on the shore of the sea so that men do not forget about him.

The cremation and the building of a mound duly take place immediately after the departure of the Ithacans from the land of the dead (at 12.8ff.). The verbal exchange between Elpenor's shade and Odysseus precedes the declaration by his mother of the role of fire in the disposal of the dead: 'for no longer do the sinews hold together the flesh and the bones, but the strong force of blazing fire destroys these, and as soon as the spirit has left the white bones, the soul, like a dream, flitters out and is gone' (*ou gar eti sarkas te kai ostea ines echousin,/ alla ta men te puros krateron menos aithomenoio/ damnai, epei ke prôta lipêi leuk' ostea thumos,/ psuchê d' êüt' oneiros apoptamenê pepotêtai*, 11.219-22).

Another aspect of this concern with cremation and the fate of the soul after death is the allusion made in *Odyssey* 10 to Pyriphlegethon, the burning river of Hades (10.513). Circe gives Odysseus advice on how best to get to Hades (10.504ff.); she tells him that 'there (beyond the stream of Ocean) into Acheron flow Pyriphlegethon and Cocytus, which is a tributary of the water of the Styx; and there is a rock, and the junction of two roaring rivers'(*entha men eis Acheronta Puriphlegethôn te rheousi/ Kôkutos th', hos dê Stugos hudatos estin aporrôx,/ petrê te xunesis te duô potamôn eridoupôn*, 10.513-5). Notions of 'hatred' (Styx), 'funereal wailing' (Cocytus), 'misery' (Acheron), and 'blazing fire' (Pyriphlegethon) lie behind the names of these rivers. The names probably evoke the grief of the living at the funeral, and the transition of the dead to Hades by means of the cremation of the body. The reference to the Underworld rivers is made by Circe at the end of Book 10, and it seems appropriate in this context because Odysseus and his companions are about to make their own transition (as living men) to the world of the dead. The absence of any reference to three of these rivers elsewhere in the Homeric poems (Styx is the exception, *Il.* 2.755; 8.369; 14.271; 15.37; *Od.* 5.185) raises the usual questions about the authenticity of the passage; as does the fact that no mention is made of them on the actual journey of Odysseus to Hades (11.13ff.).[21] As far as

Pyriphlegethon itself is concerned, it does seem to be significant that the *Iliad* provides us with a parallel image of the burning river Scamander in Book 21, and we shall have more to say about this connection a little bit later.

But the main concern in this section is with the figure of Achilles, in whose death, funeral, and passage to the afterlife the *Odyssey* takes an active interest (in Books 11 and 24). Our task is to explore references to the funeral of Achilles in the early sources (*Odyssey*/ *Aethiopis*), and how these relate to the figure of Achilles in the *Iliad*. The case will be put that the Greek sources consistently present Achilles as a figure who is immersed in fire (and sometimes in water). This happens to him as a baby, and also as a man in the full brilliance of his warrior fury, and also on the funeral pyre after his death. Immersion in fire signals his transition through life and death, but there are also attempts made by his mother Thetis, in various ancient sources, to 'burn off' his mortality altogether. Fire thus informs Achilles' immortal lineage, his special destiny, his heroism, and the fact that he undergoes a glorious cremation attended by gods and mortals together.[22] The central argument here is that the *Iliad* provides us with the earliest source for this theme of immersion in fire (Achilles in Scamander in Book 21). This passage is quite distinct from the other descriptions of his placement in fire, by virtue of the fact that in the *Iliad* he is an active adult on the field of battle, not a baby or a dead man. The poem presents us with a graphic scene of immersion in fire and water, one that has its thematic parallels in other texts. But the Iliadic immersion operates at an entirely different level by virtue of the fact that Achilles masters the physical force of fire through the sheer power of his heroic fury.

But we begin with the *Odyssey* where Achilles is an important figure in both of the descriptions of life after death in Hades. The encounter of Odysseus with the shade of Achilles in Hades in Book 11 concentrates on the latter's dejection at the kind of existence that he leads among the dead (especially the renowned statement that, if he could, he would lead a menial life on earth rather than be king of all the dead, 11.488-91). Despite his gloom about his existence in Hades, Achilles is able to take some comfort in Odysseus' story about the role of his son Neoptolemus in the final stages of the Trojan war (11.505ff.).

We next meet the shade of Achilles in the 'second *nekuia*' in *Odyssey* 24 where the focus is on his death, and the fight for his body, and then his subsequent funeral at Troy. Agamemnon's shade tells him (24.36ff.) that after his death he was laid on a bier and washed with water and ointment. The Danaans cut their hair and shed many tears over him. His mother Thetis, together with the immortal sea nymphs, came from the sea for the funeral, much as she does in the *Iliad* in his moments of despair. The sight and the sound of the immortals bewailing his death almost caused the Greeks to run away to their ships, but they were held back from doing so by the old man Nestor (24.50ff.).

Achilles is then given a lavish funeral led by the sea-nymphs and the nine muses (24.58ff.). After seventeen days of mourning, day and night, he is given over to fire on the eighteenth day dressed in clothing of the gods; and other victims and offerings are duly placed on the pyre. The pyre of Achilles is the focus of a spontaneous show of grief from the Greek warriors: 'many Achaean warriors moved in their armor about the pyre where you were burning, both footmen and horsemen, and a great noise arose. But when the flame of Hephaestus had consumed you, at dawn we collected your white bones, Achilles, and put them in unmixed wine and unguents' (*polloi d' hêrôes Achaioi/ teuchesin errôsanto purên peri kaiomenoio,/ pezoi th' hippêes te: polus d' orumagdos orôrei./ autar epei dê se phlox ênusen Hêphaistoio,/ êôthen dê toi legomen leuk' oste', Achilleu,/ oinôi en akrêtôi kai aleiphati,* 24.68-73).[23]

The *Odyssey* therefore provides us with two important passages dealing with the death, funeral and afterlife of Achilles. These two passages are obviously linked in terms of narrative continuity in that the funeral pyre is the means by which his new existence in Hades is brought about (cf. the speeches of the other dead, Patroclus, *Il*.23.69ff.; Elpenor, *Od*.11.72ff.; Anticleia, *Od*. 11.219ff.). In addition to the Odyssean description of Achilles' funeral is the likelihood that there was a more expansive account of the cremation in the lost Cyclic epic *Aethiopis*. This epic, of which virtually nothing survives, was concerned with a later stage of the war after the period dealt with in the *Iliad*, and this probably included the death of Achilles and his funeral. The surviving summary of the poem by Proclus suggests that Achilles has quite a different existence after death from what we find in the *Odyssey*: 'then they bury Antilochus and they lay out the body of Achilles. And Thetis arrives with the Muses and her sisters and sings the dirge for her son; and after this Thetis, snatches her son from the pyre and translates him to the White island' (*epeita Antilochon te thaptousi kai ton nekron tou Achilleôs protithentai. kai Thetis aphikomenê sun Mousais kai tais adelphais thrênei ton paida: kai meta tauta ek tês puras hê Thetis anarpasasa ton paida eis tên Leukên nêson diakomizei, Chrest.* 2).

Despite the un-Homeric nature of his life after death in the *Aethiopis*, on the White island rather than in Hades,[24] the placement of Achilles' body on the pyre clearly conforms to the usual funerary practice in the *Iliad* and *Odyssey*. Every Greek warrior in Homer can expect a cremation if circumstances allow, although sometimes the funeral may be a fairly basic process on account of the exigencies of their situation in a war far from home. In the *Iliad* Odysseus has an eye on the everyday demand for quick funerals. He makes the point to Achilles that things have to move on, even though men are being killed all the time: 'but it is necessary to bury him who is killed, steeling our hearts, and weeping for just one day', *alla chrê ton men katathaptein hos ke thanêisi,/ nêlea thumon echontas, ep' êmati dakrusantas, Il.* 19.228-9). This situation is not true for the best men in the war, or those connected to them, who are the beneficiaries of grand funerals: Patroclus (*Il.* 23 *passim*), Hector (*Il.* 24.707-804), and Achilles (*Od.* 24.36ff./ *Aethiopis*). Everything has to stop so that these funerals can take place, including the daily grind of the fighting. It is a sign of Achilles' greatness as a warrior that either he stops the war himself so that funerals for others can take place (as with Patroclus [*Il.* Book 23] and Hector [*Il.* 24.656ff.; 24.778ff.]); or others bring the fighting to a halt to bury him (*Od.* 24.63ff.).

Naturally, most other fallen warriors in the *Iliad* have less opulent funerals than Patroclus and Hector. In Book Seven a truce is arranged to burn the dead victims of the fighting on both sides in the war (*Il.* 7.375-7, 394-432). The burials are dealt with in economical fashion within the narrative, reflecting the comparative lack of importance of the recent victims in the fighting. These are presumably the sorts of funerals that Odysseus has in mind in his discussion with Achilles (19.228-9). The need to seek after significant amounts of firewood is put forward in the text as another factor of importance in the issue of a funeral's scale (cf. 7.417ff.; 23.110ff.; 24.663-4; 24.778ff.). There is no scope for a grand funeral in every case, bearing in mind that Patroclus' pyre is meant to be about 100 feet this way and that (23.164-5), and is so big that it burns all night (23.217ff.). In the *Iliad* there is an implicit sense that the Greeks will give to Achilles the same kind of magnificent funeral that he himself gives to Patroclus. The great importance in the *Iliad* attached to his forthcoming death (eg. 24.128ff.) is taken up in other epics where the focus turns to his actual death and the splendid funeral that honors him.

So the *Iliad* and *Odyssey* convey the notion that cremation is a general practice for fallen warriors at Troy, once their bodies have been safely acquired by family or friends; and that in some cases a grand funeral is an appropriate response to the prominence and status of the deceased. Obviously Achilles' funeral has a special importance in the ancient sources, not least because it is attended by both mortals and immortals who come together in shared grief. This united demonstration of loss and grief by individuals from different realms helps to inform the identity of Achilles in a way that we also see elsewhere in the various early sources for him. Achilles is the progeny of a mortal and an immortal (Peleus and Thetis); he is killed by a mortal and an immortal (Paris and Apollo); and his whole life is lived between these two conditions of existence (cf. the roles of Chiron and Phoenix as his teachers in the *Iliad*, and the presence of others in his earlier life, like Patroclus, and his immortal horses, Xanthus and Balius). The fact that his funeral is attended by both mortals and immortals in the *Odyssey* corresponds to the reality of his existence and the life that he leads, as depicted in the *Iliad*.

The placement of Achilles on to the funeral pyre in the two early epics, the *Odyssey* and the *Aethiopis*, also corresponds to other sources which reveal his immersion by his mother Thetis in fire and/or water whilst he is still alive. In all of these sources immersion symbolizes his transition, or the attempt at a transition, from one condition of existence to another. This is a matter of crucial importance for Thetis who is desperate to avoid eternal separation from him. Even in the gloomy world of Homer's Hades in the *Odyssey* mortal shades are often re-united after their deaths. It is understood, although never explicitly stated, that this will not be the case with an immortal mother and her mortal son. In the *Iliad* Thetis has to confront an imminent existence of grief without end, and eternal separation from her son. The other side of Achilles' 'undying renown' (*kleos aphthiton*) is the 'undying grief' (*achos aphthiton*) of his immortal mother (cf. the *ainon... achos* 'terrible grief' of Aphrodite, *HHAph.*,198-9). Time and fate dominate the lives of Thetis and Achilles like no other mother and son in the Greek myths.

Thetis's fear of the imminent loss of her son, and the prospect of eternal grief to follow, seem to explain the absence of a separation, at the emotional level, between her and Achilles in the *Iliad*.[25] Achilles is the only Greek warrior to have contact with a female member of his family in the *Iliad*, and it is significant that it is his mother with whom he communicates. It is she with whom he talks first in moments of crisis, in response to the dispute with Agamemnon (1.357ff.), or upon the loss of Patroclus (18.65ff.). The implicit notion running through the poem is that the separation of mother and son will now take place at the point of death, rather than on the usual threshold of his becoming a man and going off to war (contrast Penelope and Telemachus in the early books of the *Odyssey*).

In short, Thetis in the *Iliad* is in the awful situation of being an immortal mother with a son who is doomed to an early death and a passage to Hades (cf. Xanthus and Balius at 17.426ff., and Zeus at 17.443ff.).[26] Mortals who endure a crushing bereavement can come to terms with the death of loved ones, and then get on with their lives again. This is even the case with Niobe, who lost all her children (24.602ff.). She is a mythical *exemplum* for both Achilles and Priam, who also have to endure suffering at the loss of loved ones. The capacity of mortals to endure grief and then to return to basic human activities is an important theme in the final book of the *Iliad*. But *immortal* grief is another matter entirely, and this is the price that Thetis will pay for marriage to a mortal man (cf. 18.429ff.). The *Iliad* is not specific about how she will deal with her bereavement when it actually occurs (cf. 18.35-137; 18.429ff.; 24.120ff); but deal with it she must. The grim outlook for Thetis in the *Iliad* seems to spawn a number of variant narratives in other texts where she avoids, or tries to avoid, separation from her son, and it is in this context that immersion in fire and water is so important.

One example of the attempt of Thetis to avoid the death of her son comes from the post-Homeric *Aegimius*. It seems that in the second book of the *Aegimius* (6th cent. BC?) the story was told that Thetis immersed the first (six?) children of her marriage to

Peleus in a boiling cauldron to try to make them immortal (*ho ton Aigimion poiêsas en B phêsin hoti hê Thetis eis lebêta hudatos eballen tous ek Pêleôs gennômenous*).[27] It is not stated that Achilles himself is actually dipped into the cauldron by his mother. But the fact that the scholia refer to this story in the context of a similar immersion in the *Argonautica* might well suggest that he is immersed, or about to be immersed, when he is rescued by Peleus.

The episode in the *Argonautica* (3rd cent. BC.) has a similar resonance to the *Aegimius* except that in this case Achilles is placed in the flames themselves rather than in a cauldron. The passage describes the separation of Peleus and Thetis as a married couple. This occurred because 'Thetis was always placing (Achilles') mortal flesh in the flame of fire in the middle of the night, and day after day she would smear with ambrosia his tender frame so that he might become immortal, and that she might ward off hateful old age from his body' (*hê men gar broteas aiei peri sarkas edaien/ nukta dia messên phlogmôi puros, êmata d' aute/ ambrosiêi chrieske teren demas, ophra peloito/ athanatos kai hoi stugeron chroï gêras alalkoi*, *Arg.* 4.869-72). Peleus sees his son's immersion in the flames and gives out a terrible cry, rather like the way that Metaneira interrupts Demeter's similar attempt to make young boy Demophon immortal in the *Homeric Hymn to Demeter* (231ff.).[28] In both cases the interruption foils the planned immortality of the young lad. When Thetis is interrupted, she throws the boy down and goes away for good, thereby bringing the marriage to a premature end (4.873ff.). A combination of these two episodes in the *Aegimius* and the *Argonautica* is given by Lycophron (2nd cent. BC.) in the *Alexandra* (175ff.) who alludes to the fact that Thetis killed the first six children of their marriage by immersing them in fire (not in a cauldron, as in the *Aegimius*).[29] So the *Aegimius* and the *Alexandra* both refer to the deaths of Achilles' siblings whereas Apollonius makes no mention of the earlier born children of the marriage.

Achilles therefore is cremated after his death in the *Odyssey* and in the *Aethiopis*; and allusions of various kinds to his immersion in fire and/or water are found in four other texts (*Aegimius, Argonautica, Alexandra*, and Apollodorus' *Bibliotecha* [the last of these seems closely to follow the version of Apollonius in the *Argonautica*]). These narratives might be considered the literary parallels to the most renowned immersion of Achilles in myth – when as a baby he is taken by his mother and dipped in the river Styx. As in the other cases, his immersion in the Styx is devised by Thetis to make him immortal, but it proves to be a similar failure because she misses the left heel area, the very part of his body where he is hit later by Apollo and Paris with an arrow. The earliest extant source for this story is the Roman poet Statius (second half of the 1st century AD) in the unfinished epic *Achilleid* (1.268-70);[30] but the story itself might go back to the Hellenistic period.[31] The point however is clear that immersion in fire and/or water is fundamental to the identity of Achilles in literature, both in his very early life as a baby, and after his death. Thetis desperately tries to 'baptize' him into her own realm of existence, for anything else will mark a failure in her desperate desire for a level of continuity in their relationship.

Clearly the *Iliad* and the *Odyssey* differ from many other sources in their insistence that Achilles descends into Hades after his death, rather than obtaining for himself a more pleasant existence in a different kind of afterlife (ie. on the White island [*Aethiopis*, Pind. *Nem.* 4.49-50 *etc*], or in the Isles of the Blessed, [Pind. *Olymp.* 2.68ff.]). There is no prospect of him avoiding his fate in Hades in the *Iliad* (cf. Achilles' own statement that 'not even the mighty Heracles escaped death', *oude gar oude biê Hêraklêos phuge kêra*, 18.117). In the *Iliad* Achilles is a grown man, of course, one who is still very much alive, albeit not very far from death. Unlike the other immersion-narratives he is not a baby or a corpse, and so he is not placed passively in fire or water as in these other texts.

But it is significant that he is similarly immersed in fire and water at the river Scamander in Book 21. Indeed it does seem to be apparent that this passage (21.1-382) is the Iliadic parallel and antecedent to the later immersions which we have been examining. Moreover, the placement of nectar and ambrosia into his breast by Zeus and Athena (19.342ff.) seems to complement other episodes in which immersion in fire, and the use of ambrosia, are part of the process of transition into a different existential condition (cf. the application of ambrosia in the cases of the young boys Demophon and Achilles, *HHD*, 237; *Argonautica*, 4.869-72). Achilles' immersion in fire (Book 21) and the fact that he is sustained by the immortal foodstuffs (19.342ff.) both help to signify the extent of his transcendence of the ordinary human condition of existence.

It has been well demonstrated that Achilles in the *Iliad* has a fundamental association with fire in the later books of the *Iliad*, when he makes his return to the field of combat after the death of Patroclus.³² Thus the earlier narrative of the attempt of Hector and the Trojans to torch the Greeks ships (from Book 8 until Book 16), corresponds to the later desire of Achilles for revenge and his return to battle (beginning at 18.1ff.). Fire becomes associated with Achilles in a very important way, whereas before this it was the preserve of Hector. But whereas Hector *uses* fire as a weapon, Achilles 'becomes' a kind of fire himself. As the best warrior in the poem, and with a wrath that seems to have no bounds, Achilles is frequently depicted as the most 'heated' figure in battle.³³ His presence as the most fiery warrior on the battlefield informs his *aretê*, in much the same way as does his special spear, his divine armor, his immortal horses, and so forth. The destructive power of fire helps to convey his complete domination and transformation of the battlefield at this point (eg. 20.490ff.; 21.10ff.). And the fiery brightness of his presence, even before he acquires his new armor, creates terror in the hearts of his opponents (eg. 18.222ff.). The fire of Achilles in the *Iliad* amounts to an equivalent of the sort of (literal) fire that the Chimaera possessed in earlier times. Fire was an important aspect of the terror that this creature inflicted upon human beings (6.182); and this is why the Lycian king immediately sends Bellerophon off on a quest to kill the creature (*prôton men*...6.179). Monsters like the Chimaera are now gone from the heroic landscape, but the notion running through the last part of the *Iliad* is that the Trojan warriors, like Aeneas and Hector, have to confront somebody whose fiery presence inspires a similar kind of terror in his opponents (see Chapter 1).³⁴

Prior to his encounter with Achilles in battle, Hector reveals that he has no illusions about the task involved: 'I will go out against him, even if his hands are like fire, even if his hands are like fire, and his rage is like blazing iron' (*tou d' egô antios eimi, kai ei puri cheiras eoiken,/ ei puri cheiras eoike, menos d' aithôni siderôi*, 20.371-2; cf. 22.25ff.). But when the gods desert him, and the reality of confronting Achilles comes upon him, Hector is unable to hold on to his determination to stay and fight. And when he turns and runs from him, it is the shining brightness of Achilles' Olympian armor that causes his terror: 'in such a way (Hector) pondered as he waited, and Achilles came near to him, like Enyalius, the warrior of the glancing helmet, shaking the Pelian ash over his right shoulder, the terrible spear; and around about the bronze shone like the bright light of blazing fire or of the sun as it rises. But trembling took hold of Hector when he saw him, and he did not dare to remain there…' (*Hôs hormaine menôn, ho de hoi schedon êlthen Achilleus/ isos Enualiôi, koruthaïki ptolemistêi,/ seiôn Pêliada meliên kata dexion ômon/ deinên: amphi de chalkos elampeto eikelos augêi/ e puros aithomenou ê êeliou aniontos./ Hectora d', hôs enoêsen, hele tromos: oud' ar' et' etlê/ authi menein*…22.131-7).

The celestial brightness of the arms of Achilles had even caused trembling among those on his own side when it was first presented to him by Thetis: 'trembling took hold of all the Myrmidons and no one dared to look straight at it, but they shrank back', (*Murmidonas d' ara pantas hele tromos, oude tis etlê/ antên eisideein, all' etresan*, 19.14-15.). To friends and foe alike therefore the bright vision of the armor of Hephaestus is something to inspire a terrible fear. The reaction of Achilles to the presentation of them is quite different. The sight of it only increases the anger (*cholos*) in his heart, and his eyes flash from under the eyelids, just like fire (*hôs ei selas exephaanthen*, 19.16-17).

So Achilles has a fundamental association with fire right throughout his *aristeia*, one that helps to inform the terrible challenge that Hector actually confronts. As we have seen however it is really the battle at the river Scamander in Book 21 where Achilles' association with fire is at its most prominent. Half of the Trojans are driven to Scamander by Achilles who is completely dominant on the battlefield (21.1ff.). After it becomes clogged with bodies a dispute arises between the unhappy god and the rampant Achilles (21.211ff.). The river says that his lovely streams are full of bodies so that he is unable to pour out his waters into the sea (21.214-21). Achilles agrees to do so at first, but after a moment he leaps back in to continue the killing, whereupon Scamander tries to drown him (21.235ff.). Achilles cries out to Zeus in bitterness that he had been told by his mother that he would die in battle at the hands of Apollo, not drown in a river (21.273-83). The fury of the river is overcome only when Hephaestus enters the fray by hurling fire at Scamander at the request of Hera (21.328ff.). The fire burns the dead bodies already lying on the plain, after the carnage of Achilles; but it also burns the trees and shrubs by the river, the eels and the fish, and the water itself (21.342ff.). The effect of this Olympian attack ends the conflict within a very short space of time (Scamander actually capitulates after only 15 lines!). And so with his streams burning Scamander has no choice but to submit unequivocally to the greater force of Olympian fire (21.369ff.). It is in response to the river's plea that Hera tells Hephaestus to halt his attack.

It is hard to imagine a more graphic image than a burning river. The fighting at the river, and Scamander's subsequent struggle with the fire of Hephaestus, are sometimes thought of as one of the most memorable episodes in the whole *Iliad* (and most readers would agree that the *Iliad* is not short of memorable episodes). Moreover, it does seem to be important that *both* Homeric poems refer to burning rivers; for, as we have seen, the *Odyssey* too makes reference to Pyriphlegethon, the burning river of Hades (together with Styx, Acheron and Cocytus, 10.513-14).[35] It is remarkable that there are two rivers of fire in the *Iliad* and *Odyssey*, and no other such reference in extant Greek literature for about three hundred years. In Plato's *Phaedo* 114a (first half of the 4th Century BC) Pyriphegethon is specifically designated as the appropriate location in the Underworld for those people who strike their mothers and fathers in life. The presence of two different rivers of fire in the two Homeric poems, followed by a very long time until the next such reference, seems to provide scope for all sorts of speculations, not least the question of whether the Iliadic passage has some influence on the Odyssean reference.[36] Scamander is like a fiery river of hell after Hephaestus puts torch to it, and it is not very hard to imagine such a graphic scene influencing later poetic images of the rivers of the Underworld.[37]

There seems to be little doubt that the burning Scamander foreshadows again the fate of the city itself. The fire at the river is essentially the topographical parallel to the cremation of Hector. Troy is 'burnt' in different ways within the *Iliad*, even if the city itself is untouched by fire. We saw earlier in this chapter that the poem ends with the Trojans coming together as a community for the cremation of Hector (24.704ff.). His death and the cremation of his body seem to anticipate the fate of the whole city, not least because he is thought of by the Trojans as 'Astyanax' ('Lord of the City'). The Trojans mourn for Hector at the end of the poem, but their grief has a wider application, now that he is dead. The chain of death with which the last part of the *Iliad* is concerned (Sarpedon-Patroclus-Hector-Achilles) really looks beyond Achilles right up to the death of the city itself. At the end of the poem we anticipate the death of Achilles (24.131-2), and some time thereafter Troy itself will fall.

Just as Hector is much more than an individual Trojan warrior, so Scamander is more than just a river near the battlefield.[38] He is fundamental to the life and identity of the city (cf. 2.465ff.; 5.76ff.; 5.773ff.; 6.402; 12.19-33; 14.433-9 and 22.147-56). He provides water both for its people, and for the horses and other animals that graze on the fertile plains around Troy (cf. 24.350-1). Hector's affection for his region extends to naming his son Scamandrius (although others call him Astyanax, after Hector himself, 6.402-3).[39] In the midst of the carnage in his flow, Scamander does everything he can to protect the surviving Trojans from Achilles by hiding them in the huge deep pools (*zôous de saô kata kala rheethra,/ kruptôn en dinêisi batheiêisin megalêisi*, 21.238-9). Rivers in the *Iliad* play a great part in evoking the beauty and rustic tranquility of the Troad (and the other regions too, like Lycia, on the Trojan side).[40] Scamander's lovely waters are referred to at crucial moments in the poem, especially to evoke the beauty of life at Troy in times of peace, before the coming of the Greeks (cf. 22.147-56).[41] So the ferocity of his burning is a brutal act perpetrated by higher powers. It also stands for something much greater, something that is yet to hit the city and its people. Scamander can already see the fate of Troy for himself when he capitulates to Olympian fire and promises Hera 'never to ward off the evil day for the Trojans, not even when all Troy is ablaze, burning in consuming fire, and the warlike sons of the Achaeans do the burning' (21.374-6).

But the immediate and striking reality of the blazing Scamander is that Achilles is not burnt by the fire like everything else in the vicinity. In all likelihood the modern reader is not very troubled by the fact that the physical force of the fire has no effect on him. After all, the fire is provided to Achilles by friendly gods (Hera and Hephaestus) to counter a hostile one (Scamander). Fire saves him from drowning, which is a very unfortunate way to die for a Homeric warrior (cf. *Il.* 21.273ff.; *Od.* 5.299ff.; and Hesiod, *Works and Days*, 687, 'terrible it is to die amidst the waves' [*deinon d' esti thanein meta kumasin*]). Hephaestus' intervention in the conflict between the man and the river is meant to help Achilles, not to burn him!

But the Homeric scholia do puzzle over why the fire has no effect on him, and this at least alerts us to the very different level of existence that characterizes Achilles at this point in the poem.[42] On one level Achilles is such a 'fiery' figure himself that he is 'at one' with the surrounding fire, which therefore has no effect on him. Thus the fire of Hephaestus is an externalization of the fire that resides within him (as we see from time to time in different ways with other epic warriors, like Hector in earlier books of the *Iliad*, or the *furor* / *ardor* of Aeneas and Turnus in Vergil's *Aeneid*). And so a major distinction is drawn in Book 21 between Achilles in the fire, in a state of frenzied killing, and the world around him, which is subject to the fire in the usual fashion. Achilles, in all his brutal fury, has transcended the physical force of fire, and there can scarcely be a more graphic image of the triumphant hero than this. As we have seen, such a triumph is really at the heart of Bellerophon's victory over the Chimaera in the previous generation, and it remains a kind of heroic ideal for the warriors at Troy. Prior to venturing out on his murderous night sortie against the Trojans in *Iliad* 10 (the *Doloneia*), Diomedes says that if he had Odysseus with him 'the two of us could return even from blazing fire' (*kai ek puros aithomenoio/ amphô nostêsaimen*, 10.246-7). As it turns out, blazing fire is the least of their concerns on this mission, but the phrase does reflect the kind of heroic ideal that mastery of fire represents in the *Iliad*. It is something that only Achilles is able to achieve, and therefore it signifies his special identity in a very important way.

The description of the burning river Scamander therefore does a great deal of work in the later part of the *Iliad*. It provides the earliest and most graphic representation of Achilles in fire and water, a theme which continues to manifest itself in later literary sources. And it foreshadows the fire that Troy itself will be subjected to when the Greeks achieve their final victory. The question inevitably presents itself as to what may lie behind the narrative of Achilles in the burning river. The proliferation of the theme of immersion in fire and water in the extant versions of Achilles' life and death might well suggest the existence of pre-Iliadic accounts of some similar kind of narrative. We have already seen in Chapter 1 that the *Iliad* seems to adapt traditional accounts of the heroic confrontation with the monster to a new and very different heroic milieu. Hector and Priam both conduct quest-missions that correspond to earlier heroic encounters with monsters; but the landscape and character of the (second) war for Troy have undergone significant change, so that Achilles is really in the role of the monster that terrorizes the city.

The description of Achilles in the river of fire may also be an adaptation of an earlier narrative, either one concerned specifically with Achilles himself, or perhaps another narrative entirely. My own view on this, one which I have put forward elsewhere (see above, n. 37), is that some kind of narrative or narratives of the Underworld may lie behind the description of the river in *Iliad* 21. The graphic nature of the suffering in and around Scamander may be informed by the notion that it is truly 'otherworldly' in character, that it bears comparison with a vision of the realm of the dead. Modern discourse on the subject of war often evokes the notion of a 'hell on earth' to try to convey the horror of the landscape and the suffering of those involved. Such a notion may lie behind the burning Scamander too, especially in view of the reference to the river of Hades, Pyriphlegethon, in the *Odyssey* (cf. *Od.* 10.513 [*Puriphlegethôn*] and *Il.* 21.358 [*puri phlegethonti*]).

In the absence of much in the way of definitive evidence, especially on the subject of the pre-Iliadic Underworld, such a view is really little more than informed speculation. What we can say is that the narrative of Achilles in the river of fire is one major Iliadic episode that seems to dominate the treatment of him in later sources. The description of Scamander as a boiling cauldron (*hôs de lebês zei...* 21.362ff.), may obviously influence the story in the *Aegimius* that Thetis placed the siblings of Achilles (and Achilles himself?) in a cauldron of (boiling) water (*eis lebêta hudatos*). The action of Hera and Hephaestus in surrounding him in fire at the river (21.331ff.; cf. 21.288ff.) is clearly the adult parallel to his immersion in fire as a baby (*Argonautica, Alexandra,* Apollonius' *Bibliotecha*), and his placement on the funeral pyre after his death (*Odyssey, Aethiopis*). And the story of his immersion in the river Styx by Thetis may well have its origins in Achilles in Scamander, not least because of the 'hellish' nature of the river in *Iliad* 21. Thus it seems that Achilles' immersion in fire is a kind of Greek epic tradition that informs the passage through life and death of this greatest of warriors (it is worth comparing the figure of the horse in this context, as in Chapter 2). He is immersed in fire as a baby (*Argonautica*), as an adult warrior (*Iliad*), and as a corpse on the funeral pyre (*Odyssey/Aethiopis*). His placement in the river of fire within the *Iliad* foreshadows his placement on the funeral pyre with the same kind of certainty that Troy too will end its life in flames.[43]

Conclusion

This book has explored the notion of generational change in heroic conduct in Homer's *Iliad*. It has examined how best to 'read' the many references to the earlier generations of heroes and to the landscape in which they moved. As we have seen, stories of earlier times are scattered right throughout the poem. Sometimes they are detailed and dedicated narratives, or 'para-narratives', and sometimes they take a more oblique and abbreviated form. Collectively, they present the reader with the notion that the 'world of Achilles' is quite different from the world of earlier heroic conduct. References to the heroic past have the effect of throwing into relief the main war for Priam's Troy. As far as specific background narratives are concerned, most attention has been paid to Heracles, and to his defeat of Troy in earlier times. The broad range of references to this story, and their dispersion throughout the poem, suggest that this was a narrative that was very well known to the poet and his audience. The point was made in the Introduction that the scholarly literature devoted to the *Iliad* has evinced only a very limited interest in the background narrative of the first sack of Troy. And so a central task of this book has been to try to fill this gap. The focus on the internal evidence of the *Iliad* itself, and the absence of much in the way of speculation about earlier poetic traditions, have been part of a conscious strategy to answer the main questions asked at the very beginning. The central argument of the book has been that the *Iliad* needs to be read in the context of the heroic 'history' referred to within it. The heroic past, and indeed the future, are constructed in a very clear and coherent way in the *Iliad*, and our primary task has been to uncover the main aspects of this.

Our focus on the internal evidence does certainly not mean that the *Iliad* was composed in some kind of contextual or poetic vacuum. Indeed, as we saw at the beginning, the *Iliad*'s interest in the notion of generational change seems to be a characteristic of early Greek hexameter poetry in a much more general sense (most notably the generational development of the cosmos in Hesiod's *Theogony*, or the 'World Ages' in the *Works and Days*). Moreover, I myself am very attracted to the idea that many aspects of heroic conduct in the *Iliad*, and the *Odyssey*, consciously respond to the mythical and poetic background dealing with Heracles (see the comments on Richard Martin's arguments in the Introduction).

The first chapter focused on the way that the *Iliad* alludes to, and then adapts, 'traditional' heroic quests, like those of Heracles and Bellerophon (vis-à-vis monsters and the descent to the Underworld). And the third chapter examined the important part played by weaponry in signifying the character of the generational change that has taken place. Chapter 2 by contrast focused on some aspects of *continuity* across the generations, and the part that horses play in helping to convey this notion. Heracles' main task at Troy was to acquire the special (presumably immortal) horses that he had been promised; and it seems important in this context that Achilles has two immortal horses of his own in the war. More significant still is the fact that the central triumph of Achilles in the *Iliad* seems to 'replicate' Heraclean action, albeit in a very distinct kind of way. The poem makes it clear that Achilles, like Heracles, 'defeats Troy' as a great personal heroic endeavor. But his imminent doom means that he has to content himself with a victory in single combat over Hector, its greatest warrior, not the conquest of the city itself. In one important sense therefore Achilles repeats a Heraclean achievement - the sack of Troy; but it is a victory that is appropriate to his special identity as a doomed spearman, and one that takes place in a very different kind of heroic landscape.

It is equally clear in the *Iliad* that Agamemnon will be the commanding figure in the second sack of Troy; and so he too will bring about a kind of repetition of Heraclean action. But again it is clear that this is anticipated as a very different kind of victory from the earlier one, with much attention paid to the new level of devastation to be wrought upon the place. The text is unequivocal that Agamemnon's mind is set firmly on the utter destruction of

Troy (the most graphic example is 6.55ff.); and there are no real doubts at the end of the poem that this will be the fate of the city and its people. References to Heracles' victory over Troy therefore provide an important mythical precedent to the main action in the *Iliad*. They help to remind us that both Achilles and Agamemnon achieve new and different kinds of victories over Troy, and they therefore replicate Heraclean action in different ways. Achilles defeats the city's greatest spearman within the poem itself, whereas Agamemnon has a more general triumph after its conclusion.

All of this does not necessarily mean that the *Iliad* sets out to *surpass* the Heraclean tradition, in an agonistic kind of way, as Martin suggests (see Introduction, n. 14). Indeed I have argued throughout this book (especially Chapter 1, section 2) that the poem goes out of its way to distinguish the generations of men without necessarily giving pre-eminence to one particular period of heroic conduct. But it does certainly mean that the main action of the *Iliad* has to be viewed in a broader temporal context of heroism. The poem consciously describes the 'repetition' of earlier heroic feats, and sets them in a new and different kind of landscape.

Odysseus in the *Odyssey*, by contrast, operates in a landscape that is much more fundamentally 'Heraclean', with its monsters and cannibals and seductive women, not to mention his journey to Hades as a living man. As we saw in the first and the third chapters, the nature of the world through which Odysseus moves makes his use of the bow and arrow (*inter alia*) a fundamentally appropriate weapon. His employment of the bow seems to involve a conscious emulation by Odysseus of the heroic deeds of Heracles himself (as at 8.223ff.). All of our evidence in the *Iliad* suggests that Heracles used his special bow and arrows in the defeat of Troy, as in later sources (cf. *Il.* 5.392ff.; 5.640-54.;14.250f.); and it is probably important that Odysseus in the *Odyssey* alludes to his own use of a bow at Troy too (8.219ff.). Moreover, Odysseus' triumph over the suitors in his house with the special bow (originally from Eurytus, 21.11ff.) seems to be constructed as a parallel to the Heracles/Philoctetes-at-Troy tradition (cf. 8.215ff.). The notion of the special bow to break the 'siege' in Odysseus' house seems to recall the two defeats of Troy in the times of Heracles and Philoctetes (who use the same bow in later sources). Thus the *Odyssey*, like the *Iliad*, 'replicates' earlier heroic conduct, both in the wanderings of Odysseus, and in his resolution of the crisis in his house. But both poems respond to earlier heroism in very different kinds of ways, with challenges and weaponry that are appropriate to the two distinct heroic contexts.

One other significant difference between the two Homeric poems is the *Iliad*'s very strong interest in the *future* - in the imminent death of Achilles himself, and in the defeat of the city for the second time. The final part of the *Odyssey* has no particular interest in the future at Ithaca beyond the resolution of the crisis on the island; whereas the *Iliad* reveals a significant concern with the course of events after the actual end of the poem. As we have seen, it is made very clear that Agamemnon in particular will soon bring his own stamp to the defeat of the city the second time around. And the *Catalogue* makes it equally clear that the archer Philoctetes will play a significant part in the future defeat of Troy (2.724-5). The *Iliad*'s interest in both the heroic past and the near future has the significant effect of locating Achilles between two distinct periods. Whereas the *Odyssey* looks *back* to Heracles and Philoctetes, and their great deeds with the bow (esp. 8.215ff.), the *Iliad* situates Achilles *in between* the two of them. It recalls the career of Heracles, and foreshadows the achievements of Philoctetes. The poem makes it clear that Achilles' *heroic moment*, his special time as the quintessential spearman, is located in between two periods of great triumph over the city in which the bow and arrow is a crucial weapon. His devastating victory over Hector and the Trojans in the main action of the poem is the greatest moment in the use of the spear to defeat the city; for it is clear that other skills and other more effective weapons will need to take a primary role in the final sack of Troy (cf. 2.724-5; 16.707-9).

It is also clear that the imminent death of Achilles, at the personal level (24.131-2), corresponds closely to the coming end of Troy itself, at the monumental level. Achilles and Troy are 'at one' in the last section of the *Iliad*, not least because both are soon to meet their ends by the critical use of the bow and arrow (cf. 2.724-5 [Troy]; 21.277-8; 22.359-60 [Achilles]). Such is their greatness, Achilles as an individual warrior, and Troy as a special city, that neither can be defeated in the type of spear fighting with which much of the *Iliad* is concerned. And so the part played by archery in their imminent defeats is a signifier of just how great and imposing they are. The spear may be the weapon of the best men in the *Iliad*, but its ultimate failure to kill Achilles and to take the city of Troy (as in later sources) is even foreshadowed within the poem itself. The meeting between Achilles and Priam in the final book of the *Iliad* therefore draws some of its great power and poignancy from the fact that the two of them have endured much suffering in common, and that both will soon meet their deaths. It is also significant, especially in light of the arguments put forward in this book, that so much attention is paid in *Iliad* 24 to the subject of old age and youth. The poem concludes with an important description of the coming together of the different generations of men from the two sides in the war. And so it seems most appropriate to conclude this book with a few brief remarks on the journey of the old man Priam and his encounters with Hermes and Achilles.

We saw in the first chapter that the dispute between Achilles and Agamemnon over the prizes of war commences with the harsh treatment meted out to the old suppliant Chryses by Agamemnon (1.8ff.). And then, in the wake of the argument between the leaders over Briseis, old Nestor makes an unsuccessful plea for an end to the argument by comparing the current generation of warriors with those who went before them (Pirithous *et al.*, 1.247ff.). It is very important that old men, Chryses and Nestor, play a significant role in the action at the beginning of the poem, and that the associated notion of generational change in heroic conduct (Pirithous *et al.*) is immediately alluded to in response to the main dispute. This concern with the figure of the old man in Book 1 is then followed by a series of crucial and memorable episodes in which old men play fundamental roles - Priam in Book 3, Phoenix in 9, Nestor in 11, and so forth. The ransom mission of Priam to Achilles in *Iliad* 24 is really the culmination of the *Iliad*'s strong interest in the generations of men. The keynote of *Iliad* 24 is the restoration of the proper processes and rituals of human conduct. And one crucial aspect of this is the kind and respectful treatment provided by a young man to an old man - even to one on the enemy side in the war.

The emphasis given in Book 24 to Priam's age is such that, by my count, he is described as an 'old man' (ie. *gerôn/geraios* etc.) no less than forty-four times in Book 24 alone. The text makes it clear that such a dangerous journey is especially remarkable because of the age of the king. Moreover, Zeus is quite insistent that Priam should be escorted by a herald who is an 'older man' (*geraiteros*, 24.149, 178). Those who witness the mission are all amazed at the fact that they have dared to embark upon it. The Trojans who see them off on their way have no doubt that the mission will end in their deaths (24.327-8). And those who meet them at the other end are struck by the fact that they have embarked on something that is quite remarkable for two old men. Hermes says to Priam that 'you are not young yourself, and this one attending you is old, for warding off a man, when one initiates a quarrel' (*out' autos neos essi, gerôn de toi houtos opêdei,/ andr' apamunasthai, hote tis proteros chalepênêi*, 24.368-9). Achilles too is at pains to point out to Priam that he is aware of the fact that he has been led to him by a god, 'for no mortal would dare to come to our encampment, not even a man in the fullness of youth' (*ou gar ke tlaiê brotos elthemen, oude mal' hêbôn, / es straton*, 24.565-6). Whereas old age might normally be thought of as a weakness in the accomplishment of a heroic endeavor, it turns out, in the case of Priam and the herald, to be a significant advantage.

Just as there is great emphasis placed on the old age of the wayfarers, so there is much attention devoted to the comparative youth of those who receive them. The gods contrive that a ransom journey is undertaken by two old men, and that they are met by two young men. And so when he appears in front of them Hermes takes on the disguise of a young man in the first flush of youth (24.345-8). He is a *kouros* (24.347), and his encounter with the two Trojans is based in a fundamental way on their relative ages. Hence the youthful down on Hermes' face (24.348) is a distinct contrast to the grey head and grey beard of old Priam (24.516). Moreover the meeting between Hermes and Priam is a kind of mock verbal contest (at least on Hermes' part) of the young and the old, of a child (*tekos*, 24. 373, 425; cf. 377; cf. Achilles as *tekos*, 23.626), and a father (*pater*, 24.362; cf. 371). The nature of the encounter between them is characterized by Hermes' statement to Priam that 'you try me out old man, I who am younger than you, but you won't persuade me' (*peirai emeio, geraie, neôterou, oude me peiseis*, 24.433). The youth of Hermes, as the divine guide, complements Priam's old age in much the same way as Athena's role as the mature man Mentor complements Telemachus' comparative immaturity and naivety in the first books of the *Odyssey*.

The youthful appearance of Hermes also parallels the youth of Achilles himself. Priam's first words to Achilles call upon him to remember his own father Peleus, whose age is meant to resemble Priam's (24.486ff.; cf. 503ff., 534ff.). Throughout the *Iliad* Achilles is the quintessentially youthful warrior whose physical prowess and headstrong manner bring him into various situations of conflict and crisis. One consequence of these situations is that he is frequently on the receiving end of advice from older men – notably Nestor (1.254ff.), Odysseus (9.225ff., 19.155ff.), Phoenix (9.434ff.), and Patroclus (16.21ff.); not to mention the advice that he receives from the two goddesses, Thetis and Athena.

Achilles treats all of these older advisors with courtesy and respect. His generous treatment of older men culminates in two spontaneous gestures in the final part of the poem, one to Nestor in Book 23, the other to Priam in Book 24. In Nestor's case Achilles makes a spontaneous offer of a prize at the funeral games out of respect for his old age (23.615ff.). And in Priam's case he offers, out of the blue, to hold up the fighting so that the Trojans can bury Hector (24.656ff.). Achilles has no hesitation in offering generosity to the old men with whom he has dealings; and this even includes the old king of the enemy Trojans. In Book 23 we are told by Antilochus that the gods honor older men (23.788), and this notion is put into practice by Achilles in some important ways in the final books. As we have seen, the *Iliad* begins with an ugly incident in which an old man is roughly treated by a king of the Greeks (1.8ff.); but it ends with a magnanimous gesture of kindness and compassion from another of the Greeks who evinces a very different attitude towards an aged victim of war (esp. 24.650ff.)

In light of the arguments put forward in this book it is obviously very important that so much emphasis is placed on old age and youth in the final book of the *Iliad*. As we saw in the Introduction (15ff.), the final book of the *Odyssey* has a similar concern in its description of the three generations of men, Laertes, Odysseus, and Telemachus, coming together at the end of their various ordeals (24.511ff.). The union of the generations is fundamental to the notion of closure in both Homeric poems. And in the case of the *Iliad* it is all the more significant because the two men who meet are on different sides in the war. Priam is so old that he can remember the coming of the Amazons when he was young (3.189). Like Nestor on the Greek side, he is a kind of living memorial of the old world that Heracles tends to represent in the *Iliad*. It seems appropriate therefore that Priam should re-enact a traditional quest-journey of the 'catabatic' type. The final narrative of the *Iliad* describes a kind of traditional heroic quest, but it is one that is appropriate to the modern heroic landscape in the world of Achilles. It is re-enacted by men at opposite ends of the age spectrum, the one a survivor from the earlier time of Heracles and the Amazons, the other a pre-eminent representative of a new age of heroic endeavor.

Achilles' treatment of Priam on his ransom-mission therefore ends with a unique gesture of compassion for the enemy king and his people (24.656ff.). But notwithstanding the magnanimity of the gesture, Achilles' conduct does seem to have a rather 'traditional', or even a 'Heraclean' aspect to it. As we saw in Chapter 4, the text suggests that Heracles spared the Trojans from the most extreme violence, and he certainly refrained from burning the city. He clearly exacted vengeance on the place (note especially 5.641ff.; 5.648; 14.250-1); and we may assume quite readily that the perfidious king Laomedon was the main object of his violence, as in later sources. But equally, every effort seems to be made within the poem to stress the *continuity* of Trojan identity after the defeat of the place. There was no apparent desire for genocide and for the obliteration of the city in the previous generation. The apparent clemency of Heracles in earlier times, if we can call it that, seems to have its parallel in the compassion of Achilles for Priam within the *Iliad* itself. Priam was presumably spared when he was a youngster (by Heracles), and he is also spared when he is an old man (by Achilles).

But it is clear that compassion for the Trojan victims of war is about to come to an end. The treatment of the two old men, Chryses and Priam, in the first and last books of the *Iliad*, by Agamemnon and Achilles respectively, does not augur well for the Trojans in the next stage of the evolution of heroic conduct at Troy. After the death of Achilles it will be Agamemnon's turn again to take centre stage as the commanding figure in the defeat of Troy. His attitude to the weak and the vulnerable is very clear from within the poem, be it to an old suppliant (1.8ff), or to a pregnant woman (6.55ff.), or to the city itself (2.412ff.; 4.238-9). If Philoctetes' return to Troy represents the re-emergence of the bow as a pre-eminent weapon of war (2.724-5), so it is Agamemnon's shadow that begins to fall over the city of Troy. At the end of the poem Achilles is at least able to protect Priam and the Trojans from Agamemnon and the army of the Greeks (24.650ff., 669ff., 778ff.; cf. 683ff.). But the imminent death of Achilles is the harbinger of a new period in the war. Despite all the cruelty that is exhibited in the 'sack of Troy' by Achilles within the *Iliad* itself, the poem leaves us with the clear sense that there is much worse to come in the next and final phase of the conflict.

The *Iliad* therefore presents us with a vision in which the conduct of war seems to acquire a new and greater level of devastation through time, at least as far as Troy is concerned. The transition in just one generation is from a kind of individual victory over the city, led by Heracles with a small group of men, to a massive encounter between two vast armies. The changing landscape of heroic conduct across the generations seems to bring with it a much greater scale of conflict (cf. 3.182ff.; 5.638ff.), and a hardening in the attitude towards the execution of war. And this transition is signified by the greater importance of the spear and fire as major weapons of war. The resolve among the later generation of Greeks for the razing of the city corresponds to the divine plan for Troy's destruction; and it means that the use of fire by the characters in the poem, even by the Trojans, has the effect of anticipating the destruction of the city itself. The Trojan success in torching an enemy ship leads inexorably to the burning of their own city when Zeus switches his support to the Greek side in the war (15.599ff.).

This vision of the increasingly devastating conduct of war through time, whether it is based on historical changes in fighting practices in antiquity, or not, does seem to be remarkably 'modern' in many ways. Rightly or wrongly, a common perception in our own times is that war is more costly in human terms now than it was in the past. New military technologies have obviously brought with them the potential for greater levels of destruction, and we ourselves have seen these played out in many different theatres of war in the modern era. We are not exactly Trojans waiting for Agamemnon, but the military capacity to inflict devastating effects on human societies has never been greater. And so the *Iliad*'s vision of changes in the way the wars for Troy are fought out has a particular resonance for contemporary readers of the poem.

One aspect of Greek descriptions of the Trojan war however may seem much more foreign to us. If you think about the main narratives of the whole story of Troy, both within the *Iliad* and outside it, you can probably identify just about every imaginable atrocity: the destruction of smaller towns and cities prior to the taking of Troy, the killing of the men and the enslavement of the women and children, infanticide, human sacrifice, mutilation of a body, rape, sacrilege, and so forth. The culmination of all this is the physical destruction of Troy and the wiping out of the identity of its people. Not all of these excesses are specifically alluded to in the *Iliad* (although the story of the throwing of the boy Astyanax to his death from the city walls may lie within the poem, as at 24.734ff.). In one sense this list of horrors may not seem so remarkable because we tend rather instinctively to expect them in a war. What is remarkable however is the fact that it is the *Greeks* who are almost always the perpetrators of the worst excesses in their role as victors in the war. It is worth keeping firmly in our minds - should we ever forget - that these are Greek mythical narratives, describing Greek actions, for a Greek audience. The early Greek poets and mythmakers, and their audiences, seem to have had an unrivalled capacity to explore the darkest aspects of human conduct in war with their own people as the main agents. Homer's *Iliad* stands as the earliest extant example of this tradition, and many would say the best.

Bibliography

Alden, M.J. 'Genealogy as Paradigm: the example of Bellerophon.' *Hermes* 124 (1996): 257-63.
——. *Homer Beside Himself: para-narratives in the Iliad*. Oxford: Oxford University Press, 2000.
Andersen, Ø. *Die Diomedesgestalt in der Ilias*. Oslo: Universitetsforlaget, 1978.
Anderson, M.J. *The Fall of Troy in Early Greek Poetry and Art*. Oxford: Clarendon Press, 1997.
Andrews, P.B.S. 'The Falls of Troy in Greek Tradition.' *Greece & Rome* 12 (1965): 28-37.
Atchity, K.J. 'Horses in the *Iliad*.' In *Homer's Iliad: the shield of memory*, 299-311. Carbondale and Edwardsville: Southern Illinois University Press, 1978.
Austin, N. 'The Function of Digressions in the *Iliad*.' *Greek, Roman, and Byzantine Studies* 7 (1966): 295-312.
——. *Archery at the Dark of the Moon: poetic problems in Homer's Odyssey*. Berkeley: University of California Press, 1975.
Becker, A.S. *The Shield of Achilles and the Poetics of Ekphrasis*. Lanham, Md.: Rowman & Littlefield Publishers, 1995.
Bethe, E. *Homer: Dichtung und Sage*. Vol. 1. Leipzig: B.G. Teubner, 1914.
Boardman, J. 'Laomedon'. In vol. 6 *Lexicon Iconographicum Mythologiae Classicae*. 201-3, Zürich, Artemis, 1992.
Braswell, B.K. 'Mythological Innovation in the *Iliad*.' *The Classical Quarterly* 21 (1971): 16-26.

Bryce, T.R. 'Pandaros, a Lycian at Troy.' *The American Journal of Philology* 98 (1977): 213-18.
Burgess, J. 'Achilles' Heel: the death of Achilles in ancient myth.' *Classical Antiquity* 14 (1995): 217-45.
———. *The Tradition of the Trojan War in Homer and the Epic Cycle.* Baltimore, Md.: Johns Hopkins University Press, 2001.
Burkert, W. 'Apellai und Apollon.' *Rheinisches Museum* 118 (1975): 1-21.
———. *Greek Religion: Archaic and Classical.* Oxford: Blackwell, 1985.
Campbell, M. *Echoes and Imitations of Early Epic in Apollonius Rhodius.* Leiden: Brill, 1981.
Carlier, J. 'Apollo.' In *Greek and Egyptian Mythologies* edited by Y. Bonnefoy. Chicago: University of Chicago Press, 1992.
Catling, H. 'Heroes Returned? Subminoan burials from Crete.' In *The Ages of Homer*, edited by J.B. Carter and S.P. Morris, 123-36. Austin: University of Texas Press, 1995.
Chadwick, N.K., and Zhirmunsky, V. *Oral Epics of Central Asia.* Cambridge: Cambridge University Press, 1969.
Chirassi-Colombo, I. 'Heros Achilleus-Theos Apollon.' In *Il Mito Greco: atti del Convegno internazionale (Urbino, 7-12 maggio 1973)*, edited by B.Gentili and G. Paioni, 231-69. Rome: Edizioni dell'Ateneo & Bizzarri, 1977.
Clark, R.J. *Catabasis: Vergil and the wisdom-tradition.* Amsterdam: B.R. Grüner, 1979.
Clarke, H.W. *The Art of the Odyssey.* 2nd ed. Bristol: Bristol Classical Press, 1989.
Clarke, M. *Flesh and Spirit in the Songs of Homer: a study of words and myths.* Oxford: Clarendon Press, 1999.
Clay, J.S. 'Immortal and Ageless Forever.' *The Classical Journal* 77 (1981): 112-17.
———. *The Wrath of Athena: gods and men in the Odyssey.* Princeton: Princeton University Press, 1983.
———. *The Politics of Olympus: form and meaning in the major Homeric Hymns.* Princeton: Princeton University Press, 1989.
———. *Hesiod's Cosmos.* Cambridge and New York: Cambridge University Press, 2003.

Craik, E.M. *The Dorian Aegean*. London: Routledge & Kegan Paul, 1980.
Crissy, K. 'Herakles, Odysseus and the Bow: *Odyssey* 21.11-41.' *The Classical Journal* 93 (1997): 41-53.
Cross, T.P., and Slover, C.H., eds. *Ancient Irish Tales*. Dublin: Figgis, 1973.
Danek, G. *Epos und Zitat: Studien zu den Quellen der Odyssee*. Vienna: Österreichische Akademie der Wissenschaften, 1998.
Delebecque, E. *Le Cheval dans l'Iliade*. Paris: Librairie C. Klincksieck, 1951.
duBois, P. *Centaurs and Amazons: women and the pre-history of the great chain of being*. Ann Arbor: University of Michigan Press, 1982.
Ebbott, M. *Imagining Illegitimacy in Classical Greek Literature*. Lanham: Lexington Books, 2003.
Edmunds, L. 'Myth in Homer.' In *A New Companion to Homer*, edited by I. Morris and B. Powell, 415-41. Leiden: Brill, 1997.
Edsman, C-M. 'Fire'. In vol. 5 *The Encyclopedia of Religion*. Edited by M. Eliade, 340-6, New York, Macmillan, 1987.
Edwards, M.W. *Homer: Poet of the Iliad*. Baltimore: Johns Hopkins University Press, 1987.
———. *The Iliad: a Commentary. Volume V: Books 17-20* Cambridge: Cambridge University Press, 1991.
Eliade, M. *Myths, Dreams, and Mysteries: the encounter between contemporary faiths and archaic realities*. New York: Harper & Row, 1975.
———. *Rites and Symbols of Initiation: the mysteries of birth and rebirth*. Translated by W.R. Trask. New York: Harper Torchbooks, 1975.
Erbse, H. *Scholia Graeca in Homeri Iliadem*. Vol. 5. Berolini: de Gryter, 1969.
Escher. 'Achilleus.' In *Paulys Realencyclopädie der Classischen Altertumswissenschaft*. Vol. 1, cols. 221-45. Stuttgart, 1893.
Falkner, T.M. *The Poetics of Old Age in Greek Epic, Lyric, and Tragedy*. Norman and London: University of Oklahoma Press, 1995.
Faraone, C.A. *Talismans and Trojan Horses: guardian statues in Ancient Greek myth and ritual*. New York: Oxford University Press, 1992.

Fenik, B. *Typical Battle Scenes in the Iliad: studies in the narrative techniques of Homeric battle description*. Wiesbaden: F. Steiner, 1968.

Francis, E.D. *Image and Idea in Fifth Century Greece: art and literature after the Persian Wars*. London: Routledge, 1990.

Fränkel, H., and Heitsch, E. *Die homerischen Gleichnisse*. Göttingen: Vandenhoeck & Ruprecht, 1977.

Frazer, J.G. *Apollodorus: the Library*. Cambridge, Mass.: Harvard University Press, 1967.

Frölich, H. *Die Militärmedizin Homers*. Stuttgart: Enke, 1879.

Frontisi-Ducroux, F. *La Cithare d'Achille*. Rome: Edizioni dell'Ateneo, 1986.

Galinsky, G.K. *The Herakles Theme: the adaptations of the hero in literature from Homer to the twentieth century*. Oxford: Blackwell, 1972.

Gantz, T. *Early Greek Myth: a guide to literary and artistic sources*. Baltimore: Johns Hopkins University Press, 1993.

Garvie, A.F. *Homer: Odyssey, Books VI-VIII*. Cambridge: Cambridge University Press, 1994.

Graz, L. *Le feu dans l'Iliade et l'Odyssée*. Paris: Librairie C. Klincksieck, 1965.

Greenhalgh, P.A.L. *Early Greek Warfare: horsemen and chariots in the Homeric and archaic ages*. Cambridge: Cambridge University Press, 1973.

Griffin, J. 'The Epic Cycle and the Uniqueness of Homer.' *The Journal of Hellenic Studies* 97 (1977): 39-53.

——. *Homer on Life and Death*. Oxford: Clarendon Press, 1980.

——. 'Homer and Excess.' In *Homer: Beyond Oral Poetry*, edited by J.M. Bremer, I.J.F. de Jong and J. Kalff, 85-104. Amsterdam: B.R. Grüner, 1987.

——. *Homer: Iliad 9*. Oxford: Clarendon Press, 1995.

Hainsworth, J.B. 'No flames in the *Odyssey*.' *The Journal of Hellenic Studies* 78 (1958): 49-56.

——. *The Iliad: a Commentary. Volume III: Books 9-12*. Cambridge: Cambridge University Press, 1993.

Hall, E. *Inventing the Barbarian: Greek self-definition through tragedy*. Oxford: Clarendon Press, 1989.
Halliday, W.R. 'Note on *Homeric Hymn to Demeter*, 239ff.' *The Classical Review* 25 (1911): 8-11.
Heubeck, A., West, S., and Hainsworth, J.B. *A Commentary on Homer's Odyssey*. Vol. 1. Oxford: Clarendon Press, 1988.
Huxley, G.L. *Greek Epic Poetry from Eumelos to Panyassis*. London: Faber, 1969.
Jacquemin, A. 'Chimaira'. In vol. 3 *Lexicon Iconographicum Mythologiae Classicae*. 249-59, Zürich, Artemis, 1986.
Janko, R. *The Iliad: a Commentary. Volume IV: Books 13-16*. Cambridge: Cambridge University Press, 1992
Kahn, C.H. *The Art and Thought of Heraclitus*. Cambridge: Cambridge University Press, 1979.
Kakridis, J.T. '*Aei philellên ho poiêtês?* (Is the poet always pro-Greek?).' In *Homeric Researches*, 54-67. Lund: Publication of the New Society of Letters at Lund, 1949.
———. *Homeric Researches*. Lund: Publication of the New Society of Letters at Lund, 1949.
Kirk, G.S. *The Songs of Homer*. Cambridge: Cambridge University Press, 1962.
———. *Myth: its meaning and functions in ancient and other cultures*. Cambridge: Cambridge University Press, 1970.
———. 'The Homeric Poems as History.' In *The Cambridge Ancient History*. Vol. 2, pt. 2. Cambridge: Cambridge University Press, 1975.
———. *Homer and the Oral Tradition*. Cambridge: Cambridge University Press, 1976.
———. *The Iliad: a Commentary. Volume I: Books 1-4*. Cambridge: Cambridge University Press, 1984.
———. *The Iliad: a Commentary. Volume II: Books 5-8*. Cambridge: Cambridge University Press, 1990.
Knaak. 'Demophon'. In vol. 5 *Paulys Realencyclopädie der classischen Altertumswissenschaft*. cols. 148-52, Stuttgart, 1905.
Kosmetatou, E. 'Horse Sacrifices in Greece and Cyprus.' *Journal of*

Prehistoric Religion 7 (1993): 31-41.

Kossatz-Deissmann, A. 'Achilleus'. In vol. 1 *Lexicon Iconographicum Mythologiae Classicae*. 37-200, Zürich and Munich, Artemis, 1981.

Kullmann, W. *Das Wirkin der Götter in der Ilias*. Berlin: Akademie Verlag, 1956.

———. *Die Quellen der Ilias*. Wiesbaden: F. Steiner, 1960.

Lang, M.L. 'Reverberation and Mythology in the *Iliad*.' In *Approaches to Homer*, edited by C.A. Rubino and C.W. Shelmerdine, 140-64. Austin: University of Texas Press, 1983.

———. 'War Story into Wrath Story.' In *The Ages of Homer*, edited by J.B. Carter and S.P. Morris, 149-62. Austin: University of Texas Press, 1995.

Latacz, J. *Kampfparänese, Kampfdarstellung und Kampfwirklichkeit in der Ilias, bei Kallinos und Tyrtaios*. Munich: Beck, 1977.

———. *Homers Ilias: Gesamtkommentar*. Munich and Leipzig: K.G. Saur, 2000.

Leaf, W., and Bayfield, M.A. *Homerou Ilias*. London: Macmillan, 1908.

Lesky. 'Peleus'. In vol. 19 *Paulys Realencyclopädie der classischen Altertumswissenschaft*. cols. 217-308, Stuttgart, 1937.

Létoublon, F. 'Le messager fidèle.' In *Homer: Beyond Oral Poetry*, edited by J.M. Bremer, I.J.F. de Jong and J. Kalff, 123-44. Amsterdam: B.R. Grüner, 1987.

Livrea, E. *Apollonii Rhodii Argonauticon, Liber 4*. Florence: La Nuova Italia, 1973.

Lonsdale, S. 'A Dancing Floor for Ariadne.' In *The Ages of Homer*, edited by J.B. Carter and S.P. Morris, 273-84. Austin: University of Texas Press, 1995.

Lorimer, H.L. *Homer and the Monuments*. London: Macmillan, 1950.

Lynn-George, M. *Epos: word, narrative and the Iliad*. Houndmills, Basingstoke, Hampshire: Macmillan, 1988.

Mackie, C.J. 'Achilles' Teachers: Chiron and Phoenix in the *Iliad* ' *Greece & Rome* 44 (1997): 1-10.

———. 'Achilles in Fire.' *The Classical Quarterly* 48 (1998): 329-38.

———. 'Scamander and the Rivers of Hades in Homer.' *The American Journal of Philology* 120 (1999): 485-501.
———. 'Homeric Phthia.' *Colby Quarterly* 38 (2002): 163-73.
Mackie, H.S. *Talking Trojan: speech and community in the Iliad*. Lanham, Md.: Rowman & Littlefield Publishers, 1996.
Macleod, C.W. *Homer: Iliad, Book XXIV*. Cambridge and New York: Cambridge University Press, 1982.
Marg, W. *Homer über die Dichtung*. Münster: Aschendorff, 1957.
Martin, R.P. *The Language of Heroes: speech and performance in the Iliad*. Ithaca: Cornell University Press, 1989.
Merkelbach, R. *Untersuchungen zur Odyssee*. Munich: C.H. Beck, 1951.
Merkelbach, R., and West, M.L. *Fragmenta Hesiodea* Oxford: Clarendon Press, 1967.
Meuli, K. *Odyssee und Argonautika*. Utrecht: H&S, 1974.
Michelakis, P. *Achilles in Greek tragedy*. Cambridge: Cambridge University Press, 2002.
Moulton, C. *Similes in the Homeric poems*. Göttingen: Vandenhoeck und Ruprecht, 1977.
Mueller, M. *The Iliad*. London and Boston: Allen & Unwin, 1984.
Myres, J.L. 'The Last Book of the *Iliad*.' *The Journal of Hellenic Studies* 52 (1932): 264-96.
Nagler, M.N. *Spontaneity and Tradition: a study in the oral art of Homer*. Berkeley: University of California Press, 1974.
Nagy, G. *The Best of the Achaeans: concepts of the hero in archaic Greek poetry*. Baltimore: Johns Hopkins University Press, 1979.
Nilsson, M.P. *The Mycenaean Origin of Greek Mythology*. Berkeley: University of California Press, 1932.
———. *Homer and Mycenae*. London: Methuen, 1933.
O'Flaherty, W.D. 'Horses'. In vol. 6 *The Encyclopedia of Religion*. Edited by M. Eliade, 463-68, New York, Macmillan, 1987.
Page, D.L. *The Homeric Odyssey*. Oxford: Clarendon Press, 1955.
———. *Lyrica Graeca Selecta*. Oxford: Clarendon Press, 1968.
Parry, A. 'The Language of Achilles.' *Transactions of the American Philological Association* 87 (1956): 1-7.

Podlecki, A.J. *The Early Greek Poets and their Times.* Vancouver: University of British Columbia Press, 1984.
Preller, L., Robert, C., and Kern, O. *Griechische Mythologie.* Berlin: Weidmann, 1894-1926.
Pritchett, W.K. *The Greek State at War.* Vol. 4. Berkeley: University of California Press, 1985.
Puhvel, J. 'Vedic *ásvamedha* - and Gaulish *IIPOMIIDVOS*.' *Language* 31 (1955): 353-4.
Querbach, C.A. 'Conflict between young and old in Homer's *Iliad.*' In *The Conflict of Generations in Ancient Greece and Rome,* edited by S. Bertman, 55-64. Amsterdam: B.R. Grüner, 1976.
Rabel, R.J. 'Apollo as a model for Achilles in the *Iliad.*' *American Journal of Philology* 111 (1990): 429-40.
Redfield, J.M. *Nature and Culture in the Iliad: the tragedy of Hektor.* Durham and London: Duke University Press, 1994.
Reinhardt, K. *Die Ilias und ihr Dichter.* Göttingen: Vandenhoeck und Ruprecht, 1961.
Richardson, N. *The Homeric Hymn to Demeter.* Oxford: Clarendon Press, 1974.
——. 'The Individuality of Homer's Language.' In *Homer: Beyond Oral Poetry,* edited by J.M. Bremer, I.J.F. de Jong and J. Kalff, 165-84. Amsterdam: B.R. Grüner, 1987.
——. *The Iliad: a Commentary. Volume VI: Books 21-24.* Cambridge: Cambridge University Press, 1993.
Robert, F. *Homère.* Paris: Presses Universitaires de France, 1950.
Robertson, D.S. 'The Food of Achilles.' *The Classical Review* 54 (1940): 177-80.
Roccos, L.J. 'Perseus'. In vol. 7 *Lexicon Iconographicum Mythologiae Classicae.* 332-48, Zürich, Artemis, 1994.
Rolle, R. *The World of the Scythians.* Translated by G. Walls. London: B.T. Batsford, 1989.
Scammell, J.M. 'The Capture of Troy by Heracles.' *The Classical Journal* 29 (1934): 418-28.
Schadewaldt, W. *Von Homers Welt und Werk.* 2nd ed. Stuttgart: Koehler, 1959.

———. *Iliasstudien*. Darmstadt: Wissenschaftliche Buchgesellschaft, 1987.
Schein, S.L. *The Mortal Hero: an introduction to Homer's Iliad*. Berkeley: University of California Press, 1984.
———. 'Mythological allusion in the *Odyssey*.' In *Omero Tremila Anni Dopo*, edited by F. Montanari and P. Ascheri, 85-101. Rome: Edizioni di Storia e Letteratura, 2002.
Schrade, H. *Götter und Menschen Homers*. Stuttgart: W. Kohlhammer, 1952.
Schretter, M.K. *Alter Orient und Hellas*. Innsbruck: Inst. f. Sprachwissenschaft d. Univ. Innsbruck, 1974.
Schwartz, E. *Die Odyssee*. Munich: M. Hueber, 1924.
Scodel, R. *Listening to Homer: tradition, narrative, and audience*. Ann Arbor: University of Michigan Press, 2002.
———. 'The Modesty of Homer.' In *Oral Performance and its Context*, edited by C.J. Mackie, 1-19. Leiden: Brill, 2004.
Scott, J.A. *The Unity of Homer*. Berkeley: University of California Press, 1921.
Shay, J. *Achilles in Vietnam: combat trauma and the undoing of character*. New York: Maxwell Macmillan International, 1994.
Sheppard, J.T. *The Pattern of the Iliad*. London: Methuen, 1922.
Silk, M.S. *Homer, The Iliad*. Cambridge: Cambridge University Press, 1987.
Slatkin, L.M. *The Power of Thetis: allusion and interpretation in the Iliad*. Berkeley: University of California Press, 1991.
Smith, M.E. *The Aztecs*. Cambridge, Mass.: Blackwell, 1996.
Snodgrass, A. *Arms and Armour of the Greeks*. London: Thames & Hudson, 1967.
———. *Homer and the Artists: text and picture in early Greek art*. Cambridge and New York: Cambridge University Press, 1998.
Sourvinou-Inwood, C. *'Reading' Greek Death: to the end of the Classical period*. Oxford: Clarendon Press, 1995.
Stenger, J. 'Peleus.' In *Der neue Pauly*, edited by H. Cancik, H. Schneider and A.F. von Pauly. Vol. 9, cols. 492-93. Stuttgart: J.B Metzler, 2000.

Taplin, O. 'The Shield of Achilles within the *Iliad*.' *Greece & Rome* 27 (1980): 1-21.

——. *Homeric Soundings*. Oxford: Clarendon Press, 1992.

Thomas, H., and Stubbings, F.H. 'Lands and Peoples in Homer.' In *A Companion to Homer*, edited by A.J.B. Wace and F.H. Stubbings, 283-310. New York: Macmillan, 1962.

Toohey, P. *Reading Epic*. London and New York: Routledge, 1992.

Trypanis, C.A. *The Homeric Epics*. Warminster: Aris & Phillips, 1977.

van Leeuwen, J. *Odyssea*. Leiden: A.W. Sijthoff, 1917.

van Wees, H. *Status Warriors: war, violence, and society in Homer and history*. Amsterdam: J.C. Gieben, 1992.

——. 'Homeric Warfare.' In *A New Companion to Homer*, edited by I. Morris and B. Powell, 668-93. Leiden: Brill, 1997.

Vermeule, E. *Aspects of Death in Early Greek Art and Poetry*. Berkeley: University of California Press, 1979.

Vernant, J-P. 'A Beautiful Death.' In *Mortals and Immortals: Collected Essays*, edited by J-P. Vernant and F.I. Zeitlin, 50-74. Princeton: Princeton University Press, 1991.

Vian, F. *Apollonios de Rhodes, Argonautiques*. Vol. 3. Paris: Presses Universitaires de France, 1981.

Wathelet, P. 'Priam aux Enfers ou le retour du corps d' Hector.' *Les Études Classiques* 56 (1988): 321-35.

——. 'Les Troyens vus par Homère.' In *Quaestiones Homericae*, edited by L. Isebaert and R. Lebrun, 291-305. Louvain-Namur: Editions Peeters, 1998.

Watrous, J. 'Artemis and the Lion: two similes in *Odyssey* 6.' In *Nine Essays on Homer*, edited by M. Carlisle and O. Levaniouk, 165-76. Lanham, Md: Rowman & Littlefield Publishers, 1999.

Webster, T.B.L. *From Mycenae to Homer*. London: Methuen, 1958.

Wendel, C. *Scholia in Apollonium Rhodium Vetera*. Berlin: Weidmann, 1974.

West, M.L. *Hesiod: 'Theogony,' edited with Prolegomena and Commentary*. Oxford: Clarendon Press, 1966.

——. *Hesiod: 'Works and Days,'* edited with Prolegomena and Commentary. Oxford: Clarendon Press, 1978.
——. *Greek Epic Fragments from the Seventh to the Fifth Centuries BC.* Cambridge, Mass. and London: Harvard University Press, 2003.

Whitman, C. *Homer and the Heroic Tradition.* Cambridge, Mass.: Harvard University Press, 1958.

Willcock, M.M. 'Mythological Paradeigma in the *Iliad*.' *The Classical Quarterly* 58 (1964): 141-54.
——. *A Companion to the Iliad.* Chicago: University of Chicago Press, 1976.
——. 'Ad Hoc Invention in the *Iliad*.' *Harvard Studies in Classical Philology* 81 (1977): 41-53.
——. 'Nervous Hesitation in the *Iliad*.' In *Homer 1987: Papers of the Third Greenbank Colloquium*, edited by J. Pinsent and H.V. Hurt, 65-73. Liverpool: Liverpool Classical Monthly, 1992.
——. 'Neoanalysis.' In *A New Companion to Homer*, edited by I. Morris and B. Powell, 174-89. Leiden: Brill, 1997.

Wofford, S.L. *The Choice of Achilles: the ideology of figure in the epic.* Stanford: Stanford University Press, 1992.

Notes

Introduction

[1] Useful discussion of the issues involved in mythological allusion in the *Iliad* can be found in L.M. Slatkin, *The Power of Thetis: allusion and interpretation in the Iliad* (Berkeley: University of California Press, 1991), esp. Chapter 4, "Allusion and Interpretation', 107ff. As the title suggests the main focus of her work is the adaptation in the *Iliad* of earlier accounts of Thetis, but the study also has important implications for Homer's adaptation of other narratives. For an earlier introduction to the subject, M.W. Edwards, *Homer: Poet of the Iliad* (Baltimore: Johns Hopkins University Press, 1987), 67-70. For a recent appraisal of the subject with particular reference to the *Odyssey*, see S.L. Schein, 'Mythological allusion in the *Odyssey*,' in *Omero Tremila Anni Dopo*, ed. F. Montanari and P. Ascheri (Rome: Edizioni di Storia e Letteratura, 2002), 85-101. For epic heroism through time and across cultures, P. Toohey, *Reading Epic* (London and New York: Routledge, 1992).

[2] See, most recently, M.J. Alden, *Homer Beside Himself: para-narratives in the Iliad* (Oxford: Oxford University Press, 2000). An earlier useful study is N. Austin, 'The Function of Digressions in the *Iliad*,' *Greek, Roman, and Byzantine Studies* 7 (1966): 295-312.

[3] Lowell Edmunds emphasizes the fact that many of the stories in the poem are uttered by the heroes: *'these are not stories that Homer tells in his own voice; these are stories that Homer represents as told by the heroes'* (416-7, his italics). This is certainly true in many cases, especially of the longer 'para-narratives' told by Nestor, Phoenix, Achilles and Glaucus. The implications for the notion of heroes as storytellers in their own right are discussed by Edmunds at 418-420. L. Edmunds, 'Myth in Homer,' in *A New Companion to Homer*, ed. I. Morris and B. Powell (Leiden:

Brill, 1997), 415ff.
4 Austin, 'The Function of Digressions in the *Iliad*,' uses the term 'hortatory paradigms' for the story of Meleager and the account of Tydeus' exploits at Thebes.
5 On this episode, Ø. Andersen, *Die Diomedesgestalt in der Ilias* (Oslo: Universitetsforlaget, 1978), 33-46; Alden, *Homer Beside Himself*, 114-20. On the response of Diomedes, R.P. Martin, *The Language of Heroes: speech and performance in the Iliad* (Ithaca: Cornell University Press, 1989), 70-72.
6 J.T. Kakridis, *Homeric Researches* (Lund: Publication of the New Society of Letters at Lund, 1949); W. Kullmann, *Die Quellen der Ilias* (Wiesbaden: F. Steiner, 1960). The best summary of the main approaches, and the issues involved, is M.M. Willcock, 'Neoanalysis,' in *A New Companion to Homer*, ed. I. Morris and B. Powell (Leiden: Brill, 1997), 174-89: 'Its essential approach (ie. the approach of neoanalysis) is to see behind some of the incidents of the *Iliad* into the content of pre-Homeric poetry in the belief that it can be shown that "Homer" consciously or subconsciously reflects scenes from that broader background.'(174) Cf. more recently on the *Odyssey*, G. Danek, *Epos und Zitat: Studien zu den Quellen der Odyssee* (Vienna: Österreichische Akademie der Wissenschaften, 1998).
7 On the question of an epic or epics of Heracles lying behind the references in the poem, W. Kullmann, *Das Wirkin der Götter in der Ilias* (Berlin: Akademie Verlag, 1956), 25-35. See too, most recently, M.L. West, *Greek Epic Fragments from the Seventh to the Fifth Centuries BC.* (Cambridge, Mass. and London: Harvard University Press, 2003), 19ff.
8 M.M. Willcock, 'Mythological Paradeigma in the *Iliad*,' *The Classical Quarterly* 58 (1964): 141-54. See too B.K. Braswell, 'Mythological Innovation in the *Iliad*,' *The Classical Quarterly* 21 (1971): 16-26; M.M. Willcock, 'Ad Hoc Invention in the *Iliad*,' *Harvard Studies in Classical Philology* 81 (1977): 41-53. One probable 'invention', the story of the upbringing of Achilles by Phoenix, is discussed in more detail in Chapter 3, section 2.
9 Willcock, 'Ad Hoc Invention in the *Iliad*,' 43. Cf. M.L. Lang, 'Reverberation and Mythology in the *Iliad*,' in *Approaches to Homer*, ed. C.A. Rubino and C.W. Shelmerdine (Austin: University of Texas Press, 1983), 140-64.
10 On this subject, see Slatkin, *The Power of Thetis*, xv (and *passim*): 'The mythological corpus on which the poet draws, taken together, constitutes an internally logical and coherent system, accessible as such to the audience. The poet inherits as his repertory a system, extensive and flexible, whose components are familiar, in their manifold variant

forms, to his listeners. For an audience that knows the mythological range of each character, divine or human – not only through this epic song but through other songs, epic and nonepic – the poet does not spell out the myth in its entirety but locates a character within it through allusion or oblique reference'. For an earlier statement of similar notions, G. Nagy, *The Best of the Achaeans: concepts of the hero in archaic Greek poetry* (Baltimore: Johns Hopkins University Press, 1979), 6.

[11] M.P. Nilsson, *The Mycenaean Origin of Greek Mythology* (Berkeley: University of California Press, 1932), 189-220.

[12] For the main references to Heracles in *Theogony*, see 287-94; 313-18; 327-32; 526-32.

[13] R. Scodel, *Listening to Homer: tradition, narrative, and audience* (Ann Arbor: University of Michigan Press, 2002), 124.

[14] Alden, *Homer Beside Himself*, 24, 157-61, is an important exception. Cf. J.M. Scammell, 'The Capture of Troy by Heracles,' *The Classical Journal* 29 (1934): 418-28; P.B.S. Andrews, 'The Falls of Troy in Greek Tradition,' *Greece & Rome* 12 (1965): 28-37 (mainly on archaeological aspects); E.M. Craik, *The Dorian Aegean* (London: Routledge & Kegan Paul, 1980), 26ff., (archaeological/historical); Lang, 'Reverberation and Mythology in the *Iliad*,' 140-64, esp. 150-51; H. van Wees, *Status Warriors: war, violence, and society in Homer and history* (Amsterdam: J.C. Gieben, 1992), 193-4, deals with the fragments of Hellanicus' account and other sources, together with historical, or quasi-historical aspects of the story; Martin, *The Language of Heroes*, 228-30, argues, implausibly in my view, that Achilles surpasses Heracles as a hero. For a survey of the story with particular reference to sources in art, including further bibliography, J. Boardman, 'Laomedon', in vol. 6 *Lexicon Iconographicum Mythologiae Classicae*. Zürich, Artemis, 1992, 201-3.

[15] J. Griffin, 'The Epic Cycle and the Uniqueness of Homer,' *The Journal of Hellenic Studies* 97 (1977): 39-53.

[16] J.S. Clay, *Hesiod's Cosmos* (Cambridge and New York: Cambridge University Press, 2003), 150.

[17] See K. Meuli, *Odyssee und Argonautika* (Utrecht: H&S, 1974), (orig. publ. Berlin, 1921); D.L. Page, *The Homeric Odyssey* (Oxford: Clarendon Press, 1955), 2ff.; E. Schwartz, *Die Odyssee* (Munich: M. Hueber, 1924), 263ff.; R. Merkelbach, *Untersuchungen zur Odyssee* (Munich: C.H. Beck, 1951), 201ff.

[18] I am grateful to one of the readers of an earlier manuscript draft for some of the points mentioned about the generations in the *Odyssey*.

[19] J.S. Clay, *The Politics of Olympus: form and meaning in the major Homeric*

Hymns (Princeton: Princeton University Press, 1989), 15.

[20] For an important recent study of the myth of the Trojan war in the broader context of Homer and other sources, see J. Burgess, *The Tradition of the Trojan War in Homer and the Epic Cycle* (Baltimore, Md.: Johns Hopkins University Press, 2001).

[21] Martin, *The Language of Heroes*, 230.

[22] For a psychological approach to the parallel with modern war in the context of Vietnam, see J. Shay, *Achilles in Vietnam: combat trauma and the undoing of character* (New York: Maxwell Macmillan International, 1994).

Chapter 1

[1] E. Vermeule, *Aspects of Death in Early Greek Art and Poetry* (Berkeley: University of California Press, 1979), 184.

[2] J. Griffin, 'Homer and Excess,' in *Homer: Beyond Oral Poetry*, ed. J.M. Bremer, I.J.F. de Jong, and J. Kalff (Amsterdam: B.R. Grüner, 1987), 85ff., explores these six individuals in the context of their battles with gods. They are, he argues (97-8), figures of excess, unlike the more mild-mannered Nestor who has survived into the next generation. 'These categories of excess mark men, in Homer's world, for destruction. The mental characteristic which does make for survival is intelligence. Both Nestor and Odysseus have their tribulations, but in the end each achieves a happy ending, prosperous and surrounded by his family' (94). Fighting against gods, of course, is also a Heraclean characteristic in both the *Iliad* (5.392ff.) and the *Odyssey* (8.224-5). Cf. the sentiments of Sthenelus at *Il.* 4.404-10 about the older generation and their attitude to the gods. A useful discussion can be found in Schein (above, Introduction, n.1), 90ff., on the way that periphrases using *biê*, *is*, and a few other nouns, denote warriors of older generations in Homer (especially Heracles).

[3] F. Frontisi-Ducroux, *La Cithare d'Achille* (Rome: Edizioni dell'Ateneo, 1986), 29-30, compares Nestor's speeches with that of Tlepolemus to Sarpedon at 5.637ff., and points to the notion of 'une hiérarchie dans l'ordre des temps' that is expressed in their discourse. One argument that I put forward in this chapter is that such a hierarchy is essentially used for rhetorical purposes (with the possible exception of Nestor who may well believe in it).

[4] For the rhetorical aspects of the speech, see J. Latacz, *Homers Ilias: Gesamtkommentar* (Munich and Leipzig: K.G. Saur, 2000), 105.

[5] On the Lapiths in Homer, see G.S. Kirk, *The Iliad: a Commentary. Volume I: Books 1-4* (Cambridge: Cambridge University Press, 1984), ad. 1.263-

5.

⁶ Cf. the reference to Pirithous at *Od.* 21.295-304. The fate of Eurytion at the wedding of Pirithous is used by Antinous as a warning to the disguised Odysseus when he seeks to have a turn at stringing the bow. It is worth noting that in this particular passage, unlike the Iliadic passages, the word 'Centaur/s' is used at 21.295 and 303, and Pirithous is specifically identified as a Lapith (21.297).

⁷ On the basis that the Aeolic *phêr* is favored over the Ionic *thêr*, Kirk in his Commentary makes the plausible suggestion (ad 1.268) that hexameter poems about Centaurs, which are Aeolic rather than Ionic in character, lie behind these references to them.

⁸ Contrast *Odyssey* 21.26-30 in which Heracles is still alive and acting with considerable barbarity in the time of Odysseus. This sort of generational overlap is very 'un-Iliadic', and even those who straddle the generations (like Nestor and Priam) are clearly defined by doing their fighting among the earlier generation warriors. It is worth noting however that in the *Iliad* Chiron straddles the generations as teacher of Asclepius and Achilles (on which see below, Chapter 3).

⁹ For a complete version of the story, see Apollodorus, 2.5.9, and 2.6.4 (J.G. Frazer, *Apollodorus: the Library* (Cambridge, Mass.: Harvard University Press, 1967) with Frazer's notes to the other primary sources). For different views on the importance of the story in the *Iliad*, and how to read references to it, see above, Introduction, n. 14.

¹⁰ On the apparent contradiction between the two accounts, see Kirk's note in the Cambridge commentary to 7.443-64. G.S. Kirk, *The Iliad: a Commentary. Volume II: Books 5-8* (Cambridge: Cambridge University Press, 1990).

¹¹ Thus a parallel is clearly established between the two gods, Apollo and Poseidon, who do menial work for Laomedon, and Heracles, who also acts in the king's service (in addition to his servitude to Eurystheus). In particular, the notion of Apollo's exile, wanderings, and servitude seems to have a correspondence with many hero myths in which the young man undergoes a similar process in his early life. On this subject, J. Carlier, 'Apollo,' in *Greek and Egyptian Mythologies* ed. Y. Bonnefoy (Chicago: University of Chicago Press, 1992), 137ff.

¹² Although cf. 15.439 where there is a suggestion that Ajax and Teucer are full brothers.

¹³ Cf., on the Trojan side, the reminiscence of Priam of 'the day when the Amazons came, peers of men' (*êmati tôi hote t' êlthon Amazones antianeirai*, 3.189).

¹⁴ In addition to the passages discussed here, note the references to his birth (14.323-4 and 19.96-133); the labors (15.639-40); his oppression

of Neleian Pylos (11.690-3); Hera's persecution of him (14.250-6, 15.25-30); and his death (enunciated by Achilles at 18.117-9).

[15] On the emphasis on human form in the *Iliad*, see Griffin, 'The Epic Cycle and the Uniqueness of Homer,' 39-53.

[16] The story of Jason is referred to in a more significant way in the *Odyssey*, at 12.69-72, and it has been convincingly argued that an early *Argonautica* stands behind parts of this poem. See Meuli, *Odyssee und Argonautika*; Page, *The Homeric Odyssey*, 2ff.; Schwartz, *Die Odyssee* ; Merkelbach, *Untersuchungen zur Odyssee*, 201ff.

[17] Indeed Malcolm Willcock views the length of the speech as extraordinary, perhaps reflecting Glaucus' fear of Diomedes. M.M. Willcock, 'Nervous Hesitation in the *Iliad*,' in *Homer 1987: Papers of the Third Greenbank Colloquium*, ed. J. Pinsent and H.V. Hurt (Liverpool: Liverpool Classical Monthly, 1992), 65-73.

[18] In this passage (16.317ff.), the brothers Atymnius and Maris are both killed by Antilochus and Thrasymedes, the sons of Nestor. The two victims are the sons of Amisodorus, a Lycian who raised the unassailable Chimaera, 'an evil to many men' (*polesin kakon anthrôpoisin*, 16.329).

[19] On this subject, see M.J. Alden, 'Genealogy as Paradigm: the example of Bellerophon,' *Hermes* 124 (1996): 257-63.

[20] Kirk, ad 6.168-70.

[21] Kirk, ad 6.179-83.

[22] On 1.268, Leaf writes that 'there is no allusion in H. to the mixed bodies of the later legend, and it is possible that he conceived them as purely human beings (note, however, the opposition to *andres* in *Od*, 21.303); the myth may very likely refer to ancient struggles with a primitive race of autochthones'. W. Leaf and M.A. Bayfield, *Homerou Ilias* (London: Macmillan, 1908).

[23] The natural extension of this logic is that by including a detailed description of the Chimaera, the poet has quite possibly altered the image of the traditional Chimaera. There may be a case for this, but there are no major differences in the Chimaeras of Homer and Hesiod (*Theog.* 319ff. in M.L. West, *Hesiod: 'Theogony,'* edited with *Prolegomena and Commentary* (Oxford: Clarendon Press, 1966), ad loc.; see too *Catalogue*, fr. 43 (a) 84ff., R. Merkelbach and M.L. West, *Fragmenta Hesiodea* (Oxford: Clarendon Press, 1967). The explicit description of a creature like this in the *Iliad* does not necessarily mean that a departure from the traditional representation of its form is taking place.

[24] In artistic representations from the orientalizing period there are numerous variations in the form of the Chimaera (including variations from what we find in the *Iliad*); see A. Jacquemin, 'Chimaira', in vol. 3 *Lexicon Iconographicum Mythologiae Classicae*. Zürich, Artemis, 1986, 249-59.

25 The winged horse may well be implied in the 'signs of the gods' (*theôn teraessi*, 6.183), and in the gods' final hostility to him (6.200-3; cf. Pind. *Isth.* 7.44ff. and *Ol.* 13.92), but there is certainly no place for it in the present passage (cf. Hes. *Theog.* 325; *Catalogue*, fr. 43 (a) 84ff., Merkelbach and West, *Fragmenta Hesiodea*; and Pind. *Ol.* 13.87ff.). Two exotic creatures in the same narrative would seem to be no less appropriate than one in an episode like this, although reference to Pegasus might reduce in some way the kind of heroic character for Bellerophon that Glaucus is so keen to emphasize. All the evidence therefore does point to the poet's awareness of the story. In his Cambridge commentary, Kirk, 184, ad 6.183, has a detailed discussion of the major literature on the subject; cf., more recently, Alden, 'Genealogy as Paradigm,' 261-62.

26 Kirk's explanation for this, or at least his observation based on the character of the episode, is that the Bellerophon story may be an extract from, or condensation of, a longer poetic account. 'There is' he writes 'no good reason for regarding either the episode itself or its position here as un-Homeric.' (ad 6.119-236).

27 As we saw in the Introduction, it is worth comparing Hesiod's *Works and Days*, 156-73 (the age of 'heroes', *andrôn hêrôôn theion genos*, [159], or 'demi-gods', *hêmitheoi*, [160]). This is the 'race before our own' (*proterê geneê*, 160). Hesiod mentions those who fought at Thebes and Troy for Helen's sake (thereby conflating the pre-Trojan war generation with their sons who fought at Troy). In his commentary on *Works and Days*, West (ad. 160) contrasts *Il.* 23.790. M.L. West, *Hesiod: 'Works and Days,'* edited with Prolegomena and Commentary (Oxford: Clarendon Press, 1978).

28 Cf. Hector's prayer to Zeus and the other gods for the future of Astyanax, 'and some day may somebody say as he comes back from war "this one is much better than his father" ' (*kai tote tis eipoi 'patros g' hode pollon ameinôn'/ ek polemou anionta*, 6.479-80).

29 Cf. C.A. Querbach, 'Conflict between young and old in Homer's *Iliad*,' in *The Conflict of Generations in Ancient Greece and Rome*, ed. S. Bertman (Amsterdam: B.R. Grüner, 1976), 55-64. Querbach makes the same point: 'Diomedes rebukes Sthenelos for speaking rudely to the king, but he in no way disagrees with what Sthenelos has asserted' (58). Cf. Martin, *The Language of Heroes*, 65ff., who analyses the discourse of these sorts of encounters ('The Contested Word'): 'Diomedes knows the rules well enough to rebuke his companion Sthenelos, who has tried to counteract the insults of Agamemnon (4.404-110). The charioteer decries the knowing lies of the abuser (404) but Diomedes replies, in effect, that Agamemnon is simply playing his role correctly (413-4)' (71).

[30] Cf. Querbach, 'Conflict between young and old in Homer's *Iliad*,' 58-9, n. 28: 'the giving of counsel is the only area in which old men can still do something of value. The younger men perhaps accept this theoretically, but in actual practice they listen politely and then proceed to follow their own best judgment'.

[31] Cf. Martin, *The Language of Heroes*, 228-9: 'If we consider only quantity, Achilles, although not destined to take Troy, has already surpassed the most important hero of his father's generation. The difference in size between the two heroes' achievements is explicit in the doubling of the number at the beginning of 9.328 - twelve (cities) versus Herakles' six (ships)' (228). Martin links the Achilles-Heracles 'generational conflict' to the competing claims of Homer against a background dominated by Heraclean epic. As will become clear, I see no real justification for the view that Achilles has 'surpassed' Heracles in the *Iliad*.

[32] Cf. 5.124ff.; 5.800ff.; 6.222ff.; 14.110ff. and Andersen, *Die Diomedesgestalt in der Ilias*.

[33] It should not be inferred therefore that the previous generation (of Heracles) are all archers, any more than the later generation (of Achilles) are all spearmen, because the matter is in no way as simple as this (note, for instance, Nestor at *Il.* 4.303-9). But there does seem to be a clear distinction at work in the persons of Heracles and Achilles and the weaponry they use in their respective attacks on Troy.

[34] Cf. T.M. Falkner, *The Poetics of Old Age in Greek Epic, Lyric, and Tragedy* (Norman and London: University of Oklahoma Press, 1995), 19. 'Although the virtues of the heroes of the previous generations are sometimes praised by others (Agamemnon attempts to rouse Diomedes with a similar argument at 4.372ff.), only Nestor claims personally to embody the superiority of the past'.

[35] Cf. Odysseus at the end of his voyage near to Scheria, who expresses his fears that 'a god may even send against me some great monster from the sea, the likes of which glorious Amphitrite produces in such numbers' (*êe ti moi kai kêtos episseuêi mega daimôn/ ex halos, hoia te polla trephei klutos Amphitritê*, *Od.* 5.421-2).

[36] Clay, *Hesiod's Cosmos*, 150-1.

[37] For the material evidence for Perseus running from the Gorgon sisters after beheading Medusa, see L.J. Roccos, 'Perseus', in vol. 7 *Lexicon Iconographicum Mythologiae Classicae*. Zürich, Artemis, 1994, 340-41. As Roccos points out the flight of Perseus from the Gorgons seems to be a favorite theme in the period of our earliest sources (cf. 345).

[38] In Hesiod's *Theogony*, 319ff. the Chimaera is (probably) the child of Typhon and Echidna. As far as Achilles' divine connections are concerned within the *Iliad*, cf. 1.357ff.; 18.35ff.; 19.3ff.; 24.120ff. Thetis

of course represents only part of the divine support received by Achilles within the poem.

[39] The wild animal associations of Achilles in the final books are quite diverse, including various references to jaws, mutilation, and the eating of raw human flesh. At 19.312-3 is reference to the fact that Achilles' heart would not be comforted 'until he had entered the jaws (*stoma*) of bloody battle' (*prin polemou stoma dumenai haimatoentos*). There is an emphasis on the raw consumption of human flesh, both through the speeches of Achilles, and through his actions. For some of the main references in the final books, see 21.120ff. (Achilles flings Lycaon into Scamander saying that the fish will lick his wounds and eat his white fat); 21.200ff. (he then kills Asteropaeus and leaves him lying in the water for the eels and fishes to eat; 21.22ff. (in Scamander itself the Trojans flee from Achilles like fishes fleeing from a dolphin with a huge maw (*delphinos megakêteos*); 22.335 (Achilles says that the dogs and birds will eat Hector's flesh); 22.345ff. (Achilles states himself that he would like to eat Hector raw [cf. Hecuba, 24.212-4]); 23.20ff. (Achilles hails the dead Patroclus with pride that he has fulfilled his promise by feeding Hector raw to the dogs); 24.207 (Hecuba describes Achilles as *ômêstês*, ie. 'monstrous', 'savage', or literally, 'eating raw flesh'). It is also worth noting in this context that the adjective *ômêstês* is used to describe Cerberus and Echidna in Hesiod's *Theogony*. In the *Iliad* this is a word usually associated with the rather vicious birds and fish and dogs that seem to inhabit the vicinity of Troy (11.454; 22.67; 24.82). Likewise many of the similes have the effect of reinforcing Achilles' parallel with animals and monsters. As if conscious of his own transformed state, Achilles tells Hector that the two of them can have no level of bond or communication: 'Hector, don't talk to me about agreements you wretch; as there are no trustworthy oaths between men and lions...so it is not possible for me and you to be friends, nor will there be oaths between us'...etc. 22.261ff.). On this subject, with cross-cultural comparisons, cf. J. Griffin, *Homer on Life and Death* (Oxford: Clarendon Press, 1980), 19-21.

[40] It is worth noting that the other early description of the Chimaera, Hesiod's *Theogony* (319-20), describes it as 'breathing unassailable fire' (*pneousan amaimaketon pur*) and 'terrible'(*deinên*) and 'great' (*megalên*) and 'strong'(*kraterên*) - all admirable attributes for heroes in battle. The other important attribute referred to is its swiftness of foot *podôkea* (320). The last attribute of course has a special resonance with the depiction of Homer's Achilles (*podas ôkus*...etc). On the basis of Hesiod's description of the Chimaera, and indeed as Homer describes it, what better creature is there with which to associate Achilles, the best and most formidable warrior of his generation?

⁴¹ On this subject, see A. Kossatz-Deissmann, 'Achilleus', in vol. 1 *Lexicon Iconographicum Mythologiae Classicae*. Zürich and Munich, Artemis, 1981, 37-200, esp. 122ff. The earliest scene of his armor is the neck of the 'Melian' amphora from Delos which is dated about 670-660BC (*LIMC*, 'Achilleus', no. 506). The scene has Thetis handing over armor to Achilles, which has a prominent gorgon image on it.

⁴² For a recent discussion of Achilles and this part of the *Electra* see, P. Michelakis, *Achilles in Greek tragedy* (Cambridge: Cambridge University Press, 2002), 154-62.

⁴³ The bibliography on the shield is huge, including whole monographs devoted to its place and significance in the *Iliad*. A good place to start on thematic interpretations of the shield is A.S. Becker, *The Shield of Achilles and the Poetics of Ekphrasis* (Lanham, Md.: Rowman & Littlefield Publishers, 1995), 5, n.9. See, more recently, Alden, *Homer Beside Himself*, 48-73.

⁴⁴ It is sometimes argued that Achilles' response to the shield (19.15ff.), and indeed those of the Myrmidons (19.13-14), raise questions about the images as they are seen by the characters themselves: cf. S.L. Wofford, *The Choice of Achilles: the ideology of figure in the epic* (Stanford: Stanford University Press, 1992), 74: 'Achilles responds to the shield as if it contained images different from those Homer describes. Unlike Agamemnon's shield, Achilles' shield contains mostly images *not* of this allegorical kind, and *not* concerned with the horror, violence, or terror of war. But Achilles' response to his shield does not suggest any awareness of this difference' (on the apparent disinterest of Achilles in the shield, cf. W. Marg, *Homer über die Dichtung* (Münster: Aschendorff, 1957), 32ff. The responses of the Myrmidons and Hector to the shield of Achilles (22.131ff.), surely have much to do with the *brightness* of the Olympian armor (on which see Chapter 4).

⁴⁵ O. Taplin, 'The Shield of Achilles within the *Iliad*,' *Greece & Rome* 27 (1980): 2.

⁴⁶ An important treatment of this subject is offered in A. Snodgrass, *Homer and the Artists: text and picture in early Greek art* (Cambridge and New York: Cambridge University Press, 1998).

⁴⁷ 'Achilleus war in der Begegnung Hektors mit Andromache im Hintergrunde zugegen' W. Schadewaldt, *Von Homers Welt und Werk*, 2nd ed. (Stuttgart: Koehler, 1959), 228.

⁴⁸ Even the choice of verb here [*phthio/phthino*] may be a signal that Achilles will be his killer, through a pun on Phthia as the home of Achilles. On this subject, see C.J. Mackie, 'Homeric Phthia,' *Colby Quarterly* 38 (2002): 163-73. It is also worth comparing the juxtaposition of references to *ache(a)* 'woes' (6.413) with the name *Achilleus* (6.414).

[49] In the second volume of the Cambridge commentary to the *Iliad*, Kirk argues that the strategic awkwardness of Hector's return to the city is 'disguised by a long digression in which Diomedes faces Glaukos and elicits the tale of Bellerophon' (155). It would be severely reductionist to argue, however, that the Bellerophon story is put in place within the poem merely to alleviate this 'strategic awkwardness'. In the context of 119-236 itself, Kirk points out that 'the whole episode is inorganic, and Hektor's arrival at Troy could follow directly on 118... There is no good reason for regarding either the episode itself or its position here as un-Homeric, especially as the interruption of a narrative by an intrusive episode or diversion is typical of Iliadic composition' (171).

[50] See Schadewaldt, *Von Homers Welt und Werk*, 207-29, esp. 225ff.

[51] See J. Stenger, 'Peleus,' in *Der neue Pauly*, ed. H. Cancik, H. Schneider, and A.F. von Pauly (Stuttgart: J.B Metzler, 2000), 492-3; cf. Apollodorus, 3.13.5 together with Frazer's n.6, (Frazer, *Apollodorus: the Library*). One renowned literary account from a much later period is Ovid's *Metamorphoses*, 11.221-65. It may well be that in view of Thetis' bitterness about her marriage to Peleus (18.434), and in view of their apparent separation, the story was well enough known by the poet (thus Lesky, 'Peleus', in vol. 19 *Paulys Realencyclopädie der classischen Altertumswissenschaft*. Stuttgart, 1937, xix 298; Griffin, 'The Epic Cycle and the Uniqueness of Homer,' 41.

[52] It is worth comparing the story that Achilles was fed by Chiron on the palpitating innards of freshly caught animals (Apollodorus 3.13.6). This may, or may not lie behind the *Iliad*, but there may be a suggestion of it at 16.203ff. (with Janko's note, ad loc.); cf. D.S. Robertson, 'The Food of Achilles,' *The Classical Review* 54 (1940): 177-80; and Hecuba at *Il.* 24.207.

[53] On the parallelism of Books 1 and 24 of the *Iliad*, see J.T. Sheppard, *The Pattern of the Iliad* (London: Methuen, 1922), 205ff.; J.L. Myres, 'The Last Book of the *Iliad*,' *The Journal of Hellenic Studies* 52 (1932): 293-4; K. Reinhardt, *Die Ilias und ihr Dichter* (Göttingen: Vandenhoeck und Ruprecht, 1961), 63-8; G.S. Kirk, *The Songs of Homer* (Cambridge: Cambridge University Press, 1962), 261ff.; M.M. Willcock, *A Companion to the Iliad* (Chicago: University of Chicago Press, 1976), 266-7; C.W. Macleod, *Homer: Iliad, Book XXIV* (Cambridge and New York: Cambridge University Press, 1982), 33-4; F. Létoublon, 'Le messager fidèle,' in *Homer: Beyond Oral Poetry*, ed. J.M. Bremer, I.J.F. de Jong, and J. Kalff (Amsterdam: B.R. Grüner, 1987), 123-44.

[54] Cf. Kirk, ad 1.447-68, on the subject of the animal sacrifice here: 'this is the fullest description in the *Iliad* of this fundamental ritual act'.

[55] The same sort of thing might also be said of the minor missions

conducted by individuals along the shoreline to Achilles within the poem. These are the missions to take Briseis from Achilles (1.327-30), and the embassy of the Greeks to him (9.182-5).

[56] Cf. *Il.* 22.412ff. and 24.327-8; Hecuba at 24.201ff.; Hermes at 24.379ff.; and Achilles at 24.518ff.

[57] The journey conducted at night in Homer is one of elemental danger, whereas a daytime journey is basically free from danger. Telemachus, for instance, confronts death, especially in the form of the ambush of the suitors, on the sea at night (*Od.* 2.388ff.). His land mission however, which is conducted by day, is basically within safe territory, between the kingdoms of Nestor and Menelaus (*Od.* 3.475ff.). Similarly, the nature of the mission determines the status of the guide. Thus the dangerous night journey has a divine guide (Athena in the case of Telemachus, and Hermes in the case of Priam), whereas the day journey of Telemachus has a mortal guide (Pisistratus). In one particular case, in the territory of the Cyclopes, Odysseus' ship is enshrouded in darkness and mist (*Od.* 9.142ff.), and their success in reaching their destination is attributed to 'some god' that guides them (9.142). For night as the 'divine time', cf. Hesiod's *Works and Days*, 730 and the *Homeric Hymn to Hermes*, 68ff.

[58] The charge of cowardice that Achilles lays at the feet of Agamemnon in the dispute between the two of them (1.225ff.) is of course quite the opposite to the kind of bravery shown by Priam.

[59] Cf. Griffin, *Homer on Life and Death*, 93: 'No hero, not even the greatest, is spared the shameful experience of fear'.

[60] On this subject, see F. Robert, *Homère* (Paris: Presses Universitaires de France, 1950), 200-04; C. Whitman, *Homer and the Heroic Tradition* (Cambridge, Mass.: Harvard University Press, 1958), 217ff.; M.N. Nagler, *Spontaneity and Tradition: a study in the oral art of Homer* (Berkeley: University of California Press, 1974), 184ff.; Willcock, *A Companion to the Iliad*, 269-70; R.J. Clark, *Catabasis: Vergil and the wisdom-tradition* (Amsterdam: B.R. Grüner, 1979), 136, n.45; M. Mueller, *The Iliad* (London and Boston: Allen & Unwin, 1984), 74; P. Wathelet, 'Priam aux Enfers ou le retour du corps d' Hector,' *Les Études Classiques* 56 (1988): 321-35; J.M. Redfield, *Nature and Culture in the Iliad: the tragedy of Hektor* (Durham and London: Duke University Press, 1994), 214-15; C.J. Mackie, 'Scamander and the Rivers of Hades in Homer,' *The American Journal of Philology* 120 (1999), 485-501.

[61] On this general subject, cf. G.S. Kirk, *Myth: its meaning and functions in ancient and other cultures* (Cambridge: Cambridge University Press, 1970), 162ff.

[62] It is worth comparing the night mission of Diomedes and Odysseus into the Trojan camp in Book 10, 204ff. (the 'Doloneia'). The two heroes creep into the camp, kill enemy fighters as they sleep, and steal some prized horses (more will be said on this mission in the next two chapters). One difference worth noting here however is the fact that when Priam ventures out into the darkness the emphasis is on important symbolic landmarks, the tomb, the river etc., but not on the more usual indicators of night - lights, stars, and so forth. This can be contrasted with earlier references to darkness in the poem in which mention is made of fires (8.507ff.; 8.554-65; 9.234; 10.12; 10.418-21 and stars (10.252), and night sounds (10.13; 10.185ff.)). Cf. A. Parry, 'The Language of Achilles,' *Transactions of the American Philological Association* 87 (1956): 2. The difference appears to be that the darkness through which Priam moves is rather more eerie and mystical than these earlier descriptions. It is a kind of primordial darkness, not just night.

[63] Note the considerable attention paid in the closing lines of the poem to the gathering together of all the Trojans (especially in the use of the verb *ageiro* and its cognates [24.783, 789, 790, 802]).

Chapter 2

[1] W.D. O'Flaherty, s.v. 'Horses'. In vol. 6 *The Encyclopedia of Religion*. Ed. by M. Eliade, New York, Macmillan, 1987, 463ff. Cf. Puhvel's comment that 'the early Indo-Europeans were undoubtedly "crazy about horses" and so were the Gauls'. J. Puhvel, 'Vedic *ásvamedha* - and Gaulish IIPOMIIDVOS,' *Language* 31 (1955): 353-4.

[2] For some of the principal references to the gods and their horses in the *Iliad*, cf. 4.27-8 (Hera's horses have worked hard at Troy); 5.355ff. (the wounded Aphrodite uses Ares' horses to get back to Olympus, driven by Iris); 5.711-77 (Hera and Athena drive from Olympus to earth); 8.41-52 (Zeus drives to Mount Ida); 8.350-443 (Athena, Hera, Zeus and Poseidon); 13.23ff. (Poseidon with horses and chariot); 15.119ff. (Ares orders Terror and Panic to yoke his horses); 23.306ff. (Zeus and Poseidon as gods of horsemanship). Thus the horse has a crucial role in the divine world as a means of transport, especially between heaven and earth. Cf. too the snatching of Persephone by Hades on his chariot in the *Homeric Hymn to Demeter*, 17-18; 80-1. In the *Iliad* Hades is the possessor of glorious foals (*klutopôlos*) at *Il.* 5.654; 11.445; 16.625.

[3] Indeed the horse's role in the societies of the Greeks and Trojans in the *Iliad* is one of things that they have in common: cf. Kirk, '(the Trojans of the *Iliad* appear as) a prosperous horse-breeding people surprisingly

like the Achaeans in most of their customs'. G.S. Kirk, 'The Homeric Poems as History,' in *The Cambridge Ancient History* (Cambridge: Cambridge University Press, 1975), II. 2.834.

[4] The major reference work on this subject is the detailed analysis by E. Delebecque, *Le Cheval dans l'Iliade* (Paris: Librairie C. Klincksieck, 1951). Delebecque's comprehensive survey is divided into three principal sections: the horse in the *Iliad*; the language used to describe horses in Homer, arranged under thirty-three subject headings; and the horse in the pre-Homeric world, which includes archaeological evidence. Delebecque is much more concerned therefore with the historical and cultural context of the horse in Homer (to say nothing about questions of authorship), than with its symbolic role in the poems. See too K.J. Atchity, 'Horses in the *Iliad*,' in *Homer's Iliad: the shield of memory* (Carbondale and Edwardsville: Southern Illinois University Press, 1978), 299-311.

[5] On Diomedes and Achilles, Andersen, *Die Diomedesgestalt in der Ilias*, 14ff., and *passim*; and more recently M.L. Lang, 'War Story into Wrath Story,' in *The Ages of Homer*, ed. J.B. Carter and S.P. Morris (Austin: University of Texas Press, 1995), 149-62, esp. 154ff. For Diomedes and the horse in the *Iliad*, see esp. Book 5 (*passim*); 10. 272-579 (with Odysseus he steals the horses of Rhesus); 23. 262-513 (Diomedes wins the chariot race at Patroclus' funeral games). The epithet *hippodamos* 'breaker of horses' is used frequently of Diomedes, as is *hippobotos* 'horse-nourishing' of Argos; on these, see below, nn. 43 and 46. For Eumelus, note esp. 2.763-7 (he has the best horses after those of Achilles); and 23.262-565 (he comes last in the chariot race, but is much respected nonetheless).

[6] For Aeneas' splendid horses, see 5.221-3 = 8.105-7; 5.260-73 (with Kirk's notes in the Cambridge commentary); 23.290ff. Aeneas loses his horses to Diomedes (5.318ff.) who goes on to win the chariot race with them at Patroclus' funeral games (23.262ff.). For the quality of Rhesus' horses, note Dolon at 10.433ff. and Nestor at 10.544ff. Rhesus, the Thracian king, is killed and his horses are stolen by Odysseus and Diomedes (10.469ff.).

[7] Although one of my main points in Chapter 3 is that archers on the Trojan side, like Paris and Pandarus and Helenus, do not adopt their characteristic weapon out of any financial necessity (this is explicit in the case of Pandarus who clearly has plenty of horses and chariots at his disposal, 5.192ff.). Needless to say, Paris and Helenus have plenty of resources too. Their rejection of horses and chariots is the other side of their rejection of the spear. The lack of both accoutrements seems to say a lot about them and their outlook on war.

[8] It is worth noting in this context that Glaucus has a father with a 'horsy' name, Hippolochus, son of Bellerophon (6.206).

222   Notes to Chapter 2

9 Cf. *Od*. 4.632ff., in which a certain Noemon, son of Phronius, asks Antinous when Telemachus will return from Pylos with his ship. He says that he needs his ship to go to spacious Elis where he keeps horses and mules. Ithaca may be unsuitable for horses in the *Odyssey* (something which is implicit in the *Iliad* too), but the mainland, or parts of it, definitely have a more suitable terrain with its wider expanses of land.

10 Cf. J.B. Hainsworth, *The Iliad: a Commentary. Volume III: Books 9-12* (Cambridge: Cambridge University Press, 1993), ad 10.433-41: 'In his terror, we may imagine, Dolon reveals more (*sc.* to Diomedes and Odysseus) than he was asked. This is the turning point of the Book. At the report of Rhesos' splendid horses all thought for their original mission disappears from the two Achaeans' minds'.

11 There are places however where there is at least some sense of the chariot-charge and of fighting from chariots: cf. esp. 4.297ff.; 5.9ff.; 8.78ff.; 8.116ff.; 8.253ff.; 11.289; 11.503; 15.352ff.

12 Cf. A.J. Podlecki, *The Early Greek Poets and their Times* (Vancouver: University of British Columbia Press, 1984): 'We must leave aside the troubled question of why Homer brings his heroes into battle in chariots only to have them dismount and fight hand to hand on foot, something no historical Greek soldier ever appears to have done'(9).

13 In the third chapter of his book, and basing his argument partly on lexical analysis, Delebecque argues that Homer was well acquainted with chariot racing, but had little knowledge of war-chariots: 'En effet, si Homère et ses confrères sont parfaitement renseignés sur le char et le cheval dans leurs emplois ordinaires, c'est-à-dire essentiellement civils, ils semblent l'être infiniment moins sur la pratique de la charrerie militaire', Delebecque, *Le Cheval dans l'Iliade*, 86. For more recent literature on the subject of Homeric warfare (especially historical aspects of his treatment), see below, Chapter 3, n.1.

14 Cf. the other references to Chiron in the *Iliad*, 4.217-19, and 16.141-4 = 19.388-91.

15 On the the physical form of a Centaur, and the great distinction between Chiron and the rest (Ixion's progeny), cf. Kirk, *Myth: its meaning and functions in ancient and other cultures*, 152ff.; P. duBois, *Centaurs and Amazons: women and the pre-history of the great chain of being* (Ann Arbor: University of Michigan Press, 1982). Chiron is usually the child of Cronus and Philyra (although this is not stated in Homer), and so this presumably explains the description of him in the *Iliad* as 'most just of the Centaurs' (*dikaiotatos Kentaurôn*, 11.832).

16 Phoenix is supposed to have taught Achilles all about war in the *Iliad* (9.434ff.), and so this might be seen to include horsemanship. In this context of fatherly advice on the subject of horses, it is worth comparing

the advice of Nestor to his son Antilochus prior to the conduct of the chariot race (*Il.* 23. 306ff.).

[17] Cf. S. Lonsdale, 'A Dancing Floor for Ariadne,' in *The Ages of Homer*, ed. J.B. Carter and S.P. Morris (Austin: University of Texas Press, 1995), 278: 'The presence of a divine audience (in the 'contests' of *Il.* 22 and 23) reinforces the analogy between races involving running men and horses and the running of Hector and Achilles'.

[18] As we have seen, the horses of Antilochus and Menelaus both respond physically to the rebukes that they receive during the chariot race at Patroclus' funeral games (note 23.417-8 and 446-7), but there is no verbal response on the part of the horse to the driver. Worth noting in this context is the utterance of the hawk to his captured nightingale in Hesiod's *Works and Days*, 203ff., although this discourse is within the world of animals, not with humans.

[19] A prophetic horse also appears in a story of the death of the 'Irish Achilles', Cú Chulainn. In 'The Death of Cú Chulainn', probably composed as early as the eighth century AD, one of Cú Chulainn's horses, the Grey of Macha, warns him of his imminent death on the battlefield by turning away three times as Cú Chulainn tries to harness him. He then weeps tears of blood on Cú Chulainn's feet. On this, see T.P. Cross and C.H. Slover, eds., *Ancient Irish Tales* (Dublin: Figgis, 1973), 333ff.

[20] M.W. Edwards, *The Iliad: a Commentary. Volume V: Books 17-20* (Cambridge: Cambridge University Press, 1991), ad 17.443-5, compares 'the happy life of Poseidon's horses, whose master is immortal' (13.23-38).

[21] It is worth noting in this context that although Cú Chulainn's horse, the Grey of Macha, clearly has a sense of his master's forthcoming doom, he is both mortal (indeed the horse's death is a major part of the story), and does not have the power of speech. He must therefore convey his warning to his master by means other than direct speech (that is, by gesture). Cf. N.K. Chadwick and V. Zhirmunsky, *Oral Epics of Central Asia* (Cambridge: Cambridge University Press, 1969), 152 (and *passim*): 'Throughout Turkic literature, including that of the Kirghiz, human and superhuman faculties are attributed to horses. Not only are these generally gifted with human speech and reason, but they are...superior morally and intellectually to the heroes themselves'.

[22] M.W. Edwards, *The Iliad: A Commentary. Volume V: Books 17-20* (Cambridge: Cambridge University Press, 1991), ad 19.404-17. Cf. also Edwards, *Homer: Poet of the Iliad*, 287-8: 'This (conversation between man and horse) is closer to the fantastic than Homer usually approaches in the *Iliad* - and he very properly has the Furies swiftly put an end to such abnormal behavior - but the reminder given by the horse's words of Achilles' own approaching death is particularly effective at his

departure for battle, and gives the hero a further chance to assert his knowledge and acceptance of it. Probably such warnings occurred in other epics when Achilles or other heroes entered their last battle, and the poet has adapted the scene for the present occasion'.

23 Achilles' capacity to exchange conversation with his horses here bears comparison with the mythical role of Orpheus who has a special connection with animals. The connection between the two heroes can be seen in other ways too in Homer and Vergil, notably in the way that they deal with their emotional turmoil through song: cf. Achilles at 9.185ff., esp. *phrena terpomenon phormiggi ligeiêi*, 9.186 and *thumon eterpen, aeide d' ara klea andrôn*, 9.189; and Orpheus, Verg. *Georgics* 4.464ff., esp. *ipse caua solans aegrum testudine amorem*, 4.464.

24 A good place to start is Martin, *The Language of Heroes* .

25 Cf. M. Eliade, *Myths, Dreams, and Mysteries: the encounter between contemporary faiths and archaic realities* (New York: Harper & Row, 1975), 62-3: 'To communicate with animals, to speak their language and become their friend and master, is to appropriate a spiritual life much richer than the merely human life of ordinary mortals'.

26 He is of course, physically speaking, at the margin of the Greek army; cf. 8.222-6 = 11.5-9.

27 Telemachus conducts a land journey too, between Pylos and Sparta, drawn by the horses of Nestor (driven by Pisistratus). It is important that this land journey is a constructed as a direct contrast to the sea journey; it is undertaken by day with a human guide, not by night with a divine guide. Thus the 'rite of passage' part of the mission is the maritime part in which he confronts death in the form of a trap to kill him laid by the suitors.

28 The two are fundamentally connected in any case, most notably through Athena and Poseidon. The former is god of shipbuilding and the taming of horses; the latter god of the sea and the spirited nature of the horse. For ships as horses on the sea in the *Odyssey*, cf. 4.708-9; 5.371; 13. 81.

29 Note too the increasingly graphic nature of descriptions of horse and chariot use in the *aristeia* of Achilles. At the very end of Book 20 (490ff.) Achilles' horses trample on the bodies of the dead in such a way that the axle and the wheels become all splattered with blood.

30 See 22.395ff.; 23.24ff.; 24.12ff (note the frequentatives in this last passage).

31 J-P. Vernant's argument on this subject is very convincing, that there is a conscious attempt to destroy the memory of the victim, J-P. Vernant, 'A Beautiful Death,' in *Mortals and Immortals: Collected Essays*, ed. J-P. Vernant and F.I. Zeitlin (Princeton: Princeton University Press, 1991), 50-74.

[32] For some of the important parallels on early Greek vases, see N. Richardson, *The Iliad: a Commentary. Volume VI: Books 21-24* (Cambridge: Cambridge University Press, 1993), 181ff.

[33] Note too the fact that Patroclus was a very kind keeper of the horses of Achilles (23.279ff.), often putting oil on their manes and washing them with water (cf. Andromache at 8.185ff.). In response to his death the horses mourn his loss, and their manes trail on the ground (23.283ff.).

[34] The sacrifice of the horses has its parallels of course in the material and the literary evidence from antiquity. As far as the Greek world is concerned a connection can be made with the find at Lefkandi: cf. H. Catling, 'Heroes Returned? Subminoan burials from Crete,' in *The Ages of Homer*, ed. J.B. Carter and S.P. Morris (Austin: University of Texas Press, 1995): 'The slaughter and burning of four horses (in *Iliad* 23) makes a link with the four horses *buried at* Toumba, Lefkandi' (121). On the subject of horse sacrifice in the early Greek world and archaeological evidence for it, E. Kosmetatou, 'Horse Sacrifices in Greece and Cyprus,' *Journal of Prehistoric Religion* 7 (1993): 31-41. Note too Richardson, *The Iliad: a Commentary. Volume VI: Books 21-24*, 186-89. It is also worth noting, especially in light of Achilles' Scythian connections in post-Homeric sources (Alcaeus calls him 'Lord of Scythia', *Achilleus, o tas Skuthikas medeis*), that the Scythians indulge in frequent and sometimes massive horse sacrifices; cf. Herodotus, 4.71-72; and R. Rolle, *The World of the Scythians*, trans. G. Walls (London: B.T. Batsford, 1989), 38ff. (and *passim*). On the Alcaeus fragment, D.L. Page, *Lyrica Graeca Selecta* (Oxford: Clarendon Press, 1968), 89, fr.166.

[35] The contest of course is won by Diomedes, which is in keeping with his own horse associations in the *Iliad* (below, n.46), and the support that he receives from Athena (23.388ff.). In addition to his natural ability as a horseman, Diomedes drives the fine horses newly acquired from Aeneas (above, n.6), which were bred from those of Tros (23.290-2; 23.377-8).

[36] On this subject, see Richardson, *The Iliad: a Commentary. Volume VI: Books 21-24*, 164ff.

[37] The accounts of Achilles' funeral in other sources (*Odyssey* and *Aethiopis*) are discussed in Chapter 4, section 2.

[38] There seems to be little evidence in the *Iliad* for the view that the sacrificed horses are meant to accompany Patroclus to Hades; although it is worth comparing Lucian, *De luctu*, 14, who points out that many horses, concubines, cup-bearers, and other personal items, have been offered up as sacrifice for the use of the dead in the Underworld.

[39] On the association between the horse and death in Greek thought, and

in a wider context, see Edwards in the Cambridge commentary on 19.404-17. Worth noting too in this death/funerary context is the role of horses in taking Priam (and Hermes) to Achilles' camp and back in *Iliad* 24 for the ransom of Hector's body (note 24.279ff.; 322ff.; 349ff. etc.).

[40] *Eupôlos* is used of Troy (Ilios) five times in the two Homeric poems; at *Il.* 5.551; 16.576; *Od.* 2.18; 11.169; 14.71. It is worth noting too that the pseudo-Herodotean *Life of Homer* quotes the first line of the *Little Iliad* as *Ilion aeidô kai Dardaniên eupôlon*.

[41] Note the notion of flight here associated with horses, as elsewhere (Cf. O'Flaherty, 463ff.). Cf. the regular use of *petomai* to describe the speeding off (ie. flying onward) of horses under the lash of the charioteer (*tô d' ouk aekonte petesthên*, 'and not unwillingly the pair (of horses) flew onward', *Il.* 5.366; 5.768; 8.45; 10.530; 11.281; 11.519; 22.400; *Od.* 3.484; 3.494; 15.192.

[42] Note the fact that Anchises seems to have performed the breeding of horses himself (5.268ff.), a task that one might reasonably have expected others further down the food chain to have performed. Likewise at 24.247ff. the sons of Priam (ie. not slaves) get his horses and mules ready. The individual who prepares one's horses can inform one's status in society: cf. on Olympus where the Hours get Hera's horses ready; Poseidon takes care of Zeus's horses; and Terror and Panic are called upon to prepare those of Ares (references, above, n.2).

[43] *Hippodamos* ('breaker of horses' or 'horse-taming') is used 23 times in the *Iliad* to describe the Trojans collectively (*Trôes*). The horse-epithet used most frequently of the Greeks (*Danaoi*) is *tachupôlos* ('of swift horses'), which is used of them collectively ten times, and of the Myrmidons once (for the latter, see 23.6).

[44] See 7.38; 16.717; 22.161; 22.211; 24.804.

[45] Troy is often described as 'broad' (*eurus*, eg. *Il.* 24.256; 24.494; 24.774), a monumental city in a fertile and expansive environment. Its rivers, most notably Scamander, are a crucial part of this. As we have seen in the introduction to this chapter, the problem with Ithaca, are far as the running of horses is concerned, is that it is not broad (*Od*.13.243).

[46] Argos is frequently described as *hippobotos* in Homer ('horse-nourishing'), used of it twelve times (cf. Trica at *Il.* 4.202 and Elis at *Od.* 21.347). The suitability of Argos for horses is appropriate too in the context of Diomedes' interest in horses and the frequent description of him as 'breaker of horses' (*hippodamos*), an epithet that is used of him more than any other individual in the poem (seven times).

[47] Note that Diomedes does not specify their immortality (nor does the *Homeric Hymn to Aphrodite*, see next note), but that is certainly the

implication of the reference (bearing in mind that Achilles has immortal horses from Olympus). Immortal horses naturally convey a greater sense of continuity through the generations than mortal ones, and the *Iliad* seems to be keen to emphasize this.

[48] The account in the *Homeric Hymn to Aphrodite*, 202-17, concentrates on the response of Tros to the loss of his son (cf. Demeter's loss of her daughter to Persephone in the Demeter Hymn). He is initially overcome by grief (*penthos*, 207), but he takes pleasure in the knowledge (after he is told by Hermes) that his son would become immortal and ageless. There is little attention paid to his horses, although he is described as riding them with joy (216-7).

[49] Cf. *Od.* 4.145-6; 11.436ff.; 17.118-9; 22.226ff.

[50] An important postscript to this theme in the *Iliad* is that the *Odyssey* too is constructed on the conflict between men over the beautiful and circumspect Penelope. The nature of this situation is different again from the two disputes in the *Iliad*, but the same notion of men fighting over women is certainly germane to all three conflicts.

[51] It is worth noting the very veiled reference to the wedding of Pirithous and Hippodamia (2.741ff.; cf. 1.262ff., above, Chapter 1). The Homeric poems seem to suggest that the men of earlier times fought most especially over horses and cattle and other animals and goods (5.633ff. [horses]; 11.670ff.[cattle etc.]; and cf. *Od.* 21.22ff. [horses]). In Homer's vague references to the earlier story of Troy Heracles seems interested only in the horses of Laomedon, but not interested in Hesione, who features in later versions, and who ends up with Telamon as mother of Teucer. Likewise in the *Odyssey* Heracles kills Iphitus who comes searching for twelve mares and their young which he has lost. Heracles kills Iphitus while the latter is a guest in his house, and he then keeps his horses (*Od.* 21.13-41).

[52] On literary and visual sources for the story of the wooden horse, see A. Heubeck, S. West, and J.B. Hainsworth, *A Commentary on Homer's Odyssey*, vol. 1 (Oxford: Clarendon Press, 1988), ad 8.492-3, and, more recently, C.A. Faraone, *Talismans and Trojan Horses: guardian statues in Ancient Greek myth and ritual* (New York: Oxford University Press, 1992); M.J. Anderson, *The Fall of Troy in Early Greek Poetry and Art* (Oxford: Clarendon Press, 1997), 18ff.

[53] Note the way that in the wooden horse story Odysseus and his men are dragged across the threshold into the city in the belly of the horse. In *Odyssey* 9 by contrast they are carried out of the cave under the belly of sheep and make good their escape that way (9.424ff.). Note too the part played by wine and sleep in the defeat of Polyphemus (9.318ff.), and in the defeat of Troy (*inuadunt urbem somno uinoque*

sepultam, '[The Greeks] storm the city which was buried in sleep and wine', *Aen.* 2.265). Both Polyphemus (in the *Odyssey*), and Troy (in the *Aeneid*) are victims of the superiority and ruthlessness of Odysseus' creative intellect.

54 The story of the horse has been read as a mythologized siege engine (cf. *Aen.* 2.151), as theriomorphic of an earthquake, as some kind of horse-magic, and as a lost cultic ritual. Kirk was never very confident about the various attempts at interpretation of the narrative: 'The story of the Horse is too obscure, and none of the attempts to explain it (for example as a siege-engine) carry much conviction' (G.S. Kirk, *Homer and the Oral Tradition* (Cambridge: Cambridge University Press, 1976), 59. On the various interpretations of the story, Faraone, *Talismans and Trojan Horses: guardian statues in Ancient Greek myth and ritual,* 94-100.

55 Note the corresponding solemnity in the prophecies of the death of Achilles, and the 'death' of Troy: cf. 4.164-8 and 6.448-9 (Troy); and 21.111-13 (Achilles) with Richardson's note (Richardson, *The Iliad: a Commentary. Volume VI: Books 21-24,* ad loc.).

56 Cf. *uenit summa dies et ineluctabile tempus/ Dardaniae. fuimus Troes, fuit Ilium. Aen.* 2.324-5.

Chapter 3

1 On the subject of Homeric warfare, including a brief survey of the historical implications, see H. van Wees, 'Homeric Warfare,' in *A New Companion to Homer,* ed. I. Morris and B. Powell (Leiden: Brill, 1997), 668-93. The emphasis in the article, and indeed in most literature on the subject of Homeric warfare, is on trying to re-construct the 'actual' course of fighting as it is described in the *Iliad* (together with the historical context). Unfortunately, van Wees mentions archery only in passing, and there is no specific discussion of the wider symbolic implications of it. On the broader question of Homer and early Greek warfare, H.L. Lorimer, *Homer and the Monuments* (London: Macmillan, 1950), 132-335; A. Snodgrass, *Arms and Armour of the Greeks* (London: Thames & Hudson, 1967); P.A.L. Greenhalgh, *Early Greek Warfare: horsemen and chariots in the Homeric and archaic ages* (Cambridge: Cambridge University Press, 1973); J. Latacz, *Kampfparänese, Kampfdarstellung und Kampfwirklichkeit in der Ilias, bei Kallinos und Tyrtaios* (Munich: Beck, 1977); van Wees, *Status Warriors* ; W.K. Pritchett, *The Greek State at War,* vol. 4 (Berkeley: University of California Press, 1985).

2 Kirk, *Homer and the Oral Tradition,* 64.

3 H. Thomas and F.H. Stubbings, 'Lands and Peoples in Homer,' in *A Companion to Homer,* ed. A.J.B. Wace and F.H. Stubbings (New York: Macmillan, 1962), 300.

4 Alcinous passes over the significance of Odysseus' admission here until asking the specific question (8.577ff.) of why he weeps when he hears stories about Troy?

5 Cf. A.F. Garvie, *Homer: Odyssey, Books VI-VIII* (Cambridge: Cambridge University Press, 1994), ad 8.489-91. 'The *kleos* of the Trojan War is so great that it has already entered the repertoire of singers like Demodocus in distant Scheria, so that the tradition is in the process of formation'. It is also worth comparing Vergil's adaptation of this theme in Book 1 of the *Aeneid* when Aeneas encounters the pictures on Dido's temple (1.441ff.). Vergil's account seems to suggest an even shorter period of time in which stories of Troy establish themselves in the oral tradition.

6 *Pace* Hainsworth, ad 8.215-18: 'Schol. suggest that the present passage *prooikonomei* the massacre of the suitors, but that episode does not need the support of so distant and incidental a comment as this'. I argue here (and later in this chapter) that the speech is fundamental not incidental to the resolution of the crisis in Odysseus' house.

7 For a detailed analysis of the speech together with the Iliadic contrast, see Danek, *Epos und Zitat: Studien zu den Quellen der Odyssee*, 151-3: 'Die Odyssee postuliert also den Bogen als heroische Waffe vor Troia (und stellt sich damit für uns in Gegensatz zur Ilias), wobei der iterative Temporalsatz *hote toxazoimeth' Achaioi* einräumt, daß es sich um eine facultative Kampftechnik gehandelt habe' (152).

8 To get a sense of this, it is worth comparing some of the other references in the *Odyssey* to Greek weaponry as it was used either at Troy itself, or on his return home to Ithaca: 2.18-19 (the spearman [*aichmêtês*] Antiphus who went to Troy); 3.188ff. (reference is made here to the 'Myrmidons who rage with the spear' [*Murmidonas.. egchesimôrous*, 188] as well as to Philoctetes at Troy); 4.257 (Odysseus, dressed in disguise in Troy, kills many of the Trojans with the long blade [*tanaêkeï chalkôi*, presumably the sword or something smaller]); 9.39ff. (the battle with the Cicones is fought with chariots and spears); 10.145ff. (Odysseus takes his spear and sword to explore Circe's island); 18.261ff. (Odysseus says that the Trojan warriors are spearmen, bowmen, and drivers of swift-footed horses). At 14.222ff., in his tall story to Eumaeus, Odysseus says that he dislikes the agricultural and family life and prefers ships, wars, polished spears (*akontes*) and arrows (cf. 14.216ff.). The mixed use of bow and spear in battle is paralleled in some references to the use of the bow and hunting-spear in the hunt (cf. 9.156ff. [*kampula toxa kai aiganeas dolichaulous*]; 19. 447ff.). Overall, therefore, we may say that the *Odyssey* is a lot less rigid when it comes to the use of specific weapons than the *Iliad*.

[9] Cf. J. van Leeuwen, *Odyssea* (Leiden: A.W. Sijthoff, 1917), ad 8.219 sq. 'In *Iliade* sagittandi singularis peritia Ulixi non tribuitur (cf. K 260 sq.)'.

[10] Clay argues (J.S. Clay, *The Wrath of Athena: gods and men in the Odyssey* (Princeton: Princeton University Press, 1983), 74ff.) that the bow enhances the connection that is established in the episode between Odysseus and the Cretan Meriones (this connection is played out more explicitly in references to the background of the boar's tusk helmet, originally from Autolycus, which Meriones also gives him, 10.261ff.). Odysseus' 'Cretan' connection in the *Iliad* is then taken up in the *Odyssey*, especially in his role as storyteller: 'Only in the *Odyssey* do we learn why Odysseus came to Troy without his bow... but, in any case, archery provides yet another link between Meriones and Odysseus' (Clay, 87-8).

[11] Cf. Clay, *The Wrath of Athena: gods and men in the Odyssey*, 75-6 'It is ironically appropriate that Odysseus, the man of *doloi* par excellence, should be pitted against an opponent named Dolon... In short, the trickster, Dolon, is out-tricked'.

[12] In her work on the subject, Lorimer placed emphasis on the insignificance of the bow as a weapon on the field of battle (Lorimer, *Homer and the Monuments*, especially on 289). As we shall see, it is not nearly as effective as the heavy weaponry used by the major warriors, especially on the Greek side (although we are meant to imagine that Paris turns the tide of battle with his bow in Book 11). But archery does a lot of work in signifying differences between the two sides and in symbolizing an essentially less courageous involvement in war.

[13] Cf. Hainsworth (ad 11.263) on the subject of the spear's dominance in battle (after H. Frölich, *Die Militärmedizin Homers* (Stuttgart: Enke, 1879): 'The spear, it is clear, is *the* weapon; recourse is had to the sword when no spear is available or to give the *coup de grace*'. I have not attempted in this chapter to explore Homeric weaponry in its historical context (in the manner of van Wees, 'Homeric Warfare,' et al.). T.B.L. Webster, *From Mycenae to Homer* (London: Methuen, 1958), 123, claimed that unlike the Odysseus of the *Iliad*, who 'hardly concerns us... the Odysseus of the *Odyssey* is Mycenaean'. Part of his rationale for this is the fact that he is an archer in the *Odyssey*. Cf. Snodgrass, *Arms and Armour of the Greeks*, 23. Snodgrass speculates on whether the large spears of the Mycenaean palace period explain the prestige of the spear in Homer's *Iliad* (although on 39 he seems content to ascribe many Iliadic descriptions of spear usage to the world of the poet himself).

[14] Cf. Hainsworth, ad 11.385-95: 'Diomedes' words are an eloquent expression of the aristocratic spearman's contempt for those who fight at distance (and often anonymously) with the bow'.

[15] Cf. 2.381ff. where Agamemnon urges the men to go for their meal before joining battle. His thoughts on the accoutrements of battle are just what one would expect them to be: spear, shield, horses and chariots (2.382-4).

[16] The place of the ambush (*lochos*) is not completely clear in the *Iliad*, especially in view of 1.227 in which Achilles taunts Agamemnon with the charge that he is not prepared 'to go into an ambush with the best of the Achaeans' (*oute lochond' ienai sun aristêessin Achaiôn*,1.227). In this particular speech (uttered in the heat of the dispute between them) the ambush has virtually the same status as battle itself. But Achilles is almost certainly thinking here of lying in wait with the spear (cf. *sun aristêessin*), not with the bow and arrow. And so it would seem that specific weaponry has the same signifying effects whether it is used on the battlefield, or in an ambush.

[17] E. Hall, *Inventing the Barbarian: Greek self-definition through tragedy* (Oxford: Clarendon Press, 1989), 42.

[18] For an earlier statement of this notion, J.A. Scott, *The Unity of Homer* (Berkeley: University of California Press, 1921), 230: 'Paris was an archer, but that was no disgrace despite the anger of Diomede at being shot with an arrow'. He then cites the Greek archers who are also prominent in the two Homeric poems. Scott also put forward the view (and was supported by M.P. Nilsson, *Homer and Mycenae* (London: Methuen, 1933), 264-5, that Paris was the original leader of the Trojans: 'No people under the control of such a leader as Paris could win sympathy. Tradition furnished the Trojans with no other leader, therefore the poet must create one' (230).

[19] Kirk, ad 3.439-40.

[20] Cf. 22.359-60 (the death of Achilles by Paris and Apollo). O. Taplin, *Homeric Soundings* (Oxford: Clarendon Press, 1992), 102-3, points, quite rightly, to Aphrodite's rescue of him a little bit beforehand (cf. 3.381). But I suspect that Paris is thinking here more of active divine assistance in battle, rather than the passive assistance of Aphrodite.

[21] Cf. also Agamemnon's shield at 11.32ff., which is not only important for its images (Chapter 1), but also for its size ('sheltering a man on both sides', *amphibrotên*, 11.32); cf. the same term for a large shield used more widely, 2.389, 12.402, 20.281.

[22] Cf. E. Bethe, *Homer: Dichtung und Sage*, vol. 1 (Leipzig: B.G. Teubner, 1914), 236-7; Kakridis, *Homeric Researches*, 45ff.

[23] Likewise there is clearly a fundamental contrast in the two marriages that we witness in Troy. Paris and Helen have a childless relationship based, it seems, on appearance and sexual gratification. Hector and Andromache however have a more complete relationship with a child

at the centre of their lives. On this subject, cf. Griffin, *Homer on Life and Death*, 30.

[24] It is worth contrasting M.S. Silk, *Homer, The Iliad* (Cambridge: Cambridge University Press, 1987), 99: 'Paris, the author of the people's affliction, has more than a touch of degenerate refinement...But Paris' anti-heroics are specifically contrasted with the conduct of Hector (3.30-66, 6.318-68, 6.440-502, 503-25); and Hector is the greatest, therefore the truest, representative of Troy'.

[25] I see no reason whatever to infer from this that the two poems are by different authors (even though I have a rather strong sympathy for this view on other grounds). Different attitudes towards archery in the two poems tell us more about different thematic strategies in the *Iliad* and *Odyssey* than they do about authorship. Likewise Greek audiences must surely have been quite able to adapt to a very different heroic milieu in each poem.

[26] The treatment of weaponry is not always entirely consistent. One discrepancy seems to be the description of the Paeonians who have curved bows and are led by Pyraechmes (2.848); but later in the poem they have long spears and are led by Asteropaeus (21.139ff.). This is hardly an earth-shattering inconsistency.

[27] See Kirk's note to 2.726; on Medon in the *Iliad* more generally, see 13.693-7 (with Janko's note, ad loc); 15.332-6, in the latter of which he is killed by Aeneas.

[28] Note the further connection that both Medon and Podarces have with Phylace (Medon, 13.696, 15.335; and Podarces, 2.695).

[29] For *autokasignêtos* in the *Iliad*, cf. 3.238 (Castor and Pollux, brothers of Helen, whom the same mother bore, *autokasignêtô, tô moi mia geinato mêtêr*); 11.427 (Charops, brother of Socus); 13.534 (Polites, brother of Deïphobus); 14.156 (Poseidon, brother of Hera); 16.718 (Apollo as Asius, brother of Hecuba).

[30] One important element in the contrast is that 2.703 = 2.726, *oude men oud' hoi anarchoi esan, potheon ge men archon*, 'but his men were not leaderless, although they longed for their leader ...'.

[31] I am assuming here that Protesilaus and his cohort are spearmen, although the text does not make an explicit statement of this in the Catalogue. For Podarces in a prominent place in the fighting later in the poem, see 13.693ff.

[32] Cf. Hector at 15.486ff. who sees that Teucer has been disarmed and is very glad about it. In fact Hector describes him as one 'of the best men' (*andros aristêos*, 15.489).

[33] R. Janko, *The Iliad: a Commentary. Volume IV: Books 13-16* (Cambridge: Cambridge University Press, 1992), ad 13.177-8, argues plausibly that the poet here has confused Teucer with Ajax 'son of Telamon',

[34] Leaf, ad 8.284.
[35] Cf. his awkward exhortation of Diomedes, 4.370ff. Teucer's reply (8.293ff.) seems to suggest that he feels hard done by, in so far as he says that he has not ceased from the fighting and has hit eight of them with his bow: 'But I cannot hit this mad dog' (ie. Hector, *touton d' ou dunamai baleein kuna lussêtêra*, 8.299). The thrust of Teucer's speech seems to be 'what more do you expect'?
[36] The word *nothos* is used ten times in the poem, although there are other cases where illegitimate children are not so described: six times for Trojans (4.499 [Democoon]; 5.70 [Pedaeus]; 11.102 and 11.103 [Isus]; 11.490 [Doryclus]; 16.738 [Cebriones]; and four times for Greeks (2.727, 13.694 = 15.333 [Medon]; 8.284 [Teucer]. Two Trojan siblings, Isus and Antiphus, both sons of Priam, ride in the same chariot. The former is a bastard, the latter is born in wedlock (*gnêsion*, 11.102). The lower status of the former is implied by the fact that 'the bastard held the reins, but glorious Antiphus would stand beside him to fight' (*ho men nothos hêniocheuen,/ Antiphos au parebaske periklutos*, 11.103-4). The lower place given to the illegitimate sons of the aristocracy seems to be quite consistent on both sides. This is revealed by the fact that those described as *nothoi* tend to be charioteers on the Trojan side, and archers on the Greek side.
[37] At 15.458ff., Teucer aims an arrow at Hector, which might well have hit him, if Zeus had not broken the string on the bow just as he is about to fire. Teucer then, on the advice of Ajax, takes up the spear and the shield to fight alongside his brother.
[38] I would suggest, however, that it is one thing for a man in battle to be likened to a child when a god is assisting him, and quite another when it is his half-brother. Moreover the sweeping away of Pandarus' arrow 'like a fly' certainly makes Pandarus seem ineffective in battle. The description of Teucer reflects the realities of conflict in which the archer needs both hands to fight, and the fact that he cannot carry a shield. He must therefore try to protect himself by hiding behind some other object. Despite these realities of combat however, the simile seems to me a very unflattering one.
[39] For a useful analysis of the role of Teucer in *Iliad* 8 and the implications of it for the Homeric treatment of bastardy, see M. Ebbott, *Imagining Illegitimacy in Classical Greek Literature* (Lanham: Lexington Books, 2003), 37ff.
[40] On Meriones' status as an attendant and second-in-command to Idomeneus, see Janko's note to 13.249-50.

[41] See too 5.59ff. where he is shown fighting with the spear and kills Phereclus the craftsman.
[42] This in turn would raise the question of why the poet has failed to mention bastardy in Meriones' case when it is explicit elsewhere. But I can offer no satisfactory answer to this question.
[43] Cf. 14.479 (*Argeioi iomôroi*); 15.312ff.; 16.772ff. One other reference to archery worth noting is the fact that the Myrmidons pass their time by playing with the discus, the javelin (*aiganeê*], and the bow (*diskoisin terponto kai aiganeêisin hientes/ toxoisin th'*, 2.774-5).
[44] Although Lorimer, *Homer and the Monuments*, 301, chose on textual and historical grounds to see the passage as an interpolation.
[45] On this subject, see Hainsworth, ad 11. 263 and 11.375ff. Less fortunate however is Euchenor of Corinth (13.660ff.) who is hit under the jaw and ear, and dies instantly.
[46] Cf. B. Fenik, *Typical Battle Scenes in the Iliad: studies in the narrative techniques of Homeric battle description* (Wiesbaden: F. Steiner, 1968), 96: 'The particular insults that (Diomedes) flings at Paris here in Book 11 – that he is nothing but a weakling and a seducer – are essentially the same as those that Paris hears from his brother at 3.39: Paris' proper sphere is the company of females; on the battlefield he is worthless. On the whole, however, Paris' success in the fighting belies these charges, as Hector himself, in a calmer moment, admits'.
[47] On this, see Richardson, ad 21.113 and 276-8.
[48] On this subject, Kossatz-Deissmann, 'Achilleus', in vol. 1, 37-200 (esp.182ff. for Achilles' death); J. Burgess, 'Achilles' Heel: the death of Achilles in ancient myth,' *Classical Antiquity* 14 (1995): 217-45.
[49] Hence the interest of neo-analysts in the notion that the death of Achilles lies behind the reference (see Burgess, 'Achilles' Heel,' n.1, for references to those in favor of this and against). It is certainly not a daft idea, although it remains no more than informed speculation (see the comments in the Introduction of this book). Whatever else we may say about it, the wounding of Diomedes certainly helps us to anticipate Paris's basic conduct and what his response to the death of Achilles might be like. This may be its most important function.
[50] Cf. Teucer at 15.440-1, above and Janko's note, ad loc.
[51] For one attempt to explain this, see T.R. Bryce, 'Pandaros, a Lycian at Troy,' *The American Journal of Philology* 98 (1977): 213-8.
[52] It is worth noting that similar Apolline features characterize Odysseus when he strings his bow in the archery contest in his house (*Od*. 21.404-11; see section 4 of this chapter). He strings it without effort like a lyre player, and makes it sing like a swallow (*Od*. 21.411. Apollo's bow also twangs when he fires at the Greeks, *Il*. 1.49). For the lyre/bow parallel,

cf. Pindar, *Ol.* 9.1ff. and also Heraclitus fragment 78 (C.H. Kahn, *The Art and Thought of Heraclitus* (Cambridge: Cambridge University Press, 1979), 195ff. Cf. fragment 79, 201-2: 'The name of the bow is life; its work is death'. This plays on *biós* (bow) and *bíos* (life) which are distinguished only through accentuation.

53 Another named bowman on the battlefield on the Trojan side is Scamandrius (5.49-58), on whom see below, n.87.

54 It is worth comparing Glaucus in the following book who takes up the advice of his father Hippolochus who had told him 'always to be bravest etc.' (*aien aristeuein*... 6.206ff.). This military ethos is precisely what Hector aspires to: 'since I have learnt (presumably from Priam) to be brave and always to fight among the foremost Trojans winning great renown for my father and for my own self' (*epei mathon emmenai esthlos/ aiei kai prôtoisi meta Trôessi machesthai,/ arnumenos patros te mega kleos êd' emon autou*, 6.444-6).

55 On this subject, see P. Wathelet, 'Les Troyens vus par Homère,' in *Quaestiones Homericae*, ed. L. Isebaert and R. Lebrun (Louvain-Namur: Editions Peeters, 1998), 296-7.

56 Taplin, *Homeric Soundings*, 109, links Pandarus' breaking of the truce to his death, and to the taking of Aeneas's horses: 'Aineias loses these wonderful beasts as a result of pairing up with Pandaros. The narrative connection is direct; the ethical connection is left implicit'.

57 Note the way again that horses tend to dominate his thinking (as at 5.202). It seems that in Pandarus we have somebody with a great love and feeling for horses.

58 In post-Homeric sources Helenus has a further connection with archery. It is his prophecy that Philoctetes must return to Troy with Heracles' bow so that the city can be taken (as in Proclus' summary of the *Little Iliad* and Soph. *Philoctetes*, 604ff.; 1337ff.). He is therefore an integral figure in later sources in the thematic connection between the first sack of Troy and the main conflict with which the poem is concerned.

59 Healing scenes in the *Iliad* generally involve arrow wounds. This is the only healing scene in the *Iliad* in which the wounded man has been hit with the spear.

60 As we saw earlier in this section of the chapter Dolon is another notable Trojan archer (10.314ff. and esp. 333). As his name suggests, he is depicted as a singularly unattractive individual in the *Doloneia* of *Iliad* 10, both in physical form and in his character. His choice of weapon is in keeping with his lowly status and his overall image within the episode (as is also true, apparently, of Odysseus). He encounters Diomedes and Odysseus and quickly submits himself to their superiority.

61 Note especially the graphic image of Apollo confronting Poseidon in the *Theomachy*: 'for against lord Poseidon stood Phoebus Apollo with his

winged arrows'(*êtoi men gar enanta Poseidaônos anaktos/ histat' Apollôn Phoibos, echôn ia pteroenta*, 20.67-8).

[62] But Hall's argument is on shaky ground even without recourse to the subject of archery. Homer's *Iliad* does no favors to the broad sweep of her thesis. The conclusion to her chapter on archaic poetry is couched in the following way: 'When archaic poetry defines the Greeks' way of life - their adherence to laws, their rituals...it is not in contrast with the discrepant mores of non-Greek heroes, but with the anarchy and violence, sacrilege and gynaecocracy of the 'supernatural barbarians', the Giants, Centaurs, Cyclopes and Amazons' (54). It would be hard to argue with this statement as far as the *Odyssey* is concerned, seeing that the quest of Odysseus is to negotiate his way precisely through this kind of world. But how true is it for the *Iliad* really when one bears in mind that a defining characteristic of the poem is the marginalization of monstrosity to the generations of the past (as discussed in Chapter 1)?

[63] Part of the problem is that the discourse on this subject tends to be couched in terms of whether the poem is 'pro-Greek', 'biased', 'chauvinistic'. See J.T. Kakridis, '*Aei philellên ho poiêtês?* (Is the poet always pro-Greek?),' in *Homeric Researches* (Lund: Publication of the New Society of Letters at Lund, 1949), 54-67. Kakridis argues against the Scholia on this point; and Taplin, *Homeric Soundings*, 114: 'This (*sc.* the heavier Trojan casualties in the *Iliad*) does not, however, demonstrate the alleged chauvinism. The apparent national bias may be partly explained by a bias so tenaciously built into the poetic tradition that it was impossible to purge'. The Greeks in the *Iliad* may be a superior fighting machine, and they are certainly destined to win the war. There is never a suggestion however that they are superior as a people in any particular way; and indeed their general cruelty and rapacity in war (cf. Andromache in *Iliad* 6, *inter alia*) probably conveys quite the opposite effect. For the contrary view to Hall and Taplin, that the *Iliad* does convey ethnic difference, see Griffin, *Homer on Life and Death*, 4-5. Cf. also, on linguistic aspects, H.S. Mackie, *Talking Trojan: speech and community in the Iliad* (Lanham, Md.: Rowman & Littlefield Publishers, 1996), 161ff.

[64] On this subject, C.J. Mackie, 'Achilles' Teachers: Chiron and Phoenix in the *Iliad* ' *Greece & Rome* 44 (1997): 1-10.

[65] On mythological invention in the *Iliad*, see above, Introduction, n.8.

[66] Contrast the delightful scene in the *Argonautica* in which Chiron comes down from the mountain to the shoreline with his wife and the baby Achilles in her arms to wave off the Argonauts (1.553ff.). Needless to say, one cannot really imagine Chiron in the *Iliad* strolling along

the beach with Ajax and Odysseus to go on the embassy to Achilles' camp.

[67] On Zenodotus' athetizing of 724-5, and probably 726 as well, and the various responses to it, see Kirk, ad loc. His conclusion is that 'the elaborations of Akhilleus, Protesilaos and Philoktetes have much in common stylistically, and many points of contact with the rest of the poem; they are, in all probability by the monumental composer, Homer himself'.

[68] West, *Greek Epic Fragments from the Seventh to the Fifth Centuries BC.*, 120-21.

[69] On this subject, including other evidence, see T. Gantz, *Early Greek Myth: a guide to literary and artistic sources* (Baltimore: Johns Hopkins University Press, 1993), 459, 635ff.; Clay, *The Wrath of Athena: gods and men in the Odyssey* : 'Now, while Homer nowhere explicitly states that Philoctetes inherited Heracles' bow, it seems clear that both he and his audience knew that tradition well' (92).

[70] For Philoctetes in this regard, cf. Pindar's *Pythian* 1. 54-5, '(Philoctetes) destroyed the city of Priam, and ended the labors of the Danaans, he walked with sickly flesh, but it was the work of fate' (*hos Priamoio polin persen, teleutasen te ponous Danaois,/ asthenei men chrôti bainôn, alla moiridion ên*). For the sense of cleansing and 'healing' of the long suffering of the house of Odysseus, see below, part 4 of this chapter.

[71] This connection with Philoctetes seems to operate in addition to the Heracles/Odysseus parallel that is in evidence throughout the poem (see below, n.82).

[72] This probably reminds us of Nestor (at *Iliad* 1.254ff.), who, as we saw in Chapter 1, offers his views on the subject of the men of the past, the fact that they were superior to the men of today. Both Nestor and Odysseus offer us an idealized perception of the men of the past, that they are better than the current crop. Odysseus however, unlike Nestor, offers us a more specific comparison in which he names individuals in both the generations. Nestor's speech is uttered in the tense atmosphere of the dispute between Agamemnon and Achilles in *Iliad* 1. It is certainly not the time and place for Nestor to start telling the disputants that they are not worthy to rub shoulders with Jason or Heracles or Pirithous. And so he makes only a general comparison between the generations, being far too diplomatic to move beyond this.

[73] Contrast Sophocles' *Philoctetes* 1059, in which Odysseus claims to be the equal of Philoctetes in archery.

[74] See Hainsworth, ad *Od.* 8 224.

[75] On this subject, see R. Scodel, 'The Modesty of Homer,' in *Oral Performance and its Context*, ed. C.J. Mackie (Leiden: Brill, 2004), 1ff.

76 Note the repetition of *erizemen* (8.223) and *erizeskon* (8.225): the point is clear that contending with the earlier generations would be as fatal as it was for them when they contended with the gods. Worthy of note too is the use of the descriptive periphrasis using *biê* ('violence') and *is* ('strength'), which is used frequently of the men of the past (S.L. Schein, *The Mortal Hero: an introduction to Homer's Iliad* (Berkeley: University of California Press, 1984), 136-7, 64). Exactly with whom Heracles is meant to have contended is unclear (cf. Schein, [above, Introduction, n.1], 94ff.), although it could of course refer to the conflicts alluded to in *Iliad* 5. Another earlier generation Greek archer referred to is Idas at *Il.* 9 555ff. The story here is that Idas carried away Marpessa from her father Evenus. Apollo wanted to take the girl from Idas, and the latter even dared to confront the god. Zeus eventually broke the deadlock by making Marpessa choose between them, and she chose Idas.

77 On Heracles' bow and its use in the first sack of Troy, cf. Pindar, *Isth.*, 6.33-5; Apollod. *Bibl.*, 2.6.4, and Anderson, *The Fall of Troy in Early Greek Poetry and Art*, 96-7.

78 In Apollonius of Rhodes, *Arg.* 1.88, the bow is actually a gift from Apollo (cf. the bows of Teucer in the *Iliad* [15.440-41] and Pandarus [2.827]). This may have important implications in light of Odysseus' 'Apollonian' characteristics in the last part of the poem (below, section 4 of this chapter).

79 On this subject, E.D. Francis, *Image and Idea in Fifth Century Greece: art and literature after the Persian Wars* (London: Routledge, 1990), 77ff.

80 Worthy of note is the fact that Odysseus gave to Iphitus (21.34) a sword (*xiphos*) and a spear (*egchos*).

81 It is worth making the comment too that in the Sophoclean play *Philoctetes* the close association of Odysseus with Philoctetes has a particularly grim aspect to it. The two men have a long-standing connection based, most significantly, on Odysseus' part in the desertion of Philoctetes on Lemnos.

82 It seems to me that this siege-breaking aspect of the bows belonging to earlier archers of great renown is crucial; although it is more common to consider direct textual similarities and contrasts between Odysseus and Heracles in the *Odyssey*; cf. G.K. Galinsky, *The Herakles Theme: the adaptations of the hero in literature from Homer to the twentieth century* (Oxford: Blackwell, 1972), 10ff.; Clay, *The Wrath of Athena: gods and men in the Odyssey*, 89ff., including relevant references to poison arrows, 96; K. Crissy, 'Herakles, Odysseus and the Bow: *Odyssey* 21.11-41,' *The Classical Journal* 93 (1997): 41-53; Danek, *Epos und Zitat: Studien zu den Quellen der Odyssee*, 151ff., 247ff., 403ff; Schein, 'Mythological allusion in the *Odyssey*,' 85ff.

83 Notwithstanding the fact that Telemachus, somewhat remarkably given his immaturity and diffidence earlier in the poem, is able to string the bow (21.128ff.); but he chooses not to do so when Odysseus nods to him.

84 On Odysseus' victory in the bow-contest, it is worth noting N. Austin, *Archery at the Dark of the Moon: poetic problems in Homer's Odyssey* (Berkeley: University of California Press, 1975), especially Chapters 4 and 5.

85 A useful summary of the subject is in M. Clarke, *Flesh and Spirit in the Songs of Homer: a study of words and myths* (Oxford: Clarendon Press, 1999), 257-9.

86 In the *Iliad* Artemis is also described as killing Laodamia in anger (6.196ff.), and also Andromache's mother (6.425ff.).

87 On this subject, J. Watrous, 'Artemis and the Lion: two similes in *Odyssey* 6,' in *Nine Essays on Homer*, ed. M. Carlisle and O. Levaniouk (Lanham, Md: Rowman & Littlefield Publishers, 1999), 165-76, esp. 171ff. It is worth comparing too the death of Scamandrius by Menelaus at 5.48ff. He was a great hunter and was actually taught to hunt by Artemis herself. But Artemis is unable to help him in the fight with Menelaus, and he is quickly killed.

88 Although cf. Hecuba at *Il.* 24.757-9 who says that Hector lies there dewy fresh like one whom Apollo, Lord of the silver bow has killed with his gentle arrows (*nun de moi hersêeis kai prosphatos en megaroisi/ keisai, tôi ikelos hon t' argurotoxos Apollôn/ hois aganoisi belessin epoichomenos katepephnen*).

89 Cf. *Il.* 19.59ff. in which Achilles wishes that Artemis had killed Briseis with an arrow on the day he chose her out.

90 Cf. Odysseus in Hades who asks the shade of his mother whether she was killed by the archer Artemis (*Od.* 11.172-3).

91 For a cross-cultural analysis of the two aspects of Apollo's archery and Semitic Reshep, M.K. Schretter, *Alter Orient und Hellas* (Innsbruck: Inst. f. Sprachwissenschaft d. Univ. Innsbruck, 1974), 174-215; W. Burkert, *Greek Religion: Archaic and Classical* (Oxford: Blackwell, 1985), 145-7.

92 For the similarities between Achilles and Apollo in the *Iliad*, W. Burkert, 'Apellai und Apollon,' *Rheinisches Museum* 118 (1975): 1-21, esp. 19; I. Chirassi-Colombo, 'Heros Achilleus-Theos Apollon,' in *Il Mito Greco: atti del Convegno internazionale (Urbino, 7-12 maggio 1973)*, ed. B.Gentili and G. Paioni (Rome: Edizioni dell'Ateneo & Bizzarri, 1977), 231-69; Nagy, *The Best of the Achaeans*, 142ff; Clay, *The Wrath of Athena: gods and men in the Odyssey*, 181-2; R.J. Rabel, 'Apollo as a model for Achilles in the *Iliad*,' *American Journal of Philology* 111 (1990): 429-40; Slatkin, *The Power of Thetis*, 85ff.

[93] Burkert, 'Apellai und Apollon,' 19: 'Ein entschieden jugendlicher Held mit langem Haupthaar, dem es nicht bestimmt ist, Gatte und Vater zu werden, den auf dem Höhepunkt der Jugend Apollons Pfeil trifft, ist Achilleus'. Other similarly fateful relationships which he argues for (outside of the *Iliad*) are Iphigeneia/Artemis, Erechtheus/Poseidon, and Hyacinthus/Apollo.

[94] Slatkin, *The Power of Thetis*, 87.

[95] An important aspect of this seems to be his period as an understudy to Chiron, 11.828ff. The notion of 'healing' seems also to be 'in his blood': cf. the 'healing' role of Thetis in her dealings with other gods (1.401ff.; 6.136; 18.394ff.).

[96] Note esp. *phrena terpomenon*, 9.186 ('delighting his mind'), and *thumon eterpen*, 9.189 ('he delighted his heart'). It is also worth noting that Achilles' lyre has a 'silver bridge on it' (*epi d' argureon zugon êen*, 9.187) which might be seen to resemble the similarly silver bow which Apollo possesses (in the epithet *argurotoxos*, 'lord of the silver bow', 1.37 etc.). The lyre (*kitharis*) also features in the abuse that Hector throws at Paris early in the poem (3.54), together with the 'gifts of Aphrodite' (*dôr' Aphroditês*). This reminds us that both Achilles and Paris have their resemblances to Apollo, including the lyre and physical beauty (for beauty in Achilles' case, 2.673ff.), even if they are at opposite ends of the heroic value system and are distinguished by very different weapons.

[97] Cf. Pindar's *Nemean* 4.1ff. where this aspect is also very prominent. By way of a cross-cultural comparison, it is worth noting that Aztec doctors uttered a chant when they conducted their healing activities, M.E. Smith, *The Aztecs* (Cambridge, Mass.: Blackwell, 1996), 262-3.

[98] It is worth noting that the reason for the divine anger for the epic hero is much more explicitly stated in the *Odyssey* [with Odysseus and Poseidon] and in Vergil's *Aeneid* [with Aeneas and Juno] than it is in the *Iliad*. Poseidon's hostility is the direct consequence of the violence perpetrated against his son Polyphemus by Odysseus (1.19ff.; 9.371ff. etc.), and Juno's arises from the judgment of Paris (1.8ff.).

[99] By way of a comparison with Achilles' rejection of the bow in the *Iliad*, it is pointed out at *Od*. 7.56ff. that Rhexenor, the father of Arete, is killed by Apollo, although no reason is given for this. It could of course just be Homer's way of saying that 'he died' (of natural causes); but it is also worth bearing in mind the statement of Nausicaa that 'the Phaeacians have no interest in the bow or the quiver' (*ou gar Phaiêkessi melei bios oude pharetrê*, 6.270). There might be a suggestion of divine punishment here of a similar kind to that which we witness later in the poem when the Phaeacian ship and its crew are petrified by Poseidon, 13.125ff.

[100] It would probably be a reasonable inference that in very early pre-Homeric narratives Chiron taught his pupils how to use the bow and arrow. This would be an essential weapon for hunting animals in the wild, and one assumes that Asclepius, Achilles, Jason *et al.* learnt the skill as boys from the centaur (as the renowned hunter Actaeon presumably did). But, as we have seen, one of the very strict and emphatic codes of conduct for the leading Greek princes of the *Iliad* is that the battlefield is a domain that is quite separate from that of nature, and this is reflected in the weaponry that they use. If Achilles is a fine archer in any pre-Homeric narratives, as we might expect him to be, there is no reference to it in the *Iliad* because such an association would only diminish his stature (and the same is true for most of the other principals on the Greek side in the poem, and some of the Trojans too). Indeed, in light of the rather fixed notions evinced in the *Iliad*, and its insistence on the spear as the appropriate weapon for Greek aristocrats, it is rather difficult to imagine Achilles with a bow and arrow at all.

[101] Above, n. 78.

[102] Cf. the wine that Odysseus uses against Polyphemus which comes from Maron, priest of Apollo, *Od.* 9.195ff.

[103] Apollo as avenger is evoked frequently in later books of the *Odyssey*: note esp. 17.132ff.; 17.251ff.; 17.494; 18.235ff.; 19.86f.; 21.338ff.; 21.362ff.; 22.5ff.; cf. Apollo and the archery contest in the *Iliad*, 23.859ff.

[104] For Theoclymenus in the *Odyssey*, see 15.222ff.; 15.525ff.; 17.150ff.; 20.345ff.

[105] A critical aspect of Odysseus' strategy is to allow the suitors no opportunity to arm themselves with spears, shields and helmets (19.4ff.). This plan almost comes undone when Melanthius helps to provide the suitors with arms (22.132ff.).

[106] It is worth noting that his use of these two weapons is foreshadowed as early as the first book, by Athena in her story at 1.253ff. She (as Mentes) recalls Odysseus coming to her house 'with helmet and shield and two spears' (*echôn pêlêka kai aspida kai duo doure*, 1.256). She then tells the story that he had left his home in search of a 'manslaying drug' (*pharmakon androphonon*, 1.261) to smear on his arrow heads. Quite apart from the separate issue of using poisons in this way, the two main weapons of vengeance seem to be foreshadowed by Athena here. In Homer drugs have their positive effect, as instruments of healing, and their negative side, including the use of poisons for arrows. For the former, note esp. *Il.* 4.190-1; 4.218-19; 5.401; 5.900; 11.515; 11.741; 11.830; 15.394; *Od.* 4.220ff.; 10.287ff. For the latter, *Il.* 22.94; *Od.* 1.261; 2.329; 10.213ff. Cf. *Od.* 2.325ff. in which the suitors express fears that

Telemachus will bring back men from Pylos or Sparta, or deadly drugs from Ephyre with which to poison them.

[107] One interesting parallel to this is Odysseus' association with fire and light in later books. On this subject, see H.W. Clarke, *The Art of the Odyssey*, 2nd ed. (Bristol: Bristol Classical Press, 1989), 73-74.

[108] Achilles of course has sacked other cities before the events described in the *Iliad* itself (cf. esp. 6.414ff.; 9.128ff.; 9.325ff., on which see Chapter 4); and indeed the whole poem is anchored to a conflict that arises between Achilles and Agamemnon over the spoils of previous sackings (1.149ff. and *passim*). But there is a sense, even in the *Iliad*, one that is spelt out in other epics, that Troy itself is a very different matter from these other conquests, and that the city will not fall to the type of weaponry in which Achilles specializes. Hector's death in *Iliad* 22 is akin to the fall of Troy, but the city itself, unlike its greatest defender, will not fall to the spear.

[109] Note the 'excellent counsel' [*esthlê boulê*] of Polydamas, one which is based on defense rather than attack, 18.272ff., 18.310ff. The attacking strategy of Hector is of course a personal disaster for him and his family, and for the city and its people. But the sense of it is that the city itself can hold out for longer by adopting the sort of defensive strategy that Polydamas (and Andromache in Book 6!) puts forward.

Chapter 4

[1] Although I see no justification for the inference of C.A. Trypanis, *The Homeric Epics* (Warminster: Aris & Phillips, 1977), 80, that 'another interesting sidelight is the place of honour given to the bard (*aoidos*) in the *Odyssey*; it shows that the profession of bard has progressed since the time of the *Iliad*'. Cf. Kirk, *Homer and the Oral Tradition*, 21.

[2] A prominent discussion of the place of fire in the *Iliad* is Whitman's 'Fire and Other Elements' in Whitman, *Homer and the Heroic Tradition*, 128ff. Whitman's chapter has been especially influential on the subject of Achilles and fire. On the general subject of fire in Homer, especially on the semantics of *pur*, L. Graz, *Le feu dans l'Iliade et l'Odyssée* (Paris: Librairie C. Klincksieck, 1965). For a wide-ranging discussion of fire in a cross-cultural context, see C-M. Edsman, s.v. 'Fire'. In vol. 5 *The Encyclopedia of Religion*. Ed. by M. Eliade, New York, Macmillan, 1987, 340-6.

[3] On the building of the walls, including the role of Aeacus, cf. Pindar's *Olympian* 8.31-46. In Pindar's account Aeacus is called upon by Poseidon and Apollo to help build the walls of Troy, because the city was destined to be breached at a place where the wall was built by a

mortal hand. After the wall was built three snakes tried to jump up on to the rampart. The first two failed, but the third was successful. This omen is interpreted by Apollo to mean that Troy would be taken in the first generation after Aeacus (ie. Telamon, who was there with Heracles) and in the fourth (presumably, Neoptolemus and Epeius when one now considers Aeacus as the first generation). The same story is alluded to at *Isthmian* 5.35ff.

4 The explanation in Apollodorus for this is that Hesione chose out Priam (then called Podarces) to accompany her into exile. She ransomed him with her veil, after which he took the name Priam (after '*priamai*'= to buy) and later became king. Diodorus lays emphasis on the nobility and justice of Priam who, he tells us (4.32.5), counseled Laomedon to stick to his promise to give Heracles the horses. Heracles therefore 'gave the kingship to Priam on account of his justice (*Priamôi de dia tên dikaiosunên paradounai tên basileian*] and also entered into a bond of friendship with him (4.49.6).

5 On Heracles' role in Homer, see Kullmann, *Das Wirkin der Götter in der Ilias*, 25-35; Galinsky, *The Herakles Theme: the adaptations of the hero in literature from Homer to the twentieth century*, 9-22.

6 Note too *Odyssey*, 8.215ff. in which he too, like Eurytus, fights against the gods (although the circumstances are not stated). Heracles seems to escape punishment for this, unlike Eurytus who pays with his own life.

7 For some of the main references to the burning of Troy in *Aen.* 2, cf. 304-17; 327-30; 337; 352-3; 374-5; 431; 476-8; 505; 554-6; 600; 624-33; 664; 682-4; 705-6; 759-64. The notion of a new city rising from the ashes of an old one is implicit in Vergil's account of the foundation of Rome by the descendents of Aeneas.

8 Hence the importance of the inversion Kleo/patrê and Patro/kleês; on which see W. Schadewaldt, *Iliasstudien* (Darmstadt: Wissenschaftliche Buchgesellschaft, 1987), 140; Nagy, *The Best of the Achaeans*, 105.

9 Cf. the interest of the neo-analysts in the issue of the Meleager story and the anxiety of the Trojans about potential defeat and death, Kakridis, *Homeric Researches*, 11-64.

10 Cf. J. Griffin, *Homer: Iliad 9* (Oxford: Clarendon Press, 1995), ad 595, who points out that like Hector in this passage 'we are to think of Meleager as most moved by the thought of the fate of his wife...Tacitus says of the Germans of his own time that they were far less anxious about their own fate than that their womenfolk might be enslaved after their defeat' (*Germ.* 8).

11 The places named are Thebe (1.366 etc., the city of Eëtion); Lyrnessus (2.690-1, etc.); Lesbos (9.129); Scyros (9.668); Tenedos (11.625); Pedasus

(20.92). It is worth comparing *Od.* 3.71ff.; 14.220ff.; 17.470ff. for references to similar 'viking-style' conduct.

[12] Note Agamemnon at 4.234ff., who exhorts the Greeks with the anticipation that 'we will lead away their dear wives and little children in our ships when we have taken their citadel' *'hêmeis aut' alochous te philas kai nêpia tekna / axomen en nêessin, epên ptoliethron helômen'*(4.238-9). Slightly later in the poem, Agamemnon provides us with some even more repugnant notions when he suggests that the Greeks should even kill the unborn males dwelling in the wombs of their mothers (6.55ff.). The key aspect of his speech is that he is bent on destroying the Trojans utterly: 'let him not escape, but let all disappear together from Ilios unmourned and unseen' (*mêd' hos phugoi, all' hama pantes/ Iliou exapoloiat' akêdestoi kai aphantoi* (6.59-60).

[13] It seems clear, on the basis of other Homeric references, that the veil of Andromache is associated not just at the personal level with love and marriage to Hector, but also with the fall of Troy itself: cf. *Il.*16.100 (Achilles to Patroclus), '...that alone we two might loosen the holy veil (*krêdemna*) of Troy' (*ophr' oioi Troiês hiera krêdemna luômen*), and *Od.* 13.388. A full discussion of the various references to veils in the *Iliad* and *Odyssey* is provided by Nagler, *Spontaneity and Tradition*, 44-63. It is also worth pointing out that Hector, even before his death, is conscious that he has brought ruin to his own people (22.99ff. and esp.107).

[14] Cf. Trypanis, *The Homeric Epics*, 89: 'We know that with (Hector's) fall the Trojans will be destroyed; this is what makes the *Iliad* a real 'Iliad' and not just an 'Achilleid', or an epic celebrating the exploits of many great heroes'.

[15] It is often pointed out that the practice of cremation in the *Iliad* is one aspect of the poet's world that is very different from the Mycenaean world where inhumation was practiced. The use of fire may be driven by factors in the poet's own world; but there is no doubt that fire has a graphic poetic application that inhumation simply does not possess.

[16] Note also Zeus on the subject of Hera's desire 'to lay waste' (*exalapaxai* 4.33) the city of Troy (4.31ff.). Hera says in reply to Zeus (4.51ff.) that he himself can destroy (*diapersai*, 4.53) her cities. Note too Poseidon at 15.213ff who is very insistent that Troy must be sacked, and is very determined that Zeus should not stand in the way of this. We also learn that after the sack of the city in the tenth year Poseidon and Apollo have decided to sweep away the wall (of the Achaeans) by turning all the rivers that flow from Ida on to it. A great flood results for nine days which sweeps it away (12.13ff.).

[17] Hector's initial impulse to burn the ships is revealed at 8.180ff.; cf. Taplin, *Homeric Soundings*, 147, 67-74.

[18] This is, appropriately, Protesilaus' ship (16.286). Protesilaus was the first Achaean warrior killed on the arrival of the expedition at Troy (2.698ff.); and it is also his ship (and, as it turns out, only his ship) that is burned first by the Trojans. Taplin, *Homeric Soundings*, 173, n.34, asks the insightful question, 'since Protesilaos can never return home anyway, is Hektor's triumph undercut by burning a ship without a captain?'.

[19] Cf. J.B. Hainsworth, 'No flames in the *Odyssey*,' *The Journal of Hellenic Studies* 78 (1958): 49-56; Graz, *Le feu dans l'Iliade et l'Odyssée* : 'le rôle joué par le feu dans l'*Iliade* est fort différent de son rôle dans l' *Odyssée*'.

[20] On religious and eschatological aspects of cremation in Homer, see Clarke, *Flesh and Spirit in the Songs of Homer: a study of words and myths*, 185ff.

[21] Styx is named in three Homeric Hymns (*Dem.* 259, 423; cf.381; *Ap.* 84-6; *Herm.* 519), but the others are not named at all. Sappho and Alcaeus refer to Acheron alone of the four rivers (Sapp. 95.13; Alc. 38.2,8). On the rivers in Pindar, note Acheron (*Pyth.* 11.21, *Nem.* 4.85; fr.143) and Styx (*Paean* 10.4). Cf. Aeschylus' *Agamemnon* 1156-61, in which Cassandra anticipates her death by reference to Cocytus and Acheron.

[22] Fire, in the form of a grand funeral, therefore provides reflected glory on to the warriors (like Patroclus and Hector) who are subjected to it. Not to give the body over to the fire is of course a terrible fate, and this is what, in the first instance, Achilles does to Hector; cf. H. Schrade, *Götter und Menschen Homers* (Stuttgart: W. Kohlhammer, 1952), 216ff.

[23] It is worth comparing the brief references to the funeral in Pindar, *Isth.* 8.56ff. and *Pyth.* 3.100ff. There have (since ancient times) been many question marks hanging over the authenticity of the 'second nekuia' of the *Odyssey* (24.1-204). For a recent discussion of the issues, and an argument against authenticity, C. Sourvinou-Inwood, *'Reading' Greek Death: to the end of the Classical period* (Oxford: Clarendon Press, 1995), 94-107.

[24] See Griffin, 'The Epic Cycle and the Uniqueness of Homer,' 39-53.

[25] Contrast Telemachus in the *Odyssey* who, in the course of the poem itself, moves away (physically and emotionally) from his mother and his nurse into the male world of politics and martial conflict. Achilles enters the male world of war without ever separating emotionally from his mother. This is something that he will undergo at death. There is something of a parallel between Achilles and Telemachus in the two Homeric poems, which is seen, not the least, in the way that they are humiliated in the assemblies that they both call (in *Iliad* 1 and *Odyssey* 2). Their throwing down of the scepter in these assemblies (*Il.* 1.245; *Od.* 2.80) is a mark of their youth and frustration with the political context in which they find themselves.

26 Even Niobe was able to deal with the loss of all her children when they were killed by Apollo and Artemis (24.602ff.). They lay there for nine days before the gods buried them on the tenth. And it was then that Niobe 'took thought for food, since she was worn out with shedding tears' (hê d' ara sitou mnêsat', epei kame dakru cheousa, 24.613; cf. 602). Taking food again after the rejection of it in mourning is a Homeric signifier of a return to life (as we see most prominently with Achilles in the later books of the poem [19.303ff.; 19.319ff.; 19.342ff.; 24.122ff.; 24.472ff.; 24.601ff.]).

27 Schol. Ap. Rhod. 4.816 (C. Wendel, *Scholia in Apollonium Rhodium Vetera* (Berlin: Weidmann, 1974), 293). On the *Aegimius*, see G.L. Huxley, *Greek Epic Poetry from Eumelos to Panyassis* (London: Faber, 1969), 107-10.

28 This episode in the *Argonautica* is presumably, at least partly, a repeat of the story in the *Hymn*, 231ff. There are some important questions concerning the parallel immersions of Demophon and Achilles, including the possibility that the *Cypria* may have included a story of Achilles' immersion in fire. For an earlier article of mine on this subject, C.J. Mackie, 'Achilles in Fire,' *The Classical Quarterly* 48 (1998): 329-38. On the episode in the *Hymn*, see W.R. Halliday, 'Note on *Homeric Hymn to Demeter*, 239ff.,' *The Classical Review* 25 (1911): 8ff.; N. Richardson, *The Homeric Hymn to Demeter* (Oxford: Clarendon Press, 1974), ad 237ff.; J.S. Clay, 'Immortal and Ageless Forever,' *The Classical Journal* 77 (1981): 112-17. On the *Demeter Hymn* and the Achilles episode in Apollonius, E. Livrea, *Apollonii Rhodii Argonauticon, Liber 4* (Florence: La Nuova Italia, 1973), 273; Richardson, *The Homeric Hymn to Demeter*, 231ff.; M. Campbell, *Echoes and Imitations of Early Epic in Apollonius Rhodius* (Leiden: Brill, 1981), 77-8; F. Vian, *Apollonios de Rhodes, Argonautiques*, vol. 3 (Paris: Presses Universitaires de France, 1981), 178. On the Demophon episode and the *Cypria*, Knaak, 'Demophon', in vol. 5 *Paulys Realencyclopädie der classischen Altertumswissenschaft*. Stuttgart, 1905, col. 148; L. Preller, C. Robert, and O. Kern, *Griechische Mythologie* (Berlin: Weidmann, 1894-1926), II, 67.

29 Cf. Apollodorus (*Bibl.* 3.13.6) whose account seems to follow that of Apollonius. Both accounts describe the child 'gasping' (*spaironta*) from the experience that he endures (*Arg.* 4.874); see Frazer, *Apollodorus: the Library*, 69, n.4.

30 See too Servius ad *Aen.* 6.57. For the references to the various immersions that Achilles undergoes, Escher, 'Achilleus,' in *Paulys Realencyclopädie der Classischen Altertumswissenschaft* (Stuttgart: 1893), cols. 225-6.

31 On this subject, see Burgess, 'Achilles' Heel,' 217-43.

32 For the full list of textual references and some of the scholarly responses to them, see Richardson, ad 22.317-21; cf. Whitman, *Homer and the*

Heroic Tradition, 128ff.; Schadewaldt, *Von Homers Welt und Werk*, 320; H. Fränkel and E. Heitsch, *Die homerischen Gleichnisse* (Göttingen: Vandenhoeck & Ruprecht, 1977), 49ff.; C. Moulton, *Similes in the Homeric poems* (Göttingen: Vandenhoeck und Ruprecht, 1977), 100ff.; Taplin, *Homeric Soundings*, 226ff. Achilles, of course, is not the only Greek warrior with fire associations, any more than he is the only Greek warrior with horse associations (on which see above, Chapter 2). Cf. Agamemnon during his *aristeia* where he is compared with fire (11.155-7); and Diomedes (5.1-8) whom Athena kindles about the head and shoulders with fire. The point is however that fire is a significantly more important element in the portrayal of Achilles than any other of the Greek warriors.

[33] On the subject of warriors from many traditions being 'heated', see M. Eliade, *Rites and Symbols of Initiation: the mysteries of birth and rebirth*, trans. W.R. Trask (New York: Harper Torchbooks, 1975), 81ff.

[34] Clearly the Trojans do not have to confront the physical force of destructive fire in the same way that Bellerophon does with the Chimaera. There is no prospect of them being burnt to death by Achilles himself. But at the metaphysical level it is the elemental force of fire that helps to represent the kind of challenge that Achilles' opponents face. It is probably significant that Achilles never uses fire as a weapon in the way that Hector does. As we have seen, Hector uses fire as a weapon to try to burn the Greek ships, but for all that he is nothing like as formidable as Achilles, who never uses fire at all.

[35] Cf. 11.157 where between the living and the dead are 'great rivers and terrible streams', *megaloi potamoi kai deina rheethra*).

[36] The phrase *pyri phlegethonti* (= 'ablaze with fire') is used by Scamander himself to describe Hephaestus in the conflict: 'Hephaestus, not one of the gods can rival you, nor could I fight with you, <u>ablaze with fire</u> as you are', (*Hêphaist', ou tis soi ge theôn dunat' antipherizein,/ oud' an egô soi g' hôde puri phlegethonti machoimên*, 21.357-8). The case for a verbal borrowing would probably be stronger if it were Scamander himself, not Hephaestus, who was described as 'ablaze with fire'; but the connection between the two Homeric rivers of fire may certainly still exist. If the human suffering at the burning Scamander does influence ideas of Greek eschatology, or indeed if it plays a part in providing the nomenclature for later Underworld topography (ie. if the name Pyriphlegethon comes from *Il.* 21.358), then the Iliadic episode itself may have been 'read' in antiquity as a scene from hell. As we saw in the first chapter, the *Iliad* does seem to draw on Underworld symbolism to enhance its own narrative descriptions. This is certainly the case in *Iliad* 24 where the whole mission of Priam to get Hector's body back

has a 'catabatic' structure to it. Scamander plays an important part in the way that the passage to the afterlife is evoked in the final book of the *Iliad* (24.350-1; 24.692-3), and something similar may be taking place in the present passage in Book 21.

[37] See too Mackie, 'Scamander and the Rivers of Hades in Homer,' 485-501.

[38] In a general sense the fighting is envisaged as taking place between Scamander and Simoïs (6.4); and the river functions as one of the important topographical markers in the poem (eg. the ford of Xanthus/Scamander at 14.433-4 = 21.1-2 = 24.692-3).

[39] Cf. Simoeisios at 4.473ff., who is named after the other principal river at Troy. Indeed Simoeisios, who is killed by the spear of Telamonian Ajax, is born right beside the river as his mother came down from Mount Ida. There is also another Trojan called Scamandrius at 5.49.

[40] Rivers often help to inform the town beside which they flow; and very often a warrior's wistful recollections of home include the river: cf. Sarpedon and Glaucus and the Xanthus river in Lycia (2.876f.; 5.478ff.; 12.310-28). Note too the Axius river the water of which is described as the 'most beautiful on the earth' (2.849-50; cf. 16.288).

[41] On this subject, N. Richardson, 'The Individuality of Homer's Language,' in *Homer: Beyond Oral Poetry*, ed. J.M. Bremer, I.J.F. de Jong, and J. Kalff (Amsterdam: B.R. Grüner, 1987), 165-84: 'There are actually a large number of different phrases used of Scamander and his waters in Book XXI, and they could perhaps be said to make up a kind of loose formular system; but the poet surely still chose *erateina rheethra* here (21.218) for a purpose, to bring home to us Scamander's justified indignation at the defilement of his 'lovely waters'. It may also be significant that the phrase *kala rheethra* is only applied to Scamander: it occurs 7 times in the *Iliad*, but always in Book XXI' (171).

[42] H. Erbse, *Scholia Graeca in Homeri Iliadem*, vol. 5 (Berolini: de Gryter, 1969), ad 21.343 and 365.

[43] It is worth noting that there seems to be a corresponding solemnity in the prophecies of the death of Achilles, and the 'death' of Troy: cf. 4.164-8 and 6.448-9 (Troy); and 21.111-13, with Richardson's note, ad loc. (Achilles). See too, M. Lynn-George, *Epos: word, narrative and the Iliad* (Houndmills, Basingstoke, Hampshire: Macmillan, 1988), 209ff., on the connection between the death of Achilles and the fall of Troy.

Index of Names

A

Acheron 173, 183
Achilleid 180
Achilles see relevant sections
Aegimius 178-9, 186
Aegis 27, 46
Aeneas 1, 35, 42, 44, 48, 55, 58, 66, 68, 72, 74, 81-4, 89, 119, 122, 127-8, 130, 132, 153, 157, 159, 181, 185
Aeschylus' *Seven Against Thebes* 44, 181
Aethiopis 186
Aetolians 162
Agamemnon 4, 6, 8, 23, 28, 33-7, 39, 45-6, 53, 78, 85-6, 94, 106, 115-6, 118, 121-4, 146-7, 162-4, 166-9, 175, 178, 188-91, 194-5
Agastrophus 101
Ajax 27, 35, 37, 67, 72, 104-5, 107, 111-2, 114, 117-8, 120-3, 139, 168-70
Ajax (of Sophocles) 8, 26
Alcinous 56, 95
Alexandra 179, 186
Allecto 44
Amazons 1, 12, 30, 40, 47, 86, 90, 133, 153, 159, 193-4
Andromache 7, 33, 47, 48, 51, 74, 163-6, 170
Anteia 30
Anticleia 147, 175
Antilochus 34, 74, 80, 129, 175, 193
Aphrodite 7, 29, 83, 106, 126, 142, 148-9, 178
Apollo 4, 10-11, 26, 53-4, 70, 72, 75, 79, 84, 91, 93, 96-7, 107, 109, 119-20, 125-7, 129, 133, 138, 141, 143, 144-51, 158-60, 168, 171-2, 177, 179-80, 182, 186
Apollodorus 120, 159-60, 179
Apollonius 179, 186
Archeptolemus 117
Ares 25, 28-9
Argives 87, 138, 179
Argonautica 179
Argonauts 237
Argos 65, 68, 82
Ariadne 147
Artemis 4, 133, 145-9
Asclepius 135-7
Astyanax 48, 164, 165, 183-4, 196
Athena 13, 25-8, 35, 46, 48-9, 62, 67-8, 72, 77-8. 87, 101, 106, 108, 115, 118, 125, 127, 131, 150, 158, 166, 180, 192-3
Atreus 36, 170

B

Balius 72-3, 77-9, 88, 177-8
Bellerophon 1-2, 5, 10, 13, 14, 21, 29-34, 40, 46-9, 52-3, 67, 86, 154, 157, 181, 185, 188
Beowulf 58
Boreas 82, 84
Briseis 3, 53, 57, 62, 78, 85-6, 148, 164, 168, 191

C

Cadmeians 35
Caeneus 23
Calydon 11, 23, 162-3
Calypso 15, 78, 171
Cassandra 58
Castianeira 117
Cebriones 116-7
Centaurs 12, 25-5, 28, 32-3, 35, 39, 42, 65, 71, 76, 135-8
Cerberus 7, 25-8, 55, 161
Chimaera 5, 30-3, 41, 43-5, 47-50, 53, 76, 86, 181, 185
Chiron 32, 65, 71, 76-8, 88, 100, 135-7, 140, 144, 177
Chryseis 3, 53, 62, 146, 164
Chryses 53, 146, 148, 191, 194
Circe 173
Cleopatra 162-3
Clytius 159
Cocytus 173, 183
Coronus 24
Cretans 103
Cronus 13
Curetes 162
Cyclops 87, 172

D

Danaë 27
Dardanus 34, 82, 139, 159

Death (*thanatos*) 57, 125, 147, 179
Deipyrus 131
Demodocus 87, 97, 153
Demophon 179-80
Deucalion 120
Diodorus 160
Diomedes 3, 5-6, 29, 31, 33, 35-7, 39, 48-9, 62, 65-8, 72, 74, 80-1, 83-4, 91, 99-103, 119, 122-4, 126, 127-8, 130-2, 139, 142, 149, 153, 168, 185
Dione 7, 142
Dolon 68-9, 98-100, 185
Doloneia 98-100, 120, 185
Dryas 23-4

E

Eëtion 163
Electra of Euripides 44-6
Elpenor 172-3, 175
Enyalius 118, 181
Epeius 87
Epic Cycle 12, 17, 32, 131
Epic of Gilgamesh 77
Epicles 35
Erebus 25
Erichthonius 62, 81-3, 88
Eumaeus 147, 150
Eumelus 37, 66, 72, 80, 113
Euneus 29
Euripides 44-6, 156
Euryalus 96
Eurycleia 78
Eurypylus 124-5, 136-7
Eurytus 14, 37, 93, 96, 141-5, 147-50, 160, 189
Exadius 23-4

F

Fate (*moira*) 57, 125, 150

G

Gaea 13
Ganymede 10, 26, 83-4, 159
Gilgamesh 58-9, 77
Glaucus 1, 5, 29-34, 39, 48-9, 67, 114, 122, 128, 153, 157
Gorgon 25, 27-8, 33, 42-6
Gorgythion 116-7

H

Hades 7, 25, 27, 52, 62, 78, 142, 156, 172-8, 180, 183, 186, 189
Harpalion 119
Hector 4, 7, 19, 22, 25, 27, 32, 33, 35, 40-2, 47-55, 57-8, 62, 64-6, 69, 74-5, 78-82, 88-9, 101-2, 105-11, 114, 117-8, 121-7, 131-2, 134, 138, 148, 151, 156, 163-70, 172, 176, 181-5, 188, 190, 193
Hecuba 51-2, 113, 116, 131, 159
Helen 3, 13, 48, 62, 85-7, 106, 108, 126-8, 130, 147-9
Helenus 48, 107-8, 114, 119, 130-3, 139
Hephaestus 100-1, 155, 166, 172, 175, 182-6
Hera 7, 25, 27, 75, 101, 142, 145-6, 158, 161, 166-7, 172, 182-4, 186
Heracles 1-11, 13-8, 21-2, 25-8, 34, 37-8, 40, 44, 52, 55, 61-2, 66, 68, 83-4, 87, 89, 92, 94, 96, 109, 139-44, 151, 154-5, 157-61, 167, 180, 187, 188-90, 193-5
Hermes 44, 55, 57-8, 171, 191-2
Hesiod 9, 13-4, 16-7, 26, 42, 44, 184, 188
Hesione 8, 26-7, 84, 115, 159
Hicetaon 159
Hippodamia 24
Hippolochus 128

Homeric Hymn to Demeter 179
Homeric Hymns 17
Hypnos (Sleep) 158
Hypsipyle 29

I

Ida (Mount) 34, 159
Idomeneus 34, 99, 114, 118-20, 124, 170
Ilus 54, 83
Iphitus 143, 160
Ithaca 15, 56, 67-8, 78, 97, 144, 172-3, 190
Ixion 24

J

Jason 1, 14-5, 21, 28-9, 34, 52, 58

L

Lacedaemon 143
Laertes 16, 193
Lampus 159
Laodamas 95
Laomedon / Tros 3-5, 8, 10-11, 25-6, 34, 61-2, 68, 81, 83-4, 86, 88, 115-6, 139, 143, 154, 158-61
Lapithai 24
Latium 44
Lemnos 29, 70, 110-12, 134-5, 139-40
Leto 75, 146
Leucothea 15
Locrians 119, 121
Lycaon 116, 127-8
Lycia 5-6, 10, 29-31, 47-9, 52-3, 67, 81, 94, 114, 127, 130, 153, 159, 181, 184
Lycophron 179

M

Machaon 124, 135-7, 139
Maron 172
Medon 111-4, 116, 120-2, 133-4, 139
Medusa 28
Meleager 6, 9-10, 153-4, 162-3, 168
Menelaus 56, 67, 74, 80, 94, 106-7, 118-9, 121, 126-7, 131, 135, 147, 169
Meriones 80, 99-104, 114, 118-22, 133, 149
Messene 143
Metaneira 179
Molus 120
Muses 18, 148-9, 170, 175-6
Myrmidons 80, 182

N

Neoptolemus 87, 174
Nestor 1, 6, 9, 11, 14, 22-3, 28, 33-41, 59, 124, 129, 153, 168, 175, 191-3
Niobe 146-7, 153, 178

O

Oceanus 45
Odysseus 14-6, 18, 34-5, 37, 39, 52-3, 56, 58, 66-9, 77-8, 80, 87, 92-3, 95-100, 102, 109-10, 115, 118, 120, 124, 139, 141-5, 147, 149-52, 162, 167, 171-4, 176, 185, 189, 193
Odyssey 3, 10, 12, 14-8, 37, 39, 52-3, 56, 67, 77-8, 87, 91-3, 95, 97-9, 102-3, 109-11, 139, 141, 143-4, 147-51, 156, 160, 171-80, 183, 186, 188-90, 192-3, 197
Oechalia 18, 96
Oïleus 11-2, 121

Orion 147-9
Ortilochus 143

P

Pandarus 68, 78, 80, 83, 94, 102, 104, 111, 112, 114, 118-9, 127-33, 135, 146
Paris 4, 86, 91, 93-4, 101-9, 112, 114, 118-9, 121-34, 136, 151, 166, 177, 180
Patroclus 41-3, 51, 55, 57, 63-6, 69, 70, 72-81, 88-9, 100, 103, 107, 118-9, 122-5, 135-8, 156, 162, 165-6, 168-70, 172, 175-8, 181, 183, 193
Pegasus 32, 45
Peleus 50, 72-3, 76, 100, 135-6, 177, 179, 193
Penelope 3, 78, 147, 178
Penthesilea 86
Perseus 1, 13-4, 21, 27-8, 33-4, 42, 44, 52
Phaeacians 14, 95-7, 109, 141, 144
Philoctetes 14-6, 18, 37, 70-1, 92-3, 96, 98-9, 103-4, 109-14, 116, 134-5, 138-44, 151-2, 189, 190, 194
Phoenix 6, 71, 129, 136-7, 153-4, 161-3, 177, 191, 193
Phylace 112-3
Pindar 50, 160
Pirithous (Lapith) 1, 21-5, 28, 33-4, 37, 191
Plato's *Phaedo* 183
Pleiades and Hyades 45
Podalirius 135-7
Podarces 112-3, 134
Podarge 73-4
Polypoetes 24
Poseidon 10-11, 26, 61, 73, 84, 100, 122, 145, 158-9, 166
Priam 1-2, 4, 8, 11, 14, 22, 27, 30, 34,

Index of Names

41, 50-8, 62, 64, 77-8, 82-6, 88-90, 105, 107, 114, 116-7, 126-7, 131-2, 146, 148, 153, 155-6, 159, 160, 163, 164, 166-6, 178, 185, 187, 191-4
Proclus 139, 144, 175
Proetus 29
Protesilaus 112-3, 134-5, 170
Pylos 40, 142
Pyriphlegethon 156, 173-4, 183, 186

R

Rhesus 63, 66-9
Rhexenor 147

S

Sarpedon 6, 8, 10, 33, 37, 42, 81, 84, 102, 114, 122, 125, 132, 153, 157, 159-60, 183
Scamander 19, 101, 156, 166-7, 172, 174, 180, 182-6
Scheria 15, 95, 97
Shield of Achilles 45, 49
Shield of Heracles 44
Sibyl 44, 55
Solymi 30, 47, 86
Sophocles' *Ajax* 26
Sparta 5, 67
Statius 180
Stesichorus 142
Sthenelus 27, 36, 39, 118-9, 130
Styx 25, 173, 180, 183, 186

T

Teiresias 78
Telamon 8, 26, 84, 105, 114-6, 121-3, 158-60
Telamonian Ajax 35, 37, 72, 122, 123

Telemacheia 16, 78
Telemachus 16, 52, 67, 77, 178, 192-3
Teucer 8, 27, 102-5, 112, 114-22, 124, 13, 148-9, 158-9
Thamyris 18, 148
Thebes 6, 13, 36, 39, 44
Theoclymenus 150
Theogony 13, 17, 26, 155, 188
Theomachy 145
Theseus 23-4
Thessaly 24, 65, 82, 136, 138
Thetis 41, 50, 53, 57, 75, 100, 125, 168, 174-80, 182, 186, 193
Thracians 69
Thrasymedes 99
Titans 13, 155
Tlepolemus 1, 6, 8, 10, 25, 33-4, 37, 153, 157-8, 160
Trojan 1, 3-4, 7, 11, 15, 17, 19, 25-6, 34-6, 39, 40-2, 44, 47-9, 51-2, 61-3, 65-9, 70, 75, 78-83, 85-7, 89, 91-2, 94-8, 100, 102-11, 114-6, 118, 121-2, 124, 126-8, 131-5, 137-8, 141, 145, 149, 151, 155-6, 158-72, 174, 181, 183-5, 190, 192-5
Trojan Women (of Euripides) 156
Tros 10, 26, 62, 72, 74, 81, 83-4, 88, 159
Troy 1-8, 10-11, 13-6, 19, 21-3, 25-8, 32-4, 36, 37, 38, 40, 42-44, 46-8, 50, 53-4, 58, 61-71, 73, 77, 81-90, 93-5, 97-8, 101, 104, 105, 107, 109-13, 115, 120, 122, 123, 126-8, 132-5, 138-48, 151-67, 169-70, 172-3, 175, 177, 183-90, 194-6
Turnus 43-5, 185
Tydeus 6, 22, 29, 35, 37, 39, 68, 131, 170
Typhoeus 13, 155

Index of Names

U

Underworld 7, 25, 27, 28, 38, 44, 54-6, 58-9
Uranus 13

V

Vergil 43-5, 52, 154-5, 161, 185

W

Wooden horse 66, 70, 87-9, 144,
Works and Days 13, 184

X

Xanthus (ie. the horse, for the river Xanthus, see Scamander) 63-65, 73, 75-9, 88, 177-78

Z

Zephyr 73, 188
Zeus 6-7, 13, 17, 24-7, 36-7, 41, 56, 62, 65, 76, 83-5, 88, 108, 114-5, 123, 125, 130, 138, 148, 155-9, 162, 166, 168-71, 178, 180, 182, 191, 195

Index of Homeric Passages

This index lists the passages discussed or quoted. Not all references have been included where these are used as supporting evidence

Iliad

Book 1	**Page**
8ff.	146
254-84	6; 22ff.; 28; 33; 35; 38; 40
268	24; 32; 34
271-2	37
308-11	53
430-87	53-4

Book 2	**Page**
412-7	166
594-600	18
651	118
695-710	113-4; 134-5
716ff.	92; 99; 110-4; 134-40
724ff.	15; 112; 120; 151
740ff.	24
743	32
763-7	37; 72
768ff.	37; 72; 105

Book 3	**Page**
15ff.	106
76ff.	121
146ff.	159
182-90	34

188ff.	1; 86; 90; 159
431	106
439-40	106-7

Book 4	Page
125ff.	127
163-5	164
196ff.	94-5
219	32; 135
308ff.	23
370ff.	35; 37
387ff.	6
401-16	36; 39

Book 5	Page
171-4	130-1
193-203	128-31
202-3	68
230-8	130
265-73	10; 26; 81-4
268ff.	25
277ff.	131
302ff.	35; 39
392ff.	7; 27; 142; 161
633ff.	6; 8; 26; 33
638-51	10
641	34; 157
642	157
648ff.	26; 61; 81; 84; 158
741-2	27; 46
800ff.	35

Book 6	Page
73ff.	131
102ff.	48
116-8	32; 107-8
119ff.	49; 67
145-236	29-33; 47-8
152ff.	5; 32-3
171	49; 52
179-83	30-33; 43; 49-50; 52; 181
183ff.	86; 90

215ff.	33
232	67
237-529	33
317ff.	107-8
331	166
339	107
390ff.	47
407ff.	6; 33; 47; 51
416ff.	163
431-9	170
441ff.	47
447-9	164
450ff.	164

Book 7	**Page**
44ff.	131
206-322	168-9
219ff.	107
124ff	23
433ff.	168
446ff.	26
467ff.	28-9
451-3	10; 159

Book 8	**Page**
271-2	117-8
281-4	115-7
284	8,10; 27; 105; 120; 159
335ff.	25
349	28
358ff.	7; 25-6; 161
368	26-7

Book 9	**Page**
186ff.	148
524ff.	6
529ff.	162
600ff.	162
674	162

Book 10	Page
246-7	185
272-579	67-9; 99-100; 120
402-4	69
436-7	69
566-9	68

Book 11	Page
32ff.	45-6
36-7	28; 33
200ff.	123
349ff.	123
385-95	101-4; 132; 142; 149
497ff.	123
514-5	123
653-4	41
670ff.	23
819-21	125
828ff.	32; 71-2; 76; 136-8

Book 12	Page
88ff.	132
350ff.	114
381ff.	35; 39
405ff.	35
445ff.	35; 39

Book 13	Page
313-4	114
361	34
650ff.	118-9
712ff.	121

Book 14	Page
233-51	158
243ff.	7-8
249-51	10; 161
251	26
317-8	24
320	27

Index of Homeric Passages

Book 15	Page
25ff.	161
639-40	161
599-602	156; 170

Book 16	Page
33-5	42
112ff.	169-70
126-8	163
143	32
381	73
619	120
698ff.	171
707-9	70; 138
867	73

Book 17	Page
278-80	37
437-47	76

Book 18	Page
117-9	161
192-3	37
429-34	50
478-607	45

Book 19	Page
14-7	182
91ff.	161
114ff.	34
116	27
123	27
219	34
228ff.	80; 176
303-8	42
319-21	42
342ff.	42; 180
390	32
399-423	73-5; 79

Book 20	Page
67ff.	145

144ff.	7-8; 10; 25-7; 40; 159
147	42; 115; 159; 161
206ff.	1
215ff.	81-2; 159
231-8	10; 26; 83
286ff.	35; 39
313-7	166
315-7	88
371-2	181
434-7	108

Book 21	**Page**
1-382	180-6
238-9	184
277-8	125
331ff.	186
358	186
362ff.	186
373-6	88; 156; 166; 184
40ff.	28
441-60	10; 26
470-513	146

Book 22	**Page**
22ff.	42
38ff.	51
82ff.	51
122ff.	42
131ff.	42; 51; 182
161	165
166ff.	49
177ff.	49
203ff.	42
288	42
345ff.	42
359-60	125-6; 151
399-403	79
421-2	42
446	125
468ff.	165
487ff.	164

Book 23	Page
161ff.	80
171-2	80
274ff.	72-3
629ff.	23
740ff.	28
787-8	129
789-90	35
850ff.	98; 118-20

Book 24	Page
128ff.	57
139-40	54
149	191
178	191
201-2	51
249-62	131-2
327-9	54; 191
345-8	192
349-53	54
368-9	192
433	192
448ff.	55
486ff.	52
565-6	192
602ff.	146; 178
656-95	57
704ff.	183
804	82

Odyssey

Book 4	Page
271ff.	87

Book 5	Page
59-61	171
339ff.	15
346ff.	15
458ff.	15
365ff.	15

Book 8	Page
215ff.	92; 96-8; 109-10; 141-4
223ff.	14
492ff.	87

Book 9	Page
240ff.	56
273ff.	56

Book 10	Page
28ff.	171
513-5	173

Book 11	Page
219-22	173
523ff.	87
550-1	37
601ff.	143; 160
609-14	44
633-5	27

Book 13	Page
153ff.	15
242-3	67
397ff.	16
429ff.	16

Book 15	Page
403ff.	147

Book 20	Page
169-71	150

Book 21	Page
11ff.	143-4; 160
68ff.	98
175ff.	172
184-5	172

Book 22	Page
8ff.	150

Book 24	Page
68-73	175
511ff.	16

www.ingramcontent.com/pod-product-compliance
Lightning Source LLC
Chambersburg PA
CBHW020748160426
43192CB00006B/282